THE BEST OF

JOSEPH
X.
FLANNERY

THE BEST OF

JOSEPH
X.
FLANNERY

BY

Joseph X. Flannery

Scranton: The University of Scranton Press

Library of Congress Cataloging-in-Publication Data

Flannery, Joseph X., 1927 -
    The best of Joseph X. Flannery / by Joseph X. Flannery.
        p. cm.
    Contains Flannery's columns from the Scranton times.
    ISBN 1-58966-104-4 (pbk.)
        1. Scranton Region (Pa.) --Social life and customs--20th century--Anecdotes. 2. Scranton Region (Pa.) --Social conditions--20th century--Anecdotes. 3. Scranton Region (Pa.) --Biography--Anecdotes. 4. Lackawanna River Valley (Pa.) --Social life and customs--20th century--Anecdotes. 5. Lackawanna River Valley (Pa.) --Social conditions--20th century--Anecdotes. 6. Lackawanna River Valley (Pa.) --Biography--Anecdotes. I. Scranton times. II. Title.

    F159.S4F57 2004
    974.8'37043--dc22   2004059568

Distribution:

University of Scranton Press
Chicago Distribution Center
11030 S. Langley
Chicago IL 60628

PRINTED IN THE UNITED STATES OF AMERICA

DEDICATION

To Betty,
my high school sweetheart
and
my darling wife of fifty-four years
and
also to our six wonderful children
and
eleven grandchildren.

TABLE OF CONTENTS

Columns

BIOGRAPHY OF
JOSEPH X. FLANNERY

Joseph X. Flannery worked in local journalism for 52 years, starting as a regional reporter with the old *Scrantonian-Tribune* in 1950. During that period he did just about every job in the newsroom, from office boy to columnist. In between he was a reporter, a deskman, an editorial writer, and an associate editor of his hometown paper, the *Scranton Times*.

Mr. Flannery was born in Carbondale, Pennsylvania on December 2, 1927. He grew up in Jessup where he graduated from Jessup High School in 1945. He then went on to receive a degree in History and English from the University of Scranton in 1949.

He got his first taste of journalism as an office boy with the United Press in New York. After college he returned to New York and worked as an office boy with the *New York News*.

He was hired by the *Scrantonian-Tribune* in 1950 and he worked there for the next 10 years. While there, he won a journalism award from the *Strike It Rich* television show for a series of stories he wrote about the Little Sisters of the Poor and their home for the elderly. The sisters had been praying to a statue of St. Joseph to prevent their heating boilers from shutting down. Mr. Flannery's series of columns raised $30,000, which enabled the home to install new boilers as well as their first television sets.

In 1960 he moved to the *Scranton Times* and began covering the courthouse and writing political stories such as the election of William W. Scranton as governor of Pennsylvania. Later he traveled the country covering the unsuccessful Republican presidential campaign of Mr. Scranton.

By 1967 he began writing a weekly column. Over the years that number rose to four columns a week, in addition to a separate political column.

He also found time to write and sell stories to various newspapers and national magazines. Four of his essays appeared on the op-ed page of the *New York Times*. Others appeared in such magazines as *Good Housekeeping*, *Time*, *Life*, *Catholic Digest*, and *Family Weekly*.

He extended his career to teaching journalism at the University of Scranton for 18 years. While he has won many honors in his career, the one he prizes the most is an honorary doctorate awarded to him by the University of Scranton.

Flannery is married to the former Betty Loftus of Jessup. They have six children and eleven grandchildren.

When he retired on December 1, 2002, he estimated he had written over 4000 columns.

LETTERS OF APPRECIATION

Northeastern Pennsylvania is very fortunate to have a fine person who loves this area and its people and who can also write well. Joe Flannery has compiled a series of columns and other writings, which have always been of tremendous interest to our area. He digs up stories of people and events which we would otherwise never have known—and they are always unusual and insightful.

In this book we all have an opportunity to keep recollecting some of his stories and writings. Like so many persons here, I wish we could have them all.

This gives us an opportunity to keep remembering (because of Joe's constant interest and delving) that this area is an unusual place and has unusual, wonderful people.

We are forever grateful to him.

William W. Scranton,
Ex-Governor

For more than 50 years, Joseph X. Flannery has told ever so uniquely the stories of the ordinary and extraordinary people of the Lackawanna Valley.

This legendary scribe is a wordsmith *par excellence*. He has always managed to go behind the headlines to find the human side of the story, and somehow to often spark both laughter and tears in the very same sentence.

It has been said that history is written one life at a time. The history of our community is very much to be found in the writings of Joe Flannery as he captured the stories of the famous and the infamous, the rich and the poor, the successful and the striving. His columns have inspired us and challenged us. Through them, we have grown. And for them, we can only remain eternally grateful.

Monsignor Joseph G. Quinn,
Rector
St. Peter's Cathedral

An Appreciation of Joseph X. Flannery

"Of the making of books there is no end." These words of Ecclesiastes have been quoted *ad nauseam* since first they were espoused. However, there are some books which have to be created. One of these will now contain the collected columns and essays of Joseph X. Flannery, the noted writer of the *Scranton Times-Tribune*.

The essence of Mr. Flannery's writing is to be found in the style in which he addresses the human condition in people's "real" lives. He has been able to focus on individuals, on groups, on institutions, and on businesses in a fashion which makes the readers laugh and cry, be cynical and be joyous, empathize and be inspired. In the decade I have read Joe Flannery, unexpectedly my emotions have been touched time and time again.

For all of us, what Joe clearly provides is a look at the Damon Runyon and O'Henry characters who populate northeastern Pennsylvania. Joe is able to transform the sinner and the saint into heroic figures who breathe the same air as we do. As a stranger to this area, I have been able to feel the pulse of the local population through the words of Joe Flannery. Once I even turned the tables slightly when I had the privilege of blessing this wonderful human being while he was recovering from a car accident.

How significant it is that the University of Scranton Press has given Joe the opportunity to share his collected works, pounded out on the keyboard of life, with a much wider audience. In the Jewish tradition we say to Joe "hazak ubaruch"—be strong and be blessed.

Rabbi David Geffen, Ph.D.,
Formerly of Temple Israel
Scranton, PA

November 30, 2002

A NEWSPAPER LEGEND WALKS AWAY, QUIETLY

By Christopher J. Kelly

Almost no one noticed him go.

He slipped out the back door, quietly closing the door on 52 years of telling the stories of northeastern Pennsylvania in a voice as reliable and familiar as the seasons.

When Joseph X. Flannery was getting his start in journalism, my parents were starting junior high school. He wrote his first column the year I was born. His last will run in tomorrow's *Sunday Times*.

At 74, Joe X. retired on Tuesday. No fanfare. No cake. No speeches, presents, cards, or pats on the back. He grabbed his coat, just as he had on countless other afternoons, and simply went home.

That was the way he wanted it.

I was an intern trying to break into the business when I met Joe X. He *was* the business, a local institution with legions of readers who never missed anything he wrote. If it's possible to be famous in a town the size of Scranton, Joe X. is.

Once I was showing a woman to the elevator when he strolled by. She stopped dead. He might as well have been the pope. She practically genuflected. I ceased to exist.

Joe X. seemed a little embarrassed, but he chatted with his gushing fan for about 10 minutes before walking her out. He always had time for people, particularly those he thought he could help with his columns. There are countless such people in and around this town.

Joe X. always had time for young reporters, too. He taught journalism at the University of Scranton for 18 years, spending six as faculty advisor of the *Aquinas*, the student newspaper. When I started writing this column, Joe X. was among the first to congratulate and encourage me.

"If you can't make 'em laugh, make 'em cry," he said. When I made them mad he said, "You're stirring things up a little. That's a good thing."

It's not easy to write even a single column each week. Joe X wrote three and sometimes four. Some Fridays, I don't have a good idea, let alone a column. More than once, Joe X. caught me pacing and said, "They can't all be steak. Sometimes you have to make sausage." Sausage is made of "bits and pieces."

Joe X. wasn't always a columnist. Before he made it in newspapers, he made handbags at the Morris White Pocketbook Factory in Scranton. He hated the mind-numbing work, but I suspect it went a long way in forming the kind of perseverance and work ethic essential to meeting deadlines for more than five decades.

Joe X. spent his first 10 years working nights at the *Scranton Tribune*, jumping to the *Times* when he was offered a day job. He left the *Tribune* on a Saturday and started at the *Times* the following Monday.

"When I look back on it," he said Tuesday, "I think, 'Darn! I should have taken a vacation.'"

Joe X. covered the county courts for 18 years, and developed a niche for politics and human-interest stories. He started writing columns in 1967, beginning with the story of a down-and-out Vietnam veteran who was addicted to drugs. Tomorrow's column is number 4000. That's right —four and three zeroes.

When I heard he was leaving, I asked Joe X. to swing by my desk on his way out. I wanted to say goodbye and ask him some stupid questions to remember me by.

The "interview" went something like this:

Would you mind if I changed my middle initial to X?

"If St. Francis Xavier doesn't mind, who am I to object?"

Is there really a Betty, or is your "wife" just a creative device you use when you have writer's block?

"There is a Betty. We've been a couple since the 10th grade. I tend to do things for long periods."

What's the secret to keeping a relationship going that long?

"I know how to obey. That's key."

What do you think about the impending nuptials of J-Lo and Ben Affleck?

"They didn't invite me, so no present for them."

Can I have your Rolodex?

"I don't have one. I was never into modern things."

OK, then how about some advice?

"Never pass up an opportunity to write a column. I never started a column I couldn't finish. If you write three paragraphs, it's your duty to finish it."

What are my chances of hanging around here as long as you did?

"Pretty good, if you play your cards right. I had a good run, and there's a space to be filled there."

I wanted to stand up in the noise and bustle of the newsroom and announce that he was leaving, but he asked me not to. He wanted to go quietly.

"Journalism has been very good to me," he said. "I never got rich, but I got paid every payday, and I've always loved the pace and excitement of the newsroom. In the (pocketbook) factory, time passed so slowly, I'd swear the clock went around four or five times in a day.

"In journalism, you look up at the clock and you put your head down and go to it. You look up again, and two hours have passed, and you're an hour behind."

And everyone's so busy, almost no one notices you leave.

December 1, 2002
The Sunday *Times* Editorial

FLANNERY EXIT END OF AN ERA

To recite the history that has occurred since Joe Flannery first sat before an Underwood would be an exercise akin to singing Billy Joel's "We Didn't Start the Fire." When Mr. Flannery scratched his way into journalism Harry Truman was in the White House. Thousands of northeastern Pennsylvanians still listed their occupation as "miner." World War II had just ended. The Korean War was about to begin, and Vietnam was just over the horizon.

Mr. Flannery spent most of that career here at the *Times*, the last 35 years of it as a featured columnist. The last of his more than 4,000 columns appears on this page today.

It is impossible to calculate the change that has occurred throughout northeastern Pennsylvania over Mr. Flannery's career. But it is fair to say that, as all of that change occurred, Mr. Flannery remained our constant —a go-to guy for political coverage, a columnist who could be relied upon to get beneath the veneer of the news and tell our readers about the real life and real people of the community.

Often, the Flannery column was something of a stitch in the social safety net. When the system failed someone, Mr. Flannery often was there to not only expose the problem, but to rally the community's support to the person in need. It was journalism of the heart.

His work was also infused with a keen sense of history and human nature—especially regarding events and personalities that have shaped and continue to shape northeastern Pennsylvania. For many members of the news staff, Mr. Flannery was a living compendium of local political and social history.

That ready knowledge will be missed. And as we wish Mr. Flannery a long, healthy, and happy retirement, we know that the absence of his column from this page will leave a hole in our own journalism safety net. We'll try to fill it with the same dedication and sense of community that Mr. Flannery brought to his keyboard for the last 52 years.

FOREWORD

Dear Reader,

When I retired as a columnist for the *Scranton Times* in December, 2002, I had about 4,000 columns stashed away in plastic boxes in my basement with no particular plan for them, other than to hope my grandchildren might some day be curious enough to read them. "They might be interested in them," I told myself.

However, that game plan was changed by the Reverend Richard Rousseau, S.J., the director of the University of Scranton Press.

After meeting him one day, I was bold enough to ask if the University of Scranton Press might be interested in publishing some of my columns in book form. He immediately agreed to undertake the project. I was thrilled and began the tedious task of sorting through all my old columns and picking enough to fill a book. It wasn't easy. I was humble enough to realize that not all of them were gems. I read thousands of columns and picked those I thought were worthy of being put in the book. However, sometimes I changed my mind and took some out and replaced them with other ones. That went on for months until I finally had enough columns that I liked for the book.

One might wonder how I became a columnist.

It happened after the *Scranton Times* began publishing a Sunday paper on October 7, 1966, with the late Frank Perry as the editor. One day he came to me and said he had heard that my wife and I had spent the weekend in New York City. I wondered why our trip interested him. I didn't wonder long. He asked if I could write a column about our trip. Believing that he needed to plug a hole in the next edition, I agreed to write something, never realizing that the column I put together was the first of thousands I would write in the years ahead. While that first column was not among my best and my language is very, very outdated, I decided to start the book with it anyway.

So here is the very first column...

August 27, 1967

WHITE WAY TEEMS WITH VICE

New York City is about 130 miles from Scranton, but for a Scranton reporter it is definitely alien territory.

For the sake of this article, I am referring to midtown Manhattan—say from 40th to 59th streets.

This is an area which has the "Broadway" theatres which are not really on Broadway, famous hotels, stores ranging from the shoddiest to the classiest in the world, and a honky-tonk section that is currently known as the "gay" white way.

New York is enjoying one of its best tourist summers in history—with below normal temperatures and low humidity contributing to the happy picture. Another factor is that the city's racial situation has not really been too bad—compared to some other cities. But New York has never been more tawdry and immoral.

Take prostitution, for example. During recent months, prostitutes have been streaming into New York because of an apparent police decision not to worry too much about vice. In addition, the influx has been attributed to a new law, effective Sept. 1, which cuts maximum prison sentences from one year to 15 days.

It was just during the past few days that the New York police began a crackdown—picking up hundreds of female and male prostitutes. The crackdown was a complete reversal of previous policy.

In New York, there is a closed circuit television station—Channel 6 —aimed exclusively at persons staying at midtown motels. On this station earlier this month, this reporter heard the announcer talking openly about the prostitution situation and advising "lonely" males where they might go to find "companionship." The advice included the names of bars and cocktail lounges in the area.

Discounting the fact that the TV station's main function is to give advice and information to tourists, it was a bit shocking to hear such information being piped through a TV set in the Hotel Americana!

Mayor John V. Lindsay has tagged New York as a "Fun City" to help it out as a tourist attraction. But there is another "Fun City" that could attract the wrong kind of tourists. This is a second floor dance palace right along Seventh Ave., with wild music virtually drowning out traffic noises in the area. In the windows above the street, in scanty costumes, are go-go girls who gyrate for all to see every afternoon and evening.

Without being a prude ready to condemn such go-go palaces, there is much to be said for keeping these performances out of public view, where family groups see them whether they want to or not.

Not many doors away is the more famous Metropole, which also has been caught up in the go-go world of "mod" music. The girls are dancing endlessly here, too, but removed a little bit from the public eye. They can be seen from the street, but in the nearby "Fun City" one could not possibly miss them.

One of the first impressions one receives in New York this year is that it has more characters per square foot than any other city east of San Francisco. Miniskirts are popular in Scranton—but one seldom sees dresses as short as they are being worn on the streets of New York. One has to be a character to wear them THAT short.

The same is true for mod clothes in general, for both female and males. This may be the fashion wave of the future, but Scranton appears to be far above flood level.

Hippies are rather common in New York. In fact, only the real wild ones rate more than a passing glance as they walk by. The long hair and beards on the men go along with the ragged clothes and sandals. But for the most part, the hippies stay downtown in Greenwich Village and away from the square world of tourists.

What was once the "crossroads of the world," Broadway and 42nd Street, has degenerated into a poorly lighted area of penny arcades, book shops dealing openly with pornography, record stores dealing with "blue" party records, novelty shops dealing with sex items, and magazine shops dealing with sex publications. Without becoming a bore on the subject, it might be easier to describe the whole area as one preoccupied with sex.

The persons who congregate on the sidewalks in this area south of the old Hotel Astor—which is now being razed—are not the out-of-town tourists. They are a mixture of dope addicts, runaway delinquents, drunks, and other odd types, a policeman said candidly. He said that the main job of a cop here is to make sure tourists are not "hustled."

But for all its seedy characters, midtown New York still has the magic of Broadway shows where persons wait for months to get tickets which sometimes cost as much as $12 each. It has its splashy nightclubs, like the

Latin Quarter, where tourists see a big star and what amounts to a vaudeville revue with showgirls that might have kept vaudeville from dying.

And it has slick private clubs, such as the New York Playboy Club,
where admission is by membership key only and where entertainment is
surprisingly sophisticated and in good taste.

New York also has the highest prices in the world for tourists, with
inflated price tags being complicated further by numerous taxes and tips.

But it continues to be a fascinating place to visit.

To coin a phrase: "It's a nice place to visit but I wouldn't like to live
there."

September 10, 1967

SAD TALE OF A VETERAN OF VIETNAM

"I am sorry to have to be the bearer of bad news. . . ."

In these words, a New Jersey county prosecutor informed me recently that 21-year-old Raymond Kennedy was back in jail—this time on a marijuana charge.

The reason Somerset County Prosecutor Michael R. Imbriani was taking the trouble to pass on this information to a *Scranton Times* reporter was that the reporter had interested himself in the Kennedy case.

As detailed during the past few months in the *Times*, Kennedy was arrested in Scranton and spent some time in the Lackawanna County Prison before the story unfolded about the youth having had some tough combat experience in Vietnam.

He saw his best friend being virtually cut in half by Viet Cong machine gun bullets.

The experience led to a nervous breakdown that caused him to be shipped home and to be given an honorable discharge. But after coming home, he began experiencing nightmares in which hordes of Viet Cong continued to overrun him. Seeking an escape, he started drinking a certain type of narcotic cough medicine that produced a pleasant, careless feeling.

Then the fatherless ex-GI suffered another blow from fate when his mother was killed in an accident in New Jersey in April. It was just about a week after that tragedy that the youth left his home of Somerville, NJ, with two young friends and came to Scranton to buy some more cough medicine. But this time they were caught and charged with illegal purchase of a drug.

He was already on probation for three years in Bucks County in the same type of case. And in his home county in New Jersey, police wanted him in connection with the issuance of some $180 in bad checks.

Things looked bad for Kennedy at this point, but Atty. James J. McHale, a youthful member of the local bar, then stepped in and soon learned some reasons for his abnormal behavior. Soon he had the defendant in an examining room at the Veterans Administration Hospital in

4

Wilkes-Barre, where a physician said there was no doubt about it: Kennedy was an addict and he needed hospital care.

But the VA didn't want to get involved in the case until the criminal matters against Kennedy were cleared up. It felt this way even after it was learned that the young soldier had his first experience with marijuana while on duty in Vietnam.

So his lawyer went to work and got the court in Bucks County to agree to drop its probation against Kennedy to clear the way for him to go to a hospital. And President Judge T. Linus Hoban, an "old soldier" himself who said he knows the terrors of war, bent over backwards to be fair. He accepted Kennedy's guilty plea on the drug charge and then gave him a sentence of two months and 22 days— just the time he has spent in prison here— to permit his immediate return to New Jersey.

At this point it looked like Kennedy might have luck on his side, and might square the bad check charge in New Jersey, and get a suspended sentence to permit him to get the hospital care he needed.

But instead, the youth who had told Judge Hoban that he still had a craving for drugs was permitted his freedom on bail.

Just about anyone can guess the ending. Kennedy— already diagnosed by the VA as an addict and admitting in court here that he could not help himself— went right back to his old habits.

He was arrested with another youth in a New Jersey town, with police charging that they had a number of marijuana cigarettes in their possession. Today the ex-GI sits in Somerset County Jail in lieu of $2,500 bail.

The medical help that everyone agrees he needs seems further away than ever.

This is the way that the American justice system has taken care of one GI who fought in the jungles of Vietnam.

March 31, 1968

TAIL END OF THE TALE ABOUT TAILS

This is the tail end of the tale about Vice President Hubert H. Humphrey's tails.

Or if you don't like to play with words, it is the final story about the tuxedo that put the vice president in the soup. (Oops! There I go again.)

Just to recap the situation briefly, it will be recalled that the vice president flew here to speak at a banquet of the Friendly Sons of St. Patrick of Lackawanna County.

Unfortunately, his luggage was left at the airport in Washington. Someone—but apparently not Mr. Humphrey—decided to fly the Air Force jet back to Washington to bring the luggage here. In this way, Mr. Humphrey's tuxedo arrived on time for him to wear it to the dinner.

But Congressman H. R. Gross from Waterloo, Iowa, who has often played the role of "the spoiler," got wind of the special airplane journey and uncorked a stinging speech on the floor of Congress. Meanwhile, the Friendly Sons of St. Patrick sent a check for $704 to the Air Force to cover the cost of the trip.

This, as someone once said before, is all water over the dam. But there are bits and pieces of the story that have never been published before. Thus, this column.

First, let us check the source of the complaint. He is an ex-reporter who is known to his fellow congressmen as "Charlie" Gross.

He has built a reputation as being a man always seeking "hidden gimmicks" in legislation before the House. This could spring from his background as a reporter and editor of a newspaper in Omaha, NE, from 1921 to 1935 and a radio commentator until he was elected to Congress in 1948.

Sometimes a bit cantankerous and noncooperative with his own party leaders, Gross does have a good attendance record in the House and he expects others to be on hand, too. Thus, he frequently forced the House to adjourn by calling for a roll call to make sure a quorum was present. Because there is no quorum and a member insisted on touching this parliamentary base, the House has to quit for the day. Thus, Gross was not bashful in attacking the vice president.

In fact, Gross made headlines once by attacking President Lyndon Johnson for holding 3 A.M. White House parties and for sponsoring swinging parties at the Smithsonian Institution.

"If they want to do this, I suggest they renovate one of the burlesque halls for which Washington is fairly notorious," Gross said about the presidential affairs.

After blasting the flight to pick out Humphrey's tuxedo, Gross found himself in a debate on the subject. It began as Congressman Durward G. Hall, a Missouri Republican, asked if he was objecting to the vice president wearing a tuxedo.

Gross answered that he did not, adding: "He could wear overalls, and it would be all right with me."

This brought the comment from Congressman Thomas P. O'Neill, a Massachusetts Democrat, that he was uncertain of whether Gross was suggesting that the vice president should wear overalls at an Irish affair.

Then, Congressman Hugh L. Carey, a Democrat from Brooklyn, NY, got into a friendly exchange with Gross. Carey's interest was increased by the fact that he spoke before the Friendly Sons of St. Patrick in this city in 1966 and before the Greater Pittston Friendly Sons in 1967.

Carey asked: "Mr. Gross, I hope that you did not imply, knowing that the vice president was going to Scranton to speak to the Friendly Sons of St. Patrick, one of the oldest patriotic societies in the history of our country, that it would be all right for him in all dignity to address the Friendly Sons of St. Patrick in overalls."

Gross replied: "Why not?"

Carey commented: "Because they have long since moved out of the overall category. We reserve those for the farmers of Iowa. Many years ago we doffed our overalls and put them in Mrs. Murphy's chowder."

Gross, patching a political fence, brought the mini-debate to a close with the comment: "I have seen a lot of Irish wearing overalls in my time, and, incidentally, they were good people."

This ended the floor debate, as reported in the Congressional Record, so now the book will close on the vice president's tuxedo journey with this epilogue:

Congressman Gross is fortunate that members of the Friendly Sons of St. Patrick of Lackawanna County don't vote in his home city of Waterloo. If they could, he would meet his Waterloo. (Oops! I can't seem to break the habit.)

September 15, 1968

NO IFS ANDS OR BUTTS—QUIT NOW!

What desperate smoker has not rummaged through his ashtray, looking for a cigarette butt that holds promise of providing a few more puffs?

Or what smoker has not pulled a bit of skin off his lip while removing a cigarette from his mouth?

Or what smoker has not done a bit of arithmetic and concluded that his habit is quite expensive?

Or what smoker has not had some accident with the sparks of a cigarette burning a hole in a garment or furniture?

Or what smoker has not had a potentially more serious accident in which some small child—or even older persons—was burned by his cigarette?

Or what smoker has not singed his nose by trying to light a tiny butt salvaged from an earlier cigarette to try to avoid a trip to the store?

Or what smoker has not finally been forced to leave his house late at night to buy a fresh pack of cigarettes?

Or what smoker has not paid the penalty of excess smoking at a party by suffering the next morning from a terrible taste in his mouth?

Or what smoker has not been irked by the person who bums cigarettes from him in wholesale lots?

Or what smoker has not found himself in desperate condition by having plenty of cigarettes—but no matches?

Or what smoker has not had to take some abuse from a tidy member of the household—be it a wife, an elderly aunt, or any other person —about dirtying too many ashtrays?

Yes, there are countless annoyances connected with smoking. But it wasn't until fairly recent years that it became a reasonable assumption that cigarettes could kill you. The old adage about each cigarette being a nail in your coffin has received scientific support.

The late W. C. Fields often remarked that it was ridiculous to say that one could not stop drinking.

"I've done it thousands of times," the comedian would explain.

Many smokers can say the same thing. Most have tried to give up smoking, but only to have the resolution vanish in a puff of smoke.

As a person who smoked steadily for 22 years before finally kicking the habit, I know that it can be done without any great courage. In fact, as more and more scientific evidence is piled up against smoking, it begins to take a certain amount of courage to ignore it and to continue puffing.

The warning is on every pack of cigarettes. It says that continued use can be harmful to your health. The message is there on orders of the U.S. government. And it is backed by years of scientific research.

Look at it this way. If someone was passing out the most delicious candy pellets ever made, but warned that they could cause cancer or heart ailments, most persons would throw them away. Yet a person who smokes two packs of cigarettes a day is paying over $250 a year to increase his odds of dying early.

And just how does a smoking parent tell one of his children he should not smoke? "If Pop can do it, why can't I?" would be a normal reaction.

So how does a person quit smoking?

Instead of doing it cold turkey, give yourself a psychological buildup. Begin by reading the warning on the pack every time you take a cigarette. Read the words aloud when possible. And after a time, the message will begin to take on a more awesome meaning. "These things are killing me," you might conclude.

Then think such random thoughts as the amount of money that can be saved . . . the good example that could be set for the kids . . . the lips that won't be torn next winter . . . the accident that won't happen with furniture, garments, or children . . . the freedom from the need of always having cigarettes on hand . . . the self-respect that will be gained by not rummaging through ashtrays . . . and the pleasure of not being accused of dirtying too many ashtrays.

My own liberation came almost by accident after I went through the suggested buildup routine. In one of those periodic fits of resolve which most smokers experience, I decided to "cut down" on my smoking. (That is a famous expression that all smokers will use on an average of twice a month).

To "cut down" I switched to those small cigars with plastic tips. They proved to be very satisfying, too, and soon I was smoking them as frequently as I had previously smoked cigarettes.

But one morning, while diligently puffing on a cigar, the inspiration came to me that I might be able to live without tobacco. So I tossed the cigar away. That was two years ago. Now I have the cleanest ashtrays in town.

November 17, 1968

IT WAS JUST ANOTHER DAY OF WORK

After more than 33 years on the bench, President Judge T. Linus Hoban indicated that he will quit on January 1.

The news of an old soldier fading away was reported at that time, but there was a certain unreported drama hidden among the incidents that unfolded that morning in court.

As a reporter, I happened to be on hand as Judge Hoban presided over a term of Common Pleas Court. While he was checking on which cases were still open and what ones were disposed of, Judge Richard P. Conaboy leaned over to say: "Case No. 16 has been continued."

Judge Hoban, plagued by failing hearing, had difficulty understanding what his colleague was saying. Judge Conaboy had to repeat the message several times. Judge Hoban was obviously irked at himself.

The incident passed without this reporter attaching any significance to it. But right there was the principal reason why Judge Hoban was about to announce his decision. He was having increasing difficulty with his hearing. A broken hip had healed fine, but the hearing problem had grown progressively worse.

The judge, still showing no signs that he was about to drop a bombshell, presided over the election of a jury for a lawsuit, which he then assigned to Judge Conaboy. Only one more case remained on the trial list, so I left the courtroom as the new jury was being called. There was no news here.

As I walked down a hallway, Chief Court Officer Walter Shelinsky caught up with me and said that Judge Hoban wanted me. It was a bit unusual to be so summoned, but I thought that it must relate to some bit of court news.

As I approached the bench, Judge Hoban was writing on a tablet. He glanced up and said he was preparing a statement that would be finished in a few moments. As he wrote, I began to read the words that I was viewing upside down.

11

While I had some trouble piecing them together, I finally made out the first few: "I have concluded that I shall retire from the bench of Lackawanna County on January 1, 1969."

Judge Hoban finished the statement and handed it to me. It was just three paragraphs. As I read it I had trouble understanding a few of the words. He helped me to decode it.

At the moment I felt that I should make some kind of comment. Here was one of the leading public figures of this area saying that he was about to retire. Few persons knew of the decision. But I couldn't think of any appropriate words. So I merely shook hands with him.

The announcement was soon a news story in the *Scranton Times*. But news stories can't convey all the bits of emotion that are involved in such incidents. For example, the trouble experienced by Judge Hoban in hearing Judge Conaboy a short time before never made the news columns. But it clearly underscored the reason for calling an end to a long and distinguished career.

Moments before the day's court session began, Judge Hoban informed Judges Conaboy and Otto P. Robinson of his decision. While his retirement plans had been subject to speculation for a year or so, the two jurists were still surprised when they heard the news so abruptly.

It would seem that a career of such length should be ended with more of a flourish.

Yet, the quiet way in which he signaled the end is indicative of the type of man Judge Hoban has always been. He doesn't believe in making a big flourish about himself.

Right after he made his retirement decision public, he presided over a "hinky-dink" court case that involved damages of just about $300. And later that afternoon he heard testimony in a case of a store trying to do business on Sundays.

As far as Judge Hoban was concerned, it was just another workday.

December 15, 1968

SANTA IS A "PRETTY FAR-OUT GUY"

Does it make you uneasy to see a longhaired hippie?

Well, relax and take another look at Santa Claus. If ever there was anyone who flaunts tradition with his clothing and beard, it is happy, jolly St. Nick.

Imagine parading around in a red velvet suit trimmed in white fur. Then throw in a white flowing beard and a pair of patent leather boots. It's almost too much for the mind to comprehend. The average hippie would be afraid to wear such outlandish garb.

In fact, when one takes a really critical look at Santa, he does seem to be a pretty far out guy.

For instance, kids may take trips with LSD, but I've never heard of any of them flying around with eight reindeer. Their trips aren't THAT wild, even with the help of hallucinogenic drugs.

Now before this goes any further, I want to make it clear that I like Santa. In fact, I spend a lot of money at this time every year to make him look good in my own home. The only point I want to make is that if we can get used to someone like Santa Claus, we might teach ourselves not to stare at hippies.

To put Santa in perspective, I would like to place him on a witness stand in a courtroom. It might go something like this:

Q. Please state your name, age, and address.

A. My main name is Santa Claus, but I have several other aliases including St. Nick, Kris Kringle, or just plain Santa. I have no age. And I live at the North Pole.

Q. Do you really expect this court to accept those answers without being held in contempt? I insist that you treat these proceedings more seriously. Now, what is your occupation?

A. I make toys and give them away.

Q. I never heard anything more ridiculous in my life. No one gives things away without having some angle. Now, what's your angle, Mr. Claus?

A. To make people happy.

13

Q. Your honor, I must ask you to warn the witness that he is to answer my questions truthfully. The last answer is so obviously false that it offends the dignity of the court. (At this point the court directs Mr. Claus to answer the questions to the best of his ability, but the prosecutor also is warned against badgering the witness.)

Mr. Claus, you said earlier that you live at the North Pole. Now everyone knows that the United States has sent many scientists to the North Pole and that it flies planes over the North Pole, but no one has ever found your house or your toy factory. Isn't that a bit unusual?

A. No.

Q. Now, I have read that you tour the world on Christmas Eve, traveling in a sled pulled through the air by eight reindeer. Do you expect us to believe that?

A. It's true and I'd like you to believe it.

Q. But reindeer can't fly!

A. Mine can.

Q. I'll pass that and ask you how you can carry toys for millions of children in one sled?

A. It isn't easy starting out, but things are a bit more comfortable after I'm half through. I don't have doll legs sticking in my neck.

Q. Another thing I read about you is that instead of entering homes by doors, you land on rooftops and slide down chimneys. Are you going to stick with that story?

A. Oh. That's a bit exaggerated. I still use the chimneys in some houses, but it's a dirty business and I'd prefer to use the regular entrances when there isn't any chance of being seen. You see, I'm kind of stuck with the legend myself. People expect me to use the chimney, so that's what I do when I figure there is any chance of being watched.

Q. If you slide down chimneys and then, by some magic, you fly back up, how come your suit is such bright red?

A. Mrs. Claus, God bless her, is in charge of keeping my suits clean.

Q. I notice that throughout this questioning, you have had a pipe in your mouth. Don't you think it would be more dignified if you avoided smoking in a court of law?

A. I'm not really smoking. I gave that up for health reasons centuries ago. But the pipe is another part of the Santa bit, and I feel I owe it to my public to keep it in my mouth.

Q. If this court rules that you are what you say you are, what will you do for me on Christmas Eve?

A. Stuff your stocking with coal!

AN INSTITUTION WITH TRADITIONS

A truly inventive man is one who can call his wife from the office every day and have something new to say.

But the average man has such a stereotyped conversation that he could put it on a tape recorder and play the tape when his wife answers the phone.

The words may vary, but they would go something like this: "Hi! What are you doing? Anything new? How are the kids? Any mail? Need anything on the way home? See you later."

On the theory that such conversations need not always be the same, one might strive to be more interesting by throwing in such snappy remarks as these: "Town certainly is crowded today." Or for more variety: "Town certainly is quiet today." Or—and this admittedly is reaching —one might remark: "Town is just about normal today."

Of course, not all the blame for conversations being conventional should rest on the male. Wives do their bit by giving uninspired answers to the male's dull questions. Thus, this produces this type of office— home conversations:

Husband: "Hi. What are you doing?"

Wife: "Nothing exciting."

Husband: "Any mail?"

Wife: "Just a few bills."

Husband: "Nothing else to report?"

Wife: "No."

Husband: "How are the kids?"

Wife: "Making trouble as usual."

Husband: "Need anything on the way home?"

Wife: (Optional answers:)

"No."

"Yes, we're low on bread."

"Yes, we're almost out of milk."

"Yes, we need milk and bread."

As commonplace as these conversations may seem, the calls are absolutely essential to husband and wife. Failure to call causes many men to feel they have somehow failed one's marriage vows. And with most wives, the lack of a phone call virtually proves that love is either fading or is completely gone.

When one of the youngsters answers the phone, the calls can take on new dimensions. Depending on how busy Dad happens to be when he places the call, the children seem to sense how much time he can afford to spend on the phone and then begin a filibuster aimed at exceeding the time limit.

Almost without exception, the children will show a marked reluctance to calling their mother, and will ask Dad to buy something on the way home from work. And it won't be milk or bread.

Most men make a habit of calling home about the same time every day. To vary this routine causes all kind of consternation.

A call from the office to the home ahead of schedule immediately requires explanations:

"What's wrong?" is one possible reaction. Or: "How come you're calling so early?"

The "just thought I'd call" explanation sounds rather weak, but it is the truth. One may go into detail by adding something like this: "Oh, I'm having a slow day for a change and I thought I'd surprise you." This isn't very exciting or sparkling, but the truth should have some value.

A later-than-usual call requires similar explanations. The "too-busy-to-call-earlier line" is not too helpful in this situation.

The regular telephone call can be started and concluded in about two or three minutes, but there are times when the calls run into a snag. For instance, a busy signal has been known to drive some men to tears. And a phone that is not answered is an invitation to the imagination to think up thousands of reasons why the wife could not pick up the receiver. Most of these, naturally, are very sinister.

Suffice it to say that the office-to-home call is an institution with its own traditions. More could be written on the subject, but right at this moment the author has something important to do. He has to call home.

June 1, 1969

DEPUTY READY FOR DUTY

After all, I never pretended to be sophisticated. So it was a bit of a thrill to be sworn in last week by Sheriff Joseph Wincovitch as Special Deputy No. 814.

Sure, there are hundreds of persons who have been deputized by the current sheriff and his predecessors. It's not exactly an exclusive honor.

But I could still feel the surge of authority as I took the oath to obey and defend the laws of the Commonwealth of Pennsylvania. Special Deputy No. 814 was ready for duty.

Yet in all fairness I must point out that there are a few reservations to my availability. For instance, if it's all the same to the sheriff, I'd rather not get called out at night or weekends. And if there is any danger of violence, I think some of the more experienced deputies should be sent out. Don't give the rough jobs to the new men.

Then there is this matter of guns. I never did like them very much, and I have no intention of carrying one now. I'd rather be the deputy who stays behind in town when the posse rides out after the bank robbers. After all, someone has to look after things at home.

Another hang-up that I feel the sheriff should know about is that horses and I have never been very friendly. If the new job means galloping off to Dodge City, I'd rather go in my station wagon. I tried riding horses some years ago, but could never feel comfortable in a saddle. And I always had the impression that the horses weren't very comfortable either.

So if all these things are clear to the sheriff and he still wants me, Special Deputy No. 814 is ready for duty.

While I'm waiting, however, I intend to let my imagination work out the details of my career as the country's newest lawman.

The first vision I came up with was of Chester limping down the road in search of Matt Dillon. That wasn't quite what I had in mind so I clicked to a different channel. Then I saw Gabby Hayes riding over a dusty trail on a jackass. Again, it was the wrong image. Obviously, I was going to have trouble with typecasting.

I decided to begin the transformation by teaching myself to think like a lawman. Here I had a bit more luck. I began to see violence from a policeman's viewpoint. And I wondered why the average cop risks his life for a very modest pay.

This line of thinking brought me to the stark realization that being a special deputy carries no salary. My resolve not to get involved in any violence became stronger. After all, the only weapon I have is a card in my wallet, and I doubt whether this would help me through a riot. A can of mace might be more useful.

Dreaming about a career as a lawman involves a lot of random thoughts. I wonder what a good horse would cost—and whether I could keep him in my garage. Then, too, how much would a pair of six shooters cost? Also, don't forget to get a good Zane Grey book at the library. And make a note to watch all the western shows on TV. Check the late shows on TV to see if any of the old Western movies are being shown. And saunter down to the saloon as often as possible.

Being a lawman opens up other lines of thought. As a father, I wonder whether I might use my new authority at home. For instance, when a kid steps out of line, charge him with disturbing the peace. I could clog the courts with such cases.

Special Deputy No. 814 has no intention of protecting homesteaders, sheep ranchers, or the small ranch owner who is being squeezed by the crooked banker. I'll leave those jobs to the sheriff.

I'm just going to meander down to the corral with my portable typewriter. My true ambition in life is to have the fastest typewriter in the East.

June 22, 1969

COUNSEL ON PART-TIME JOBS

The season of part-time jobs and temporary employment is here again.

And with a bit of experience in the field, I'd like to do some counseling on pitfalls to be avoided.

The first rule: Never become a potato sorter.

Some years ago, with a few friends, I signed up to sort potatoes on a railroad car in Scranton. The owner had bought the carload cheap because the shipment was going bad. It was our job to get rid of the decaying potatoes.

Anyone who has ever smelled a rotten potato can imagine what the working conditions were aboard an enclosed boxcar parked in the hot sun.

On the way home to Jessup that evening, we potato sorters had the rear of the bus to ourselves, although there were people in the front. When I arrived home, I was informed that my career as a potato sorter had ended and—to make the decision conclusive—my mother threw out my cruddy working clothes.

The second rule: Never become a delivery boy for a shoe repair shop unless you first study the world's major religions.

As a youth, I signed on to deliver shoes for a downtown Scranton repair shop. In due time, I was dispatched to a home in East Scranton to make a delivery.

The woman of the house responded to my knock on the door by yelling for me to let myself in. Then, from some corner of the house that I couldn't see, she directed me to go to a closet and find her purse. She told me to take the money I needed along with a ten-cent tip. The voice then told me to let myself out.

At the time, I thought she was some kind of a nut who endangered the contents of her purse with a kid she couldn't even see. How was I to know that my customer was an Orthodox Jew and could not handle money on Saturday, her Sabbath?

Thus, it's a good idea to get checked out on religious matters before starting to deliver shoes.

The third rule: If you are going to work as a railroad laborer, pick a nice day to start.

I went to work for the Erie Railroad on July 28, 1945. It was a miserable day, with frequent showers drenching the crew and the temperature well below comfortable levels. After a shift of carrying rails and swinging a sledgehammer, I went home cold, wet, and exhausted.

When the alarm went off the next day, I made a snap decision to roll over and abruptly end my career as a builder of railroads. Instead, I decided to go to college. After all, someone has to write the newspaper columns and this work is done indoors.

I can remember the date of my one-day railroading career because it occurred on the same day that a plane slammed into the Empire State Building. It was just a bad day all around for American transportation.

My sporadic work record included many other posts, including dishwasher at resort hotels, clerking in grocery stores, operating a teletype machine at a newspaper, operating a cutting machine in a pocketbook factory, and serving as an office boy for newspapers and wire services.

Without exception, these posts prove my final rule: Don't expect to get rich with temporary employment.

But a variety of jobs sometimes help a person find his vocation.

As a paperboy, my newspaper career was at jeopardy right at the outset. On a cold, windy, winter day I fell on ice as I was delivering along my route. The seat of my pants was wet because I broke through the ice on a small puddle. With tears in my eyes, I watched the wind blow the papers in every direction.

I abandoned the papers and went home, making a lot of customers quite unhappy. But it was only a temporary retreat.

Now, after years of experimentation, I know that once the bug of journalism bites, newspaper work is a hard habit to shake.

CHILDREN WINNING THE BATTLE

In the constant war that is being waged between children and adults, the driveway ranks among the major battlegrounds.

And, I am sorry to report, fathers and mothers are losing valuable ground right under the eaves of their homes.

I know that I have already lost this battle, and now my children let me use the driveway—provided I acknowledge it to be their territory. And much the same applies to the garage, which was once my very own.

Parents are apt to lose such battles simply because they are too complacent. The first thing they must recognize is that children don't fight orthodox wars. They harass, subvert, propagandize, and wear down the opposition. In other words, they kill off your spirit even before you know you are engaged in a fight.

Now take this matter of a driveway, for instance. The kids never announce that they want to own that narrow strip of land. Instead, they open the war by littering it with a wide assortment of items such as bicycles, baseball bats, sweaters, and baby brothers. They know that some parents may survey this scene of assorted litter and immediately park in front of the house.

But if the parent is made of more hardy stock, he will bark commands to the nearest children to clear the driveway. Most of the children will melt into the foliage. But the ones who are caught out in the open will adopt strategy No. 2. They will resort to harassment, by picking up items as slowly as possible, and invariably will try to overlook one or two stray pieces.

Another trick they might employ is to obey the letter of the command by moving everything as ordered—but violating its spirit, by moving everything just inches off the driveway. Children will fight with every weapon, including endangering their own lives, to carry out a war of nerves. This has many variations, but the chief method is to stand so close to a moving car in the driveway that the driver loses his nerve to continue. Or they may race alongside or immediately behind the moving car to achieve the same result.

While much of the war is fought in the driveway, the real prize is in the garage. If it is a two-car garage, the children will scorn their assigned side in favor of the side where the family car is supposed to be parked. And if there are two cars in the family, only one is permitted into the garage. Formal studies have been made to try to determine why children want the garage space reserved for the family car, and about the most logical explanation is that they love the oil slick on the floor.

One of the things that adults must realize about the driveway war is that children will disarm the opposition with a pretense of friendliness. Thus, their shout of "Hey, Mom! Dad's home," is really a coded message that means: "Here he comes! To the barricades!" Then they line up—some on foot and some on bicycles—and block the entrance to the driveway.

The first wave of troops will fall back as the car approaches, but will be prepared for many distracting maneuvers. For instance, kids will dart across in front of the car, content in their knowledge that fathers will never really run them down. Or they may drive their bikes ahead of the car, just to slow the car's pace.

It matters not that the car is eventually parked in the garage. The point of the battle is that Dad has been worn down a bit more, and the children have come a day closer to the time when he will park the car on the road and leave the driveway to them.

The best that a parent can do is try to hold the driveway until the children grow up and own their own cars. Then they will park their vehicles in the driveway and the war will be officially concluded.

If one wants a more immediate end to the fight, then get rid of the family car. This seems to placate the kids and they never go near the driveway.

February 1, 1970

MAN WHO SMASHED MOLLIES

On Friday the 13th of December 1889, a 53-year-old industrialist closeted himself in a hotel room in Washington and killed himself.

The bullet that slammed into the brain of Franklin B. Gowen ended the life of the principal figure in the destruction of the Molly Maguires.

Gowen died 20 years after Pennsylvania had hanged the twentieth person who was alleged to have committed a crime while a member of the Mollies.

His death touched off a rumor that some former members of the secret society murdered him to avenge the deaths he had caused on the gallows. But the facts were so clear that he had shot himself that the theory evaporated.

What recalls this bit of history is that a movie had its world premiere in this area last week. It tries to tell the story of the Molly Maguire movement. But in some ways, the story is just too big for a movie screen.

For instance, Gowen is only briefly pictured in the movie as a spectator at an Irish football game. But one could easily forget that he was even in the film. Yet, without Gowen, there could never have been a story about the Mollies.

As an industrialist, he built the Reading Railroad into one of the largest corporations in the nation. And as head of a firm that had big investments in anthracite mining, he hired the Pinkerton Detective Agency to break up a lawless element which was terrorizing the area. It isn't by accident, however, that most of the terror was directed at coal companies and their bosses.

One could very easily question Gowen's motives. While he fought the Mollies on the pretext that he wanted to save the people of the area from the terroristic organization, it's clear that most of the acts blamed on the Mollies were directed against the mining interests.

Gowen was elected district attorney of Schuylkill County in 1862, and several violent crimes went unsolved and unprosecuted during his term. No crusader then, he found little challenge in the prosecutor's job, and resigned in 1864 to devote full time to his private law practice.

As a Pottstown attorney making about $18,000 a year, he bought his way out of serving in the Union Army. But tragedy struck him in 1865, as his only two sons died of illness and a brother in the army was killed.

A legal staff position with the Reading Railroad opened the door for Gowen to climb to the top of that firm. He guided its growth as a major producer and hauler of anthracite.

By standards of that day, Gowen was not considered to be too violent an enemy of labor. In fact, he talked other operators into accepting a contract that was the first written agreement drawn up between miners and operators in America. But the deeper he became involved in corporate affairs, the more he became troubled by the lawlessness that so often was directed against the industry.

Finally, in 1873, he hired Allan Pinkerton to break up an element of Irish immigrant workers whom he referred to as the Molly Maguires. In this era the same workers, banded together in secret terror groups, were called the Buckshots, or Sleepers. Back in Ireland, where the enemies were the landlords, the advocates of revolution by terror were also known as the Mollies, the Ribbonmen, and the White Boys. But by any name, Gowen wanted to get rid of them.

A Pinkerton agent, James McParland, became the undercover spy for Gowen. For three years he supplied enough information, for $12 a week, to hang 20 men and imprison 26. In addition, some workers who wanted to escape the gallows pointed accusing fingers at others and helped to convict their friends—while being granted immunity from prosecution.

In the process, many an innocent person was convicted and some guilty ones were turned free. But Gowen, who actually went into court to serve as a public prosecutor, achieved his goal of smashing the opponents of the mining companies.

Gowen's career tumbled in the years ahead. The Reading Railroad went into bankruptcy and slipped from his control. He wound up his career working as a lawyer.

Ironically, while Gowen ended his own life—some say because he was haunted by the men he had hung—McParland, the undercover spy, remained with the Pinkerton firm and lived to the ripe age of 75. He died 50 years ago—on May 18, 1819—in Denver.

Now that the Mollies are being glorified on film, there is a danger that the truth about the period of capitalism verses unionism will be further obscured by myths.

The story of the Mollies simply cannot be understood without first knowing about Franklin B. Gowen.

June 7, 1970

MONGREL LACKS CLASS
BUT RESPECTS COLUMN

One recent evening, while viewing the animals in a local pet shop, I noticed a very fancy French poodle bearing a price tag of almost $100.

Then I happened to notice that there was newspaper beneath her cage—for hygienic purposes.

Now I would consider this a very ordinary arrangement in most instances. But in this case the newspaper happened to be the *Sunday Times*, and it was opened to a page carrying my column. And the column area was very definitely darker than the rest of the page.

I considered the discovery an affront, because while I don't mind studied criticism, I don't like having my spirits—or my column—dampened. And that goes double when the dampening agent is a French poodle.

Now, before I am set upon by a pack of poodles or their owners, let me say that every person has a right to this own likes and dislikes. I happen to prefer mongrel dogs who let their hair grow the way nature intended. It's OK with me if someone else prefers dogs that would trade character and dignity for a fancy haircut. I am ready to concede that I have the most homely mongrel in the world. But this blob of mixed genes, flab, and shaggy hair is too interested in the people in our house to be concerned about her looks. And my Candy may not have much class, but she wouldn't desecrate one of my columns. (At least, I like to cherish that thought.)

My dog does very little besides sleeping, eating, and barking at squirrels. If I were to give her a haircut and manicure, put a jeweled collar on her neck, and call her "Fifi," I'm sure she would bite me. And it would be a well-deserved bite.

Candy should not exclude any sex appeal because—as sophisticated dog owners put it—she has been "fixed." The only trouble with this arrangement is that we have several swinging dogs in our neighborhood with questionable moral codes. They would like to make our Candy into an ordinary strumpet, but they are wasting their time. She's not THAT kind of dog.

In fact, these dogs would be better off seeking some fancy "Fifi" and let Candy free to chase squirrels.

I haven't figured out whether Candy actually has a high moral code or a terrible ignorance, but whatever it is, she's a clean-cut, all-American mongrel, and I don't want her falling in with bad company.

During the recent Democratic primary election, Ed Lavelle, Archbald's gift to politics, wanted to use Candy as a prop in pursuing his campaign for governor. He had read about the dog in the previous column and figured it would be cheaper to borrow her than to buy a new animal.

Since Lavelle was an also-ran in the contest, my refusal to loan out my pet apparently did little to change the course of the state's political history. As much as I respect Candy, I don't think she could have helped the Lavelle campaign. And since Candy doesn't warm up quickly to strangers, she might actually have bitten Mr. Lavelle. So it probably all worked out for the best.

In any case, Candy is uninterested in politics, sex, and many other things. But when I come home from work and the kids are too engrossed in television to say hello, Candy always waddles over and jumps up on me —even though it's hard for her to defy the law of gravity. So I can forgive her disinterest in haircuts, manicures, jeweled collars, and other fancy finery.

In fact, the only demand that I do make on her is that she keep her thoughts to herself on my writings. There are just too many "Fifis" in this world who are ready to criticize something before they read it. If they must be so vulgar, let me desecrate their own pedigree papers. Candy doesn't need any fancy papers to prove her worth.

June 21, 1970

ICE BOXES DISCOURAGED
BETWEEN-MEAL SNACKS

In looking around for a way to illustrate how life has changed in the past few decades, one could not find a better point of reference than the kitchen refrigerator.

This gleaming metallic monster—usually the biggest single item in the kitchen—permits families to stock perishable foods in large amounts, making it possible to do the marketing as little as once a week.

Now consider the old iceboxes that chilled milk, butter, and a bit of leftover roast in small storage compartments, making it mandatory to buy perishable foods almost daily.

The replacement of the icebox by the refrigerator changed the buying habits of American homeowners.

"You have to go to the store to get something for supper," was an order that broke up many a ball game or marble contest. (I use the word "supper" because that was what the evening meal was called in that era.) But now the freezer compartment has a variety of foods ready for several evening meals.

Refrigerators today are stocked with cold drinks, popsicles, and ice cream in such a routine fashion that such treats have lost some of their appeal. The old iceboxes might have contained a pitcher full of lemonade and a hunk of watermelon, but popsicles and ice cream were available only at the store.

The automatic refrigerators have replaced iceboxes so thoroughly that the relics of another era are hard to find—except for those still being used in spartan cottages. In fact, millions upon millions of iceboxes have disappeared with barely a trace. They don't clutter up the landscape like used refrigerators, because they were made of wood and they have been chopped up for firewood or have rotted into nothingness.

As iceboxes were phased out of existence, one never heard of them becoming menaces to human life—probably because they were too small for children to hide in and accidentally close the door. In any case, they probably weren't airtight. But abandoned refrigerators frequently became

27

tombs for children, as careless adults leave them unguarded with doors intact.

Iceboxes may be hard to find these days, but their memory lingers on. And the most vivid part of the memory is the work that they involved. Ice had to be deposited in the top compartment and the pan of water on the floor had to be emptied regularly.

No person who ever performed the job can forget the skill that was required in carrying a pan—filled to the brim with water—from the icebox to the kitchen sink. The penalty for forgetting the job was to find a puddle of water on the kitchen floor in the morning.

The icebox was based on the scientific principle that ice absorbs heat and hot air rises. Thus, as the ice in the top of the box absorbed heat, the cooled air flowed downward to the food compartments. (There also was an economic principle that only the affluent families bought ice in the winter, because there was plenty of natural refrigeration available on windowsills, back porches, and other such places.)

I checked an encyclopedia to find out how long ice has been harvested in the winter for use in the warm weather, and found that the Chinese were doing it in 1000 B.C. And New England shipowners were hauling ice as far away as India in the 1800s. So there was nothing uniquely American about the icebox. Yet it was never as big a business anywhere else as it became in America.

The iceman—who was often the coal man in the winter—carried blocks of ice to kitchens on his daily rounds. Some companies passed out cards that were hung in windows to tell the ice man how big a piece of ice was needed. If the ice block was too large, the top wouldn't close on the icebox, and a dishtowel would have to be draped over it to slow down the melting.

Youngsters may not have had home freezers stuffed with summer treats, but they did have hunks of ice given to them by generous icemen. So there were compensations for living in an era when kids were pulled out of a ball game to buy meat and other items for supper.

Don't get me wrong. I like our big refrigerator with its large freezer. But it was easier to stay on a diet in the days of the icebox. That's really what caused me to write this piece.

MEMORIES OF ROOSTER
RULE OUT FARM LIFE

I would make a terrible farmer, because I'd get too friendly with my animals to ever be able to send them off to be slaughtered.

I know that dumb beasts were put on earth to serve man, and that one should try to keep his perspective about such things. That's why I am not a vegetarian and I hold no grudges against persons who raise animals to be slaughtered.

But if you don't mind, I'd rather not get too close to any animal that I might wind up eating for dinner.

I don't have to consult a psychiatrist to uncover any subconsciousness. It is "Whitey," our old rooster.

In going back to my childhood, I can remember clearly the few chickens that an older brother began to raise as a hobby. Now most of the chickens knew they were chickens, but Whitey acted more like a member of the family. He pranced around our yard as though he had purchased it.

Whitey could chase away a cat or repel a dog with mighty wings flapping, a few rapid pecks, and a great deal of loud clucking and screeching. And his other claim to fame was that he could perch himself on a clothes-line for a couple of minutes before losing his balance and flapping down to the ground in a storm of feathers.

The miniature chicken farm produced an occasional egg, some crowing early in the morning, and a lot of work. The population also included another rooster and about four hens, in addition to Whitey.

But a neighbor's dog cut down the hen population on several forays, one chicken got sick and died, and the general nuisance level of the surviving birds outweighed their value. So some person in authority—I was never sure who it was—gave the order to phase out the chicken farm.

Being practical, the plan involved placing poultry on the family's menu on several occasions. But the idea proved to be difficult to carry out. For instance, no one in the house had the courage to serve as the executioner, so a hardy neighbor was drafted on the job. (Naturally, as a youngster, I was not old enough to be consulted on family matters. I did not know of the wipeout plans while they were being framed.)

Thus, the day came when a delicious meal was placed on the table. It included stewed chicken, dumplings, and other mouth-watering foods. But everyone began skipping the chicken. I forget how it happened, but the word was finally passed that the chicken on the platter was actually "Whitey."

The meal was a disaster. No one would nibble on the family mascot. So if the body of "Whitey" was desecrated, at least his spirit was treated with honor.

The lesson I learned from this incident was never to get involved with any sort of animal that might wind up on your dinner table.

In that era most chickens were bought complete with feathers and innards. Thus, meal preparation included plucking feathers loosened by hot water.

But chickens today come in plastic packages that are so neat and sterile that a youngster might get the idea that chickens are made in a factory instead of raised on a farm. There is no danger of anyone becoming emotionally involved with a precut, prepackaged chicken that is often in so many pieces that a surgeon could not put it back together again.

But these nameless ex-birds lined up neatly in the supermarket meat case probably had very little talent or character. I bet not one of them could sit on a clothesline or chase a cat or dog out of the yard.

Yes, I can remember the day when a chicken was REALLY a chicken. And I remember "Whitey."

HOUSEPLANTS SURVIVE
EVEN THOUGH SLIGHTED

If there were any medical centers with intensive care units for house-plants, I could recommend a few emergency cases.

Plants at our home have seen the face of death many times, but somehow escape its final cold grasp.

In fact, if there were such a thing as a Society for the Prevention of Cruelty to Houseplants, its officers would probably surround our home and make us surrender all our plants immediately—or face a shoot-out.

It's not that our plants are not loved; it's simply that they are so taken for granted that they don't always get the best care. If God had given them vocal chords, they might force a cry for help out of their parched water ducts. But instead, they suffer with the silence of medieval mystics.

Our plants grow in soil that at times takes on the characteristic of Vermont granite. But then they are watered and the soil becomes like something out of the Okefenokee Swamp. In fact, our plants have come close to death from dehydration so often that they probably regard their watering process as some sort of plant-world last rites.

Through the rigors of such a cycle, our plants have shown such a tenacious grip on their plant souls that scientists interested in uncovering the mysteries of life might very well begin by studying them. The efforts to start life in a test tube have been exceeded in reverse in our house by philodendron that absolutely refuse to die.

It's true that from time to time, during some terrible droughts, one or more leaves may shrivel up and die, but the main portion of the plants live on. Some of our specimens have survived for many years in this manner. It's not a record to rival that of the California Redwoods, but it must be some sort of record in the houseplant world. (The only trouble is that nobody keeps such records on the lowly houseplant.)

There was a time, before our house was so heavily populated, when our plants were actually pampered. They were bathed regularly, had their leaves shined, had their wild branches trimmed, and had their roots fed all sorts of nutrients. But as the competition for time became more

31

intense, the plants lost more and more ground to children. Yet, for such pampered little things, they did show amazing ability to face hard times.

The hazards are not merely those of neglect. There are the overt acts of aggression, such as one of the children shredding a few leaves when there isn't anything better to occupy his time. Or there is the careless knocking over of a plant, spraying the room with dirt.

Yet our plants have withstood the theft of their leaves with barely a shudder. And many times, a de-potted plant has been picked up off the floor, its leaves bearing more soil than its roots. Then, with broom and a dustpan, the soil is regathered and sprinkled around the roots. Finally, the plant is doused with water and placed on a windowsill to await the healing hand of nature. About the only extra help it receives is a quick prayer. Then—oh, sweet mystery of life—it starts growing again.

There are persons who lean toward plastic plants. But I have the feeling that plastic plants would somehow die in our house.

Anyway, I prefer the come-from-behind live plants that can survive in our home and—at certain magical moments—can even burst into bloom. Humans can learn something from this kind of spartan determination.

We all can learn how to become hardy soil brothers.

OLD MOVIE MONSTERS
NO LONGER TERRIFYING

I looked forward, with fearful anticipation, to seeing a late show TV presentation of the old movie, *The Invisible Man*.

I clearly recalled seeing this Claude Raines thriller when I was a youngster and it scared me half to death. And I mean SCARED.

To put this in its proper perspective, bear in mind that the movie was a hit more than three decades ago. I went to see it with an older brother, but I spent a good part of the show hiding behind the seat in front of me. Though I missed much of the movie and I had completely forgotten the plot, the memory of my terror will remain with me forever.

Now the movie was going to be shown on TV and I could hardly wait to enjoy a fresh infusion of fear. I felt that the years had matured me so that I could watch the movie without flinching. But I also anticipated being scared again. It was like waiting in line to ride on a big roller coaster.

But, a horror of horrors, the ancient film wasn't at all as I had remembered. As Claude Raines materialized and dematerialized, I could not understand why the film had frightened me so much when I was a child. The disembodied bandages floating about the screen seemed oddly cornballish in 1971. In fact, it was about as frightening as TV commercials showing enzymes chewing into dirt and a disconnected arm emerging from a washing machine, clutching a bleach tablet.

This disappointment with *The Invisible Man* was about the biggest I have experienced by watching TV revivals of films I had remembered as being very scary. But it was far from my ONLY disappointment.

Consider the old movie, *The Picture of Dorian Gray*. It had a scene involving a sudden presentation of a horrible face on a canvas, all distorted by age and evil. The first time I saw the film the scene stood my hair on end. You couldn't ask for better entertainment.

But when I caught the movie on TV, the scare factor was gone. I'm not certain of the reason, but it could be because so many other movies have used that same gimmick—the sudden showing of a horrible face—

that the trick has lost its effectiveness. Or maybe I've simply become more used to ugly faces.

Then there was the old movie, *Jane Eyre*. There was a moment I could recall when a horse and rider came thundering through the English fog, and everyone in the theatre thought they were about to be trampled to death. But when I caught the show on TV, the zip was gone. In fact, I've seen more exciting scenes on the Lassie show.

Seeing another scary movie classic on TV also convinced me that Dr. Frankenstein's monster is just too well-known to frighten anybody again. And seeing Count Dracula in an old movie would not cause me to hold my hands on my neck for precautionary reasons. And Dr. Jekyll's other self, the Wolfman, and even King Kong just don't have it anymore.

Yet, there is a scene in which a tomato is shown on the Sesame Street TV show—accompanied by some eerie kind of music—that scares my four-year-old twins today. They take off and hide behind some piece of furniture until the tomato leaves the screen.

But don't ask me to explain why they are afraid of the Sesame Street tomato. (Being modern kids, maybe they fear that it has been sprayed with DDT or has been grown with nonorganic fertilizers.)

As for myself, very little I see on the screen can frighten me anymore. But one notable exception is the TV news show that depicts wars, riots, and other such things. Now that is SCARY!

June 20, 1971

SQUARE DAD NOT HIP
TO FOOTWEAR COMFORT

"No one wears THOSE THINGS anymore!"

That's a typical remark from a child after being told to put on a pair of overshoes.

"Everyone will laugh at me!" is the dire warning of another child when presented with the same problem.

It seems that the younger generation has banned overshoes, finding them to be too closely related to persons of the older generation to be acceptable to their feet.

"If I walked into school with those on my feet, I'd be laughed out of the building," is the way one of my kids explained the social problem involved.

"But they'll keep your feet dry," was my lame comeback.

"I'd rather have wet feet and friends than dry feet and be lonely," is the way my logic was defeated.

Anyway, most kids maintain that despite the weather, their feet will not get wet. "I don't need them to keep dry," they say despite the fact that rainwater is running six inches deep on the street.

"But your shoes will get wet and you'll catch cold," is another way of trying to reach the young with reason. All too often, however, they use even more deadly reasoning by answering: "So?"

In the midst of winter, when the slush goes halfway to their knees, girls will wear waterproof boots because they are fashionable. But boys will still insist that they don't need overshoes. It's as though someone has tipped them that the social disgrace involved is worse than pneumonia.

"Pneumonia can be cured with drugs, but there is no cure for the outcast label I'd have if I wore overshoes," is the explanation I once received.

With a twinge of envy for the independence of today's kids, I remember my own youth when a child wore overshoes if the sun had not evaporated all the morning dew off the grass. Of course, there was no social stigma attached because all the kids wore them. But I do think that our feet were overprotected from the elements.

What worries me most about this overshoe revolution is that it seems to be spreading to shoes and socks. More and more youth have abandoned socks—except for graduation ceremonies and other such events. And shoes are something that they keep trying to get rid of by losing them in the house.

"I can't find my shoes," is a common complaint in any house that has youthful occupants.

"Have you tried looking for them in the breadbox, or under your pillow, or in the china closet?" is my usual answer. But I really know that they are: (1) on the floor of the bathroom; (2) under the living room couch; or (3) under a bed. Actually, the only time shoes are really "lost" is when they are on a shoe rack in the child's closet. They may be there for months before they are found.

Dr. Freud would probably say that the reason children keep losing their shoes is that they really don't want to wear them anymore. In fact, I might say the same thing, judging by the number of bare feet one sees on today's youth.

"You'll step on a tack, get blood poisoning, and die," is a warning I sometimes issue when I see one of my offspring running around without shoes. But I get about as far with this warning as I do with my warning about overshoes and pneumonia.

And yet, when I try to go modern, things don't work out so well. I put on a new pair of sandals the other day, but made the mistake of wearing them over a pair of socks. "Dad, you shouldn't wear socks with sandals," I was told. Now I ask you, how should I know that such a rule even existed?

Oh, for the uncomplicated days when even white socks were socially acceptable.

MOHR AND GRUBER TOLD
THEIR SONG IS CORNY

The scene: The Triple Funk Music Co. in New York's Tin Pan Alley. A songwriting team, Father Joseph Mohr and Frank Gruber, are present with a copy of a new song. They are trying to sell it as a Christmas novelty number to Joe Snook, regarded as a genius in recognizing potential hits.

Mohr: "This little number came to me as I walked through the snow-covered hills in my native village in Austria on Christmas Eve in 1818."

Snook: "That's very nice, Father, but a song must have some gimmick—trick words, a new sound, or a shocking message—if it's ever going to climb the charts. It's got to go 'Pow!' Your number is too traditional."

Mohr: "Well, it tells the story about the birth of our Lord."

Snook: "That market's being saturated with 'Jesus Christ Superstar' and a lot of other Jesus stuff. They're killing a good thing. That's one of the problems of the music business—whenever anything clicks, everyone overdoes it."

Gruber: "I wrote the music for this number and I do think it has a quality that could make it an all-time favorite. And the fact that it was written for the guitar should make it more marketable with today's kids."

Snook: "Maybe you're right. I won't argue. But I can tell you that every composer that walks through that doorway says he has a tune that is certain to become next year's Golden Oldie. But there are only a few numbers like 'White Christmas' and 'Rudolph.'"

Mohr: "But this is more a religious song, a hymn, that could become a hit in every Christian country in the world."

Snook: "There just isn't a market for that kind of stuff anymore. It doesn't relate to what's happening today. Maybe if you could work in a drug theme it would have a chance. But your lyrics are too corny. Take the line, ". . . round yon Virgin Mother and Child . . . ." That's too corny for today's kids. With my apologies to you Father, I have to say that virginity is not a very big subject for songs these days."

Gruber: "Let me tell you of the reaction we've had on the song in our parish. Father Mohr worked out the words in his mind as he walked through the stillness of the Salzach Valley. Then he gave them to me, because in addition to teaching school in Oberndorf, I also play the organ at St. Nicholas Church. I worked up the tune, but because the organ was broken, I did it with my guitar. We introduced it at midnight Mass and it was a smash. The people loved it. They left the church humming the tune and some even were singing the simple words. So I say that if it clicked there, it would click on the open market."

Snook: "I don't want to kill your enthusiasm, but it takes more than that to make a hit tune. It's got to be done by a good group to start with. So we'd have to get someone like Three Dog Night or the Fifth Dimension to do the number. And somehow I can't see either showing any interest. You've got to get a record company to buy it and you've got to get radio stations to play it. All that involves a lot of hard selling. You just don't understand the business."

Mohr: "You mean we came all the way to New York just to be turned down?"

Snook: "Well, I don't want to give you any false hopes, Father. But I'll tell you what I'll do. If you can do certain things with the song, then come back and we'll talk business. First, try to get the Singing Nun to record it. That would help sell it. Then make a few changes in the lyrics. Try to work in some message about drugs or sex or something."

Mohr: "Well, I guess I could try . . . ."

Snook: "Oh yes, one other thing. Change the title. 'Silent Night' just doesn't hit me right. Maybe you could make it 'Son of Superstar.' That just might sell. Yea, I like that . . . ."

MEMORY FOR OLD AGE:
I SAW OSMONDS SING

You simply wouldn't believe the screams!

In fact, there isn't much else you would believe either about a concert featuring a singing group that appeals primarily to young girls—say from 4 to 14.

When the Osmond Brothers take the stage, it's billed as a concert, and I'm not about to quibble over the meaning of the word. If they say that all that amplified noise and foot stomping is a concert, then a concert it is.

I can remember the way the girls swooned over Frank Sinatra and the way they moaned over Elvis Presley, but I still was not psychologically prepared for the mass screaming that the Osmonds generate. The worshipping is so intense that I believe that if 14-year-old Donny Osmond was to order the girls to march on the nation's capital, the march would begin instantly.

I caught the Osmonds in concert at the Allentown Fair. My mission was to buy the tickets for my three daughters and a neighborhood pal, drive them to Allentown, and them drive them home. Since I couldn't very well do this without going myself, I got to see the Osmonds in person. While that was not very thrilling to me, it was educational.

For instance, I learned that Donny, the group's superstar, sends the girls into ecstasy by wiping sweat from his brow and then throwing the tainted towel into their midst. What the lucky girl who gets the towel does with it at home is something I haven't figured out yet. But two girls left the concert with such sweaty souvenirs.

I also learned that at the tender age of nine, Jimmy Osmond can stir female emotions with such earthy tones as "Long-Haired Lover From Liverpool" and "I Got a Woman." Due to his youth, he spends only a short time on the stage—an arrangement I am glad to endorse.

An Osmond Brothers' concert should be billed as a Heywoods-Osmonds concert because the Heywoods—"picked specially by the

Osmonds"—do the first half of the show. All the while they are on the stage, they lie about the momentary arrival of the Osmonds. Meanwhile, hawkers sell books to read about the Osmonds ($2), large posters depicting the Osmonds ($2), and binoculars to see the Osmonds ($1.50).

While the Heywoods, to untrained eyes and ears, are very much like the Osmonds, most of the thousands of girls at the concert treated them as obstructionists who were merely delaying the arrival of the real stars of the show.

Sad to say, persons who put on such concerts have borrowed an old trick from burlesque houses on how to peddle merchandise. During the intermission, they announce over the loudspeaker that Hershey bars being sold for 50 cents each include a few with lucky coupons good for an album of the bands' music. The trick worked, too, because many Hershey bars were sold. (I failed to find one winner in the crowd—making it appear that they adopted the old burlesque technique completely).

When the Osmonds ran onto the stage, I was somewhat limp after an hour of the Heywoods and about 15 minutes of intermission. But the sharp screams made me sit straight up again. Here, before my very eyes, were Alan, 23; Wayne, 21; Merrill, 19; Jay, 17, plus the more famous Donny. (Jimmy came a bit later).

Police had a hard time keeping the girls from swarming in front of the stage. After all, you can't use mace on a 10-year-old or use the nightstick on a 12-year-old. But the book hasn't been written on how cops are to regulate a mob composed entirely of sweet little girls.

Thousands of flashbulbs gave evidence of all the pictures that were being taken from the stands while the Osmonds were performing. (As usual, ours didn't turn out very well).

In number after number, there was instant recognition in the audience of the tune—but most were new to me. The speakers occupied a larger portion of the stage than did the performers. They threw sound waves right at me, making me wonder if I would ever have normal hearing again. But as I looked around, the danger to our hearing didn't seem to be worrying any of the girls in the audience. In fact, the only ones I could find to relate to were some elderly women sitting in wheelchairs in a special reserved section. They had been brought to the show as a "treat." But they glanced at each other with a bit of alarm in their faces, making me think that they were really going to enjoy the solitude of their usually lonely rooms later that evening.

As the Osmonds sang, their movements reminded me of Indians doing a war dance, African natives performing a tribal rite, a group of puppets moving on the same strings, or some sort of coordinated ant stomping.

But all that goes to show that I am much too old-fashioned to feel the magic of the Osmonds. When Donny sings his big hit, "Sweet and Innocent," he's unintentionally describing what you have to be to enjoy their shows.

In fact, maybe I should have bought one of those 50-cent candy bars. I might have won one of the albums. And then I could play it over and over to make myself like the music. But I still would do it wrong. I'd play it at a low noise level. And that would ruin the whole thing.

September 3, 1972

ANGRY HORNETS CAUSE
A FAMILY MELODRAMA

I became an expert on hornets a few evenings ago—but I did it the hard way.

I found myself in the midst of a swarm of them after one of my youngsters fell onto their ground-level nest, causing them to attack.

Now that it's over, it's easy to discuss it rationally, but while the attack was in process, it was like a scene from a horror movie. Thank God, it ended without anyone being seriously harmed. But it has made me swear that I will never laugh again at the sight of hornets chasing someone in comic strips or in movie cartoons. It's not a laughing matter.

One person who observed our family melodrama from a safe distance thought he saw a man beating a child, I learned a few days later. What he actually saw was me trying to swat hundreds (or were there thousands?) of the mean and stubborn wasps from my six-year-old son, Tom.

Since it's always best to tell a story from the beginning, let me start by setting the scene. I went with my family to visit relatives at a cottage at Newton Lake one evening last week. It was just about twilight when I went for a walk with my children down to the lake and amusement park.

After walking a few hundred yards, an approaching car forced us to move into the weeded area adjoining the roadway. Just then I happened to meet a friend walking in the same direction and we paused to talk. My back was turned to the children as they continued to walk along the road. Then the quiet was broken by a chorus of screams from my youngsters. As I turned, I saw them swatting at themselves and at each other—with their frantic behavior punctuated by many screams.

The light was too dim to be sure of what was happening. It was only after I ran to Tommy—who seemed to be the focal point of the excitement—that I could see scores of dark bugs on him. Because they were so hard to brush off, my first notion was that they were some sort of leeches that had attached themselves to the skin.

At a moment like this, one does not spend too much time thinking. Instinct takes over. It was this that caused me to rip off my nylon jacket and to use it to swat the bugs that I now could see on all the kids and in the air. Still unaware of the nature of the attack, I suddenly became aware of pain in my own left arm. I yelled for everyone to run back to the cottage. Tommy's arm was virtually covered with the "things," so I kept swatting at them. Then I scooped him up, wrapped him in my jacket and dashed for the cottage.

As we fled like an army under fire, many of the bugs continued to inflict painful bites. It seemed like hours before the cottage was reached —but it was only a few seconds. As we dashed inside, they must have thought we had all lost our minds. We couldn't even explain immediately what had happened because we didn't even know that we were being attacked by hornets. But we carried about eight of them into the cottage with us, so in the bright light we were able to identify the enemy.

During the next few hectic minutes, some of the terror of the attack remained as we hunted down and killed the stray hornets. Poor Tommy continued to cry and squirm until we removed his trousers and found a hornet trapped inside.

Aware that insect bites—and particularly the poisonous stings of hornets—can cause shock and even death, we sweated out the next few minutes. But while the bites caused some swelling, ice cubes and regular insect bite medication helped to ease the pains and return the situation to normal.

It was difficult to take an accurate inventory of the bites. Because some were so close together, it was hard to count all of them. Tommy was the most damaged with about eight stings. I had about four. Tommy's twin, Tim, had about two. Erin had two, Maureen had one, and Eileen escaped completely. Even the friend I had been chatting with received one.

A few days later, I met a cottager from the lake who had heard about the hornet affair. He also told me of the other story he had heard—the report that a person viewing the scene from a distance was sure he saw a man beating his child. That story hurt almost as much as my hornet bites.

NOTHING BEATS POTATO ROASTED ON OPEN FIRE

One of the joys of my childhood was to roast a potato in an open fire. But most kids are deprived of such a pleasure today.

Unaccompanied by adults, a group of youths would go to a clearing in an area far removed from homes. We would then build a nice fire, using wood, which was easy to gather in the general vicinity. We generally did it about this time of year, when the evening air is snappy.

Everyone would bring one or two potatoes and they would be put right into the flames. Mixed among the burning embers, they would be burned black on the outside.

But once pulled from the fire and cooled enough to handle, they would be cut open with a penknife—revealing a steaming mound of luscious white food that somehow tasted much better than a potato served at home.

Our only supplies would be a few spoons or forks and a saltshaker borrowed from home, plus the ever-present penknives.

A professional chef might faint at the sight of our blackened potatoes, and today's average child would have his parents arrested if they ever served them any such thing—but after all these years, my mouth still waters at the thought of this delicious treat.

Common sense also tells me that they must have been good, because there we were, a group of youths with no parents to dictate to us, and we ate them with great enjoyment.

As we ate them, our fingers and clothing became quite dirty from the charred potato skins. Inevitably, some of this smudge would get on the steaming white interior. And just as inevitably, the core of the very large potatoes would be still rather firm because they were not cooked long enough. But who ever said that a potato had to be mushy anyway?

At these impromptu potato roasts, we sometimes went a bit further by adding hot dogs to the feast. They were cooked on long sticks thrust into the flames or held over the glowing embers. Sometimes they got a bit charred, too—but they were always eaten anyway.

I even recall a few times when we brewed some coffee in a large tin can on the open fire. Using cups borrowed from home, we drank this terrible brew without sugar or milk, and with grounds that refused to settle to the bottom. Yet this also was relished as a treat.

Now, I know that organized youth groups may be doing much the same thing today—with a much higher degree of sanitation. But there is something special about a group of children getting together and doing this sort of thing on their own—without adults interfering. That adds to the appeal.

Obviously, it would be harder to do today, and we're all to blame. First of all, in cities and suburban areas, it's almost impossible for kids to find a nice safe spot where they could build a pleasant fire without being arrested by the police, being chased by neighbors, or being suspected of holding a cigarette, booze, or pot party. And even in rural areas, some of these same threats exist.

Secondly, the average parent—myself included—would fear that: (1) a child may be burned seriously while playing around a fire; (2) the food would not be sanitary; and (3) anyone drinking coffee cooked in a tin can should be sent to a hospital immediately to have his stomach pumped .

And finally, kids wouldn't eat a blackened potato, a burned hot dog, or a cup of black coffee with grounds. They have too many other goodies available to them in their own home freezers or cupboards to go to all that trouble.

Besides, how would one go about roasting powdered mashed potatoes that come in a box?

Let's face it. The potato roast is a victim of our modern way of living. It's sad, but true.

November 26, 1972

A BARK IN NEWSROOM
WOULD REVEAL SECRET

This is a true story. Honest, it is.

It began a few weeks ago in our newsroom at the *Times*. One of our reporters, who takes his lunch to work in a brown paper bag, left the lunch on his desk.

Another newsman, who's inclined towards practical jokes, thought it would be a dandy one to take the lunch and eat it.

So that's what he did. As he smacked his lips after wolfing down the sandwich and dessert, he casually told the hapless victim that his lunch was not only gone—but that it was really delicious.

Everyone had a good laugh, except the owner. He had to put his coat on and head for a nearby restaurant, where he mumbled almost incoherently through his new lunch, vowing to get even.

The victim went home and relayed the story to his wife. She didn't think it was very funny at all. It was bad enough that she had to pack a lunch for her husband, but packing one for an office prankster was carrying things too far.

Ordinarily, the story might have ended here—with the newsman being careful to put his lunch in his locker in the future.

But that would not take into account the inventive mind of the victim's wife. She was determined to strike back. So the next time she went to the store, she bought a can of Alpo dog food. That's a 100 percent meat preparation that looks and smells very much like an ordinary can of sandwich spread for humans.

She then used about half the contents of the can, spread it generously over a slab of bread, added a bit of lettuce and topped it with another slice of bread. It looked like a delicious sandwich made with a filling not unlike chopped ham.

The sandwich was carefully wrapped in wax paper and slipped into a brown lunch bag. A Hershey bar was added for desert. Her husband then carried the "lunch" to work and parked it in a very conspicuous spot on his desk. The hook was well-baited.

A few other newsmen were brought into the conspiracy, with their task being to urge the person who had stolen the first lunch to strike again. But as things often go with practical jokes, this didn't work according to the plan. The practical joker who was now the intended victim was reluctant at first to do anything. Then, just to satisfy the conspirators, he consented to take the lunch. But instead of eating it, he merely hid it.

To almost everyone's disappointment (by now, just about everyone in the office knew about the gag), the intended victim seemed determined to avoid the trap. He even grew weary of having the lunch hidden, so he retrieved it and returned it to the owner's desk.

Now you might think that the story ends here, but it didn't. From here on, fate began to guide the destiny of the botched practical joke.

The owner of the lunch gave up on trying to even the score—at least for the moment. Without meaning to be too corny, it might be said that he gave up because his intended victim "did not bite." So the brown bag containing the Alpo and lettuce sandwich and the Hershey bars was forgotten due to the press of deadlines. Thus, the lunch was still on the desk as the daytime workers went home.

The next day the lunch was still in the office—although on another desk. This caused some of the jokers to suggest that the trick be revived to again try to get the intended victim to eat the bag's contents.

Someone went to retrieve the bag, which was now beginning to look a little mangled. To try to make it look as good as possible, someone opened it up to straighten out the contents.

Then the discovery was made. The Hershey bar was there, alright. But half the Alpo sandwich was gone.

Now here we are, weeks later, trying to figure out who ate half of the Alpo sandwich. But maybe it's better that we never learn the person's identity.

However, if anyone in the office starts to bark one of these days, I think we'll at least have a prime suspect.

SUPPERTIME RULE:
EAT FROM THE MENU

Following is a typical conversation around the supper table of a family that includes six children, a wife, and a newspaper columnist:

What's for supper?

Steak, mashed potatoes, and green beans.

I hate green beans.

I don't like gooey mashed potatoes.

I hate steak.

Why can't we ever have anything good like hot dogs?

Yuck, I hate hot dogs.

Can I make a peanut butter sandwich?

No, you're going to eat what's on the table.

How come I get more beans than anyone else?

Like heck you do. I got two more than you did.

She just put some beans back when she thought no one was looking.

Please swallow what you have in your mouth.

May I be excused?

Not until you clean your plate.

But that's not meat—it's just fat.

There's more meat there than fat and I want you to eat it because there are kids in the world who . . .

I know . . . they are hungry. But it's not going to make them feel any better if I eat all that dumb stuff.

Eat it or sit there all night.

What these kids need is a good Depression to make them appreciate good food.

We forgot to say grace.

Great. Well, let's say it now.

(Many voices) Bless us, Oh Lord, and these thy gifts which we are about to receive through the bounty of Christ, our Lord, Amen.

We should say, which we ARE RECEIVING.

No, we should say, which we HAVE RECEIVED because I'm finished.

No, you're not. Not until you eat all of your meat.

But that's all fat.

I'm on a diet. Do I have to eat my potatoes?

Yes, you do. If you're on a diet, give up your dessert.

What's for dessert?

Nothing fancy. Just pudding and cookies.

I don't like pudding.

Well, don't eat it.

But that's not fair. Everyone else is getting dessert except me. I should get something else.

You might very well get SOMETHING ELSE if you keep it up.

These beans are cold.

They were hot when you got them an hour ago.

Boy, does Dad exaggerate. We're just sitting down here for a few minutes.

Long enough for your beans to get cold. If you ate them at the start, they'd be warm.

But I hate them.

This dessert is good.

Something is actually good. I think I'm going to faint.

Why can't we ever get through one meal without someone spilling a glass of milk?

It's all over my pants.

May we be excused before we get milk in our laps?

Yes. You, change those pants. You, get a sponge to clean up the booth.

Someone should feed the dog and someone else should do the dishes. Hey, where did everyone go?

Never mind. Let them go. It's so nice and quiet here. Let's enjoy this moment.

Candy, quit looking at me like that. I'll feed you now.

At least she likes what's on the menu.

October 28, 1973

HALLOWEEN WAS GREAT
IF YOU WEREN'T CAUGHT

It's a miracle we didn't get ourselves killed or at least put in jail.

The way we marked Halloween a few decades ago puts the lie to the claim that kids today are wilder than their parents.

Actually, I think just the opposite is true when it comes to Halloween —that holiday for pranksters which is due again on Wednesday.

Consider the night that we knocked over Farmer Paul's outdoor toilet. What we didn't know when we did it was he was in it.

First, I must write a few words about the victim of this Halloween prank. Now dead for a number of years and with no survivors, this farmer was known to get nasty only when he was drinking. But that covered a good deal of the time.

Often the victim of Halloween pranks, Pauly was not above picking up a couple of good size stones and throwing them in the direction of a group of fleeing boys who had thrown one of his own pumpkins against his door, or who had nailed shut the door to his outhouse—the only such facility in town.

On this certain Halloween night, a group of about seven neighborhood boys decided to have some fun spooking the neighbors.

We knocked on a few windows and it scared the daylights out of a few housewives and young kids. Some fright also was generated by a device fashioned from a large wooden spool from a sewing box. With notches carved in the ends of the spool, a stick of wood stuck through the middle, and a length of cord wrapped around it, the device could make a terrible racket on a window, as the string was pulled and the notches whirled against the glass.

At a few other homes, we marked-up windows with soap; we threw leaves on the front seat of parked cars; we rolled a large stone across a few porches; we dropped a few balloons full of water onto cars passing under a railroad bridge; we moved a pile of leaves onto the roadway to create a one-lane road; and we hid behind hedges until a pedestrian walked by and then we yelled like a bunch of wild men to scare the hapless person half to death.

Then, with our imagination just about exhausted, we wandered up to Pauly's farm to examine the possibilities there. Someone saw the outhouse glowing in the moonlight and thought that it might be worth trying to tip over.

So, quiet as mice, we crawled under the wire fence of the farm, made our way through the fields, and finally arrived at the outhouse. We remained quiet because we assumed Pauly was in the nearby farmhouse. Then, all assembled on one side, we gave a might push and over it went. Naturally, we were fleeing before it came to rest.

As we looked back over our shoulders, we could see Pauly crawling from the stricken building—somewhat dumfounded by the events, but still able to let out a few oaths in our direction that gave us the general idea that it would be prudent to continue running.

Pauly never did catch us. Indeed, he never even tried, because he was still having trouble hitching up his pants over his long underwear when we last saw him. But we still ran until we were exhausted on the chance that he might still be after us.

Exhausted because of our full evening of pranks, we went to our homes and went to bed—with most dreaming that Pauly was still chasing us.

To the best of my knowledge, Pauly never did find out who did this terrible trick. Indeed, if he had, I'm sure we would have paid a dear price. A powerfully built man who sometimes had to be restrained by police when he became drunk, he might have bashed in a few of our skulls in retaliation.

Fortunately, we escaped. But if one of my kids did anything like that today I'd think that they were out of their minds. And I'd punish them severely.

Do as I say—not as I did.

December 9, 1973

SHORTAGES BESETTING
HEAVENLY POPULATION

One might think that everything is perfect in Heaven.

But no, the inhabitants there are having their problems with shortages, too.

By peeking under the edge of a cloud, the following little drama was observed last week;

Angel No. 1: "If we can't find ways of slowing down the population growth here, there won't be a cloud left to sit on."

Angel No. 2: "Yes, they must have really relaxed the rules down there, judging by the way people are streaming through the pearly gates these days."

Angel No. 1: "What really worries me, though, isn't the crowded conditions, but the way we're running out of things. Just the other day I heard that they might start rationing harp strings."

Angel No. 2: "And they say that we are going to be able to enjoy the Beatific Vision only every other day because of scheduling problems."

Angel No. 1: "Remember the good old days when there were only a few people around and we angels had Heaven pretty much to ourselves."

Angel No. 2: "Yes, and at the start when they opened Heaven to humans, they said it would involve only a few high-type saints. But now they don't care who they let in, it seems."

Angel No. 1: "They say that this is because hardly anything humans do these days is regarded as sinful. So if they can't sin, they zip right up here as soon as they die."

Angel No. 2: "It makes one wonder if the Old Boy really knows what he's doing these days."

Angel No. 1: "I got a taste of the shortage problem the other day when I went to get some glitter on my wings. The operator of the shop said he's been out of glitter for a week and isn't sure when he'll get more. He tried to give me some spray paint that he said everyone is using instead of that old glitter. But I told him I would take real glitter or nothing. Then I walked out."

Angel No. 2: "They're having a lot of shortages down on earth and it makes me wonder if this is God's plan for preparing humans for the shortages up here."

Angel No. 1: "No, I think it's a general condition all over. I've heard that it's even happening in Hell. They say that there is a fuel shortage there that is so bad that the inhabitants are starting to wear sweaters."

Angel No. 2: " Well, I can tell you I'm having a little trouble getting used to Heaven being a chilly 68 degrees all the time. I hate myself for having such thoughts, but I can't help but wonder on cold nights if the fallen angels might be a bit more comfortable than we are. So, if they are having a fuel shortage there, I can't help being happy over it, at least."

Angel No. 1: "At the risk of being sacrilegious, why can't the Boss simply perform a bunch of miracles to cure all the shortages—especially those up here?"

Angel No. 2: "You'd better watch the way you talk, because I understand some of the clouds are bugged these days. Lucifer would never recognize the old place."

Angel No. 1: " I still say that the Boss could cure our problems with a barrage of miracles. And don't worry about this cloud being bugged. I checked it before I sat here."

Angel No. 2: " Well, if you're absolutely sure that it's safe to talk here, I can let you in on something that is really top secret. I have it right from an archangel that He can't produce all the miracles we need these days."

Angel No. 1: "You mean . . .?"

Angel No. 2: "Yes, he has used up so many of them in the past that there's a shortage of those, too."

December 29, 1973

SCROOGE'S THRIFTINESS
ANSWER TO OUR WOES

Could it be that Ebenezer Scrooge was merely the victim of bad public relations?

Is it possible that being a mean, miserly businessman, he was actually a man ahead of his time who knew that mankind was going to have to tighten its belt to survive?

True, Scrooge does not look too good in the Charles Dickens book, *A Christmas Carol*, but that may be only because he was espousing causes which were not popular in his era but which have since grown in popularity.

For instance, consider how right he was in trying to save fuel. His clerk, Bob Cratchet, no doubt would have thrown plenty of coal on the fire in his stove in the quarters of Marley and Scrooge if he were not afraid of Scrooge raising an objection. So Cratchet heated his hands at a candle so that he could keep his fingers nimble enough to continue writing in the ledgers.

Oh, how America could use more employers like Scrooge today as we struggle to save fuel. So what if a few employees suffer from frostbite? We would achieve the main goal of saving fuel.

Indeed, Scrooge might have made a wonderful fuel czar for the United States if he were alive today. He would have known how to put down those millions of Bob Cratchets who want nothing but creature comforts.

Scrooge might also have been a good person to put in charge of our welfare programs. In the story, he warned Cratchet and his own nephew that nothing—not even Christmas—was a substitute for an honest day's work. Today, President Nixon calls that the American work ethic, but it's the same thing.

If put in charge of our welfare programs, he no doubt would drastically cut benefits. Remember when solicitors visited his office and sought a contribution to help the poor? He asked if the jails and workhouses were still open. When assured that they were, he chased the solicitors away after saying that he was doing his bit for the poor by helping to finance the jails and workhouses.

Wouldn't this philosophy be music for some ears if it were espoused today? So what if a few Tiny Tims starved to death? The main goal of economy in government would be achieved.

Scrooge could even be put into higher government positions. For instance, wouldn't he make a wonderful secretary of labor? After a bit of whip-cracking, he could turn American workers into mass copies of Bob Cratchet—not only ready to work long hours in cold offices for low wages, but also ready to drink a toast to their employers on Christmas Day.

But since he was a businessman, Scrooge might have made a better secretary of commerce. With his high regards for the rights of business, he'd make sure that government didn't get too restrictive in enforcing its laws. Then we'd have no more scandals, because whatever businessmen did would no longer be considered to be wrong.

The talents of Scrooge might have made him a good person to enforce this year's White House request to douse the lights of Yule decorations. His classic comments of "Bah" and "Humbug" would help to put the holiday season in its proper perspective.

Scrooge also was ahead of his time in warning about the population explosion. He favored the idea of letting the poor die off as a way of curbing the crowded conditions of the city. What a marvelous idea!

I realize, of course, that Scrooge might have his enemies even today. There would be those who would fault him for believing in ghosts, for instance. But that would be a minor point compared to the good he could bring to government.

The alternative is to let some fuzzy-thinking liberals such as Bob Cratchet, Scrooge's own nephew, or old Mr. Fezziwig run our public affairs. Or, horror of horrors, we might even wind up with someone like Tiny Tim waving his cane around and uttering such nonsense as: "God bless us, every one."

Yes, Mr. Scrooge, we have finally reached the point in mankind's history when a person of your talents can really be appreciated.

SOCKS SHOULD COME IN THREES,
NOT PAIRS

Every sock drawer in America has in it some single socks that are doomed to remain forever separated from their mates.

Just how it happens that pairs of socks become divorced, with one disappearing, is a mystery that many great minds have pondered, but never have solved. Most of this pondering, incidentally, is done quite early in the morning as people get dressed for their daily tussle with life.

Maybe socks should be sold in groups of three instead of pairs. Then, when the day came when one disappeared, there'd be a pair left. (There are other more dramatic cures for the problem, too, but we'll get to those later.)

When socks come into a home, they arrive in perfectly matched pairs. Then they are worn as a pair and are thrown into a clothes hamper as a pair. From here they are moved to a washer and possibly to a dryer; they then are rematched, rolled into a neat ball, and placed in the sock drawer.

At least, that is the way it is supposed to work.

But there are times when the system breaks down and socks reach the sock drawer without their mates. So as the months and years go by, the sock drawer begins to fill up with single socks. There are times, of course, when a stray sock reappears as mysteriously as it disappeared. Then pairs can be reunited again. Maybe the stray sock was actually rolled up with an incorrect mate. Or maybe static electricity had caused it to stick to some other article of clothing, such as a shirt or blouse.

But more often than not, when a missing sock reappears, it does so as mysteriously as it disappeared—leaving no plausible explanation of where it has been for days, weeks, or even months. They just go away, some forever and some temporarily.

Not being superstitious, I'm not about to suggest that there are sock fairies running around the world, stealing at random. Nor do I believe that there is such a thing as a sock monster that devours them, clean or dirty. Nor do I believe that there are troubled spirits of dead humans prowling around the world, seeking the socks they were deprived of when they were alive. And despite the popularity of the movie *The Exorcist*, I refuse to put the blame on spirits from hell that steal socks instead of souls.

No, I think there is a much more logical explanation for the disappearance of socks. For instance, maybe the washer or dryer eats them. Or maybe the sock companies make some socks from vanishing yarn to spur their sales. Or maybe there are such things around as sock burglars. Since it's obviously impossible to solve the mystery here, maybe it would be a good idea to attack the problem from the other end: What can we do with single socks?

Well, communities could set up Single Sock Centers, which could serve as clearing houses for persons who want to clean out their sock drawers. One would try to match single socks there to create new pairs. But where this proves to be impossible, single socks would be left behind for other persons to try their luck.

The ultimate answer, however, will require passing a law requiring all sock manufacturers to produce a single style sock. It would be made of stretch yarn so that one size would fit all feet. And it would be produced in a single color. Thus, they would be identical in all respects.

This new universal sock would no longer have to be matched to a mate because it would match all the other socks, too. So if a sock disappeared, it could easily be replaced.

It may sound radical, but really, it's the only solution. So write to your legislators and sock it to 'em.

February 10, 1974

IN A FLASH,
HEARTBEAT OF REASSURANCE GONE

It was warm and comfortable in the womb. The baby didn't have a developed thinking process yet, but she knew what she liked and what she didn't.

For instance, when she got into an uncomfortable position, she knew that a good swift kick, a jab with an elbow, or even a poke with a fist could quickly correct the situation.

Maybe "knew" is too strong a word to describe the baby's mental abilities. But after four months in the womb, she could sense what she liked and what she didn't like as well as any baby three or six months after birth.

In the warm blackness, she loved the "thump, thump, thump" of her mother's heartbeat. She could feel it all around her as the blood coursed through her veins—and it made her feel secure.

In fact, if she ever entered the outside world, the heartbeat sound would still make her feel good in her first few years if her mother would cuddle her. And she wouldn't understand the reason then anymore than she does now.

At this time, in the womb, she was perfectly content. It wasn't a bad life, aside from being put into an uncomfortable position or being squeezed too much on occasions. And she already knew how to fight those things. She was never hungry. She was never frightened. She was warm. In other words, she was happy.

There was no way that this tiny unborn baby could know that her mother had problems. The mother was young and unmarried and she had become pregnant "by accident," as she put it.

Terrified at the prospect of having a baby, she had already left home and was living in a lonely room in a lonely city many miles from her parents—without the slightest notion of what she was going to do.

The baby, now fully formed, with blue eyes, blond hair, and rather long fingernails, had no way of knowing that she was a problem to the person who was carrying her. She still heard her mother's heartbeat and everything seemed normal. Although the act was involuntary, it often caused her to smile in the darkness.

How much did this tiny baby actually know about life? Well, whenever there was a quick movement of the womb, she recoiled to protect herself. And while she had it in her power to begin the birth process, she knew now that she should remain where she was—knowing that it was not yet time to make her debut.

The mother carried this bit of life with her one day to an address given to her by a person who had befriended her. The person had said that an abortion was the answer to all of her problems. In a few days, she'd be free of this terrible "problem" which she was carrying in her womb, and then she could return to her home and resume a normal life.

As the mother entered the white sterile world where more than germs are killed, the baby in the womb had no way of knowing that its hours were numbered. The "thump, thump, thump" of her mother's heartbeat was a bit faster than normal, but that meant nothing to her. It was still a reassuring sound and she loved it.

Then the horror began. Light entered the womb and it diffused through her closed eyelids. Cold steel entered, also. The baby dug her fingernails into her palms. But she had no way of resisting the tongs that dragged her out into the bright light.

There was a split second when she began to believe that she might be able to survive in the light. But it passed quickly as the chord was cut. Then the "thump, thump, thump" was gone.

And another bit of protoplasm was sent to the hospital's giant incinerator.

September 22, 1974

ED LAVELLE:
A MASTER OF GATE-CRASHING ART

Ed Lavelle was a true character in every sense of the overused word.

Ed, who died a week ago yesterday, departed from this world without much of the publicity that he so dearly loved. In fact, he was buried before newspapers reported his death. But if he had been involved in it, his wake surely would have been a spectacular affair.

In life, Ed always had displayed colossal nerve. Once, while running one of his many political races, the League of Women Voters sought out the biographies of the candidates to have them printed in a brochure. Ed submitted material spiced with outrageous claims, such as identifying himself as a world famous horse breeder and as a graduate of England's Oxford University. The material was printed as it was submitted, much to the embarrassment of the League of Women Voters, but much to the delight of Mr. Lavelle.

One of the difficult things to do in discussing Ed Lavelle is to pick out the facts from the fiction, which he was only too willing to have you believe. For instance, I know that the story of the election brochure is true because I saw it. And I know that he once had himself listed in the Scranton telephone book as "Governor Edward Lavelle," conning the telephone company with a fancy spelling of the office, which he once actually did seek.

I also witnessed Ed employing his mastery of the fine art of gate-crashing. The incident occurred during the inauguration of William W. Scranton as governor. Ed was in Harrisburg with many other Scranton residents, and he bravely announced that he planned to attend every function—tickets or no tickets.

Someone was foolhardy enough to bet him that he could not get into the fundraising event that was being held at Harrisburg's Zembo Temple. Well, the meal was barely under way before Ed was inside ready to collect his bet. He didn't explain how he got in without a ticket, but a clue was furnished by the fact that he was wearing an ornate fez and red blazer—the same costume that was being worn by other members of the order that owned the temple.

At any number of political-social affairs, when determined efforts were made to bar him, he would slip inside carrying his violin—an instrument that he could really play. Once inside, he would put the violin away in a safe corner and mingle with the crowd. But he delighted in telling the story of the night that he was squired directly to the bandstand and had to play half the night in the band before he was able to slip away and enjoy the party.

No affair was too big to frighten him away. For instance, he loved to go to the Democratic National Conventions, even though security there was a test of his ingenuity. The story is told that he once bet the late County Commissioner Michael F. Lawler that he would get into the convention hall. Then, due to really strict security, the Pennsylvania delegates —Mr. Lawler included—had great difficulty getting to their own assigned seats. But when they finally arrived, who was there to greet them? That's right, it was Ed Lavelle.

Ed knew the shock value of some of the more outrageous stories he told about himself. He claimed to have parlayed a racetrack accident—a horse stepping on his foot—into a court settlement that enabled him to buy a Cadillac. Then, he delighted in telling how gasoline station attendants looked at him in wonder as he pulled up in his big black car and asked them if they would cash a welfare check.

While he had the same car, he claimed that he hired a professional chauffeur, complete with uniform, just to drive him to church in his native town of Archbald. The whole point was to give the folks in Archbald a chance to see a successful native on a return visit.

Ed ran for many offices, including governor, and he even held out the possibility that he might take a whack at a presidential race someday. But beneath the veneer of pure gall was an amazing knowledge of politics. On occasions, he was able to take on an undercover political job for some candidate or party, although it was generally hard to tell when he was so engaged. I once told him I doubted a story he had told me about working for a certain political figure. So he enlightened me by showing me a $500 check he had received from the person.

There was nothing incongruous in Ed's eye in running for governor while hitchhiking to Harrisburg, wearing a dapper homburg hat. So if I received a postcard from Hyannisport, Mass., with Ed claiming he was there for a meeting "with the Kennedys," I felt it was an obvious bluff. Yet, I know that he once crashed a presidential inaugural ball and wound up dancing with Margaret Truman and the wife of Tom Clark, then U.S. attorney general. So who was to say he couldn't crash the Kennedy family circle?

Ed often sends me postcards from places such as Miami, New Orleans, and Boston, with short messages, such as that he was checking on his investments or was about to close some major "deal." And on a fairly regular basis he attended the annual dinner of the Pennsylvania Society of New York at the Waldorf-Astoria Hotel. In fact, he often invited me down as his guest.

"Stay at my suite in the Waldorf," he would say, adding, "I'll show you how to have a big weekend without spending a penny."

And I have no doubt that he's giving some similar line to St. Peter right now.

November 3, 1974

GROCERY NOT THE PLACE
FOR A BOY IN A HURRY

It was one of hundreds of such stores in this area in the 1930s and early 1940s, but I remember this one in particular because I was sent there so often as a child.

It was a neighborhood food store operated by a foreign-born grocer as an extension of his home.

When one walked in, the door triggered a bell, and if no one were in the store at that moment, the sound of the bell would bring some family member from the residence.

At any given time, any member of the family might be put into service to take care of the customers, but it was the grocer himself who usually presided over the meat block.

Other members of the family might be able to slice liver or grind up hamburg, but when a customer wanted a fresh cut of beef, such as a steak or roast, it was the grocer who lugged the heavy side of beef from the cooler to the block to cut it as ordered. This took time, of course, but people weren't in such a hurry then as they are today.

In fact, this casual approach to time was part of the character of the grocery story. It was no place to be if you were in a hurry.

Most of the items in the store were on shelves out of the reach of customers. So the customers merely stood in front of the front of the counter and read off a list of wanted items. The person or persons behind the counter usually fetched the items one by one, frequently walking from one part of the store to another to do this—only to have to make the same trip again for another item.

If an item was on a high shelf, a long pole with a clamp device on one end and a handle on the other was used to reach it—an invention that goes all the way back to Benjamin Franklin.

Then, if the telephone rang and someone called in an order for delivery of a few items, everything stopped while the order was taken.

Most of the time, the grocer was the only one on duty behind the counter, so if several customers arrived at about the same time, there was nothing to do except to wait patiently to be served. And young children had a tendency to be overlooked if their heads did not reach more above the counter level—which was my problem.

If a customer bought a lot of meat—for instance, a roast that had to be tied up with string, some round steak that had to be ground, or a pork loin that had to be cut into chops—then there was certain to be a long delay for all the other customers.

Few of the things in the store came prepackaged. Thus, all produce had to be bagged and weighed, cookies had to be measured out on a scale, pickles and sauerkraut had to be taken from barrels, butter would be taken from a wooden tub, and eggs were loose, and all different sizes, sometimes speckled with tiny bits of feathers and even sometimes warm from the henhouse behind the grocer's home.

Most people who bought there bought "on the book," which was the charge account system that enabled many families to live day-to-day because the grocer trusted them. Unfortunately, it caused many grocers to go broke when too much credit was extended and jobs could not be found. But most God-fearing people paid their grocer as faithfully as they gave to their churches.

The store actually was rather dark and dingy by today's standards. It had few lights to brighten it and the shelves and woodwork were usually of a dark color. There was no air-conditioning, but there were some overhead fans that turned around at a leisurely pace, more to chase away the odors of strong cheese and the garlic in the sausage than to provide cooling.

If nothing else, a child sent to such a store learned patience and how to shift from one foot to another as he waited his turn, and as the grocer spoke in a strange tongue to some older customers.

It was not exactly a loved chore for a child, but it was one that had to be done just about every day.

February 23, 1975

HOME HAIRCUTS WERE A
PAINFUL EXPERIENCE

As a tot, I rarely had the pleasure of getting a professional haircut.

Instead, my late mother—who cooked, baked, sewed, cleaned, and did scores of other household tasks—was our barber.

The shearing was done on a kitchen chair, with tools that included a scissors that needed sharpening and a hand clipper with a few missing teeth.

It was the clipper that actually made the home haircut such an ordeal. It pulled out almost as many hairs as it cut—or at least it seemed that way. And it was this hair pulling that made a haircut about as welcome as having a tooth extracted.

The ordeal occurred every few weeks because that was an era when boys wore their hair shorter than the girls. Once cornered and backed into a kitchen chair, a dishcloth—sometimes a former flour bag—was pinned tightly around the neck with a big safety pin.

Unfortunately, it was never possible to get the dishcloth tight enough to prevent tiny bits of hair from slipping down behind the collar and down the back. So it was certain that the ordeal of a haircut was going to be followed by an ordeal of back itch that would not end until the hair was washed away in a bathtub.

The clipper, no doubt, had once been new and had smoothly snipped hair without discomfort. But at this point it had a few broken teeth. So when it was supposed to clip the hairs, in the spots where the teeth were missing, it merely pulled them out. And there was no way to escape this torture.

The home haircut was administered primarily for economic reasons. True, a child's haircut might have cost only 25 or 35 cents, but that was a great deal of money at that time.

(Now with children's haircuts costing over $2 and family budgets being attacked daily by inflation and recession, it is just possible that we may be on the edge of a new era of home haircuts. But even if that happened, chances are that there would be more sophisticated tools today—including smooth electric clippers with a full set of teeth.)

I vividly recall that point in my life when I became too old for home haircuts. So I went to a barber shop and luxuriated in the comforts there —even if I did have to sit on a small stool placed in the regular barber's chair for a year or so, and wasn't able to read some of the shop's girly magazines.

What was enjoyable here was the expertise of the barber. Whether using the assortment of scissors at his fingertips or one of his several electric and hand clippers, he could trim the hair without causing pain. And the shave at the back of the neck was wonderfully painless, too. Finally, there was the hair massage and the liberal dousing of the locks with some fine-scented perfume—just the right thing to make a boy feel that he could match the aroma of any lilac or rose.

Of course, over the years, haircuts became more of a chore than a pleasure as the memory of the home haircuts faded. And then came the era of longer hair when periods between haircuts became greater and the barbers—in self-defense—had to boost prices again and again, just to stay in business.

Now the hair of tots is so long that I find it possible to administer an occasional haircut myself. But this involves merely cutting it with a scissors, so no major skills are needed. Still, even this is hated by tots, I find. When I mention trimming someone's hair, that child usually vanishes quickly.

I wonder what would happen if they had to face my mother's old hair clipper with the broken teeth.

March 16, 1975

A LETTER TO BOBBY
RECALLS VISIT HERE

Dear Bobby:

You probably won't remember me. I'm a reporter who covered you when you made a visit to Scranton to give a St. Patrick's Day speech 11 years ago.

I realize that you are now dead—the victim of assassination—but I am sure that this message will reach you. Indeed, if we can still address messages to St. Patrick, more than 500 years after his death, I find nothing strange in addressing one to you a mere eight years after your death.

What prompted me to write you is that I happened to mention your trip to Scranton one day recently at home. One of my twin sons—age eight—asked if he had been born at that time. My initial thought was that he must have been because this was just a few years ago. But when I began to count the years, I realize that this had occurred in 1964—two years before my twins made their debut. (Years do have a way of telescoping, I find.)

I vividly recall that after your brother, John, was shot on Nov. 22, 1963, you spent a great deal of time in seclusion. When you accepted an invitation to come here, it was one of your first public appearances after that terrible tragedy. It still sticks in my mind that the very day you flew here, stopping at John's grave at Arlington Cemetery was one of the last things you did before you left for Scranton.

One reason you came here, you said, was that you remembered the way this area had turned out in support of John when he campaigned for the presidency in 1960. Nobody before or since has caused such great crowds to gather here. In fact, when John was about to make a trip to Ireland in 1963—as the first Irish Catholic president of the United States —he told you that he expected the crowds there to be just about the same as those he had met in Scranton. You, yourself, told us that story. I'm pleased that he went to Ireland with his Scranton visit on his mind.

And the Kennedy magic worked for you, too. When you arrived at the local airport, you were mobbed by some 3,000 persons. The cops were frightened that you'd be hurt, but I got real close to you then and remember you saying over and over again, "I'm OK. Don't push them. I don't want anyone to get hurt."

Even as you were getting into your car, I can recall hearing you tell the driver to be careful not to hurt anyone. One doesn't forget such things.

A little later, when you dedicated the site for a new school in Scranton that now bears the name of your brother, there were about 5,000 persons there to greet you. But it was to the kids that you addressed most of your remarks. I recall you delighting them by telling them that when the president encountered such groups during his campaign, he always winked at the kids and said: "Remember who it was who got you out of school."

Your next stop was at the Federal Building, where another 2,500 persons mobbed you. My most vivid recollection of this stop was riding up in the elevator with you and you recalling that your brother was "enthusiastic" about Scranton and its people. This sticks in my memory as though you said it yesterday.

Later, as you went to the Hotel Casey, you were mobbed by about 300 persons in the lobby. You were probably getting a little tired of crowds at this point and I couldn't say that I could blame you. You finally escaped to your room and had the first bit of privacy in quite a while.

At this point, I timidly asked an aide if I could have a photograph —the property of a neighbor—autographed. I thought he might take it to you himself, but he amazed me by ushering me into the room.

As I entered, you were shaving in the bathroom and your aide introduced us through the closed door. You made a joke about not expecting to meet an Irish reporter here. You made a few more remarks about how your brother liked this area and how he owed it so much. And you said you'd be happy to autograph the picture.

A moment later you came out wearing only your underwear and I really felt like an intruder. But you didn't seem to mind a bit.

That night, you wowed audiences at St. Patrick's dinners at Pittston and Scranton. Then you left smiling—giving us a perfect example of how one must carry on in the face of adversity.

Now, 11 years later, I just want to assure you that some memories resist fading, and the visit by you to this area is in that category. You found that this is far from a perfect world, but like St. Patrick, you did your best to improve it. And that's why I'm thinking of you on this eve of St. Patrick's Day.

Prayerfully yours,
Joe

BUSES USED TO WAIT FOR TARDY PASSENGERS

I met a retired driver of the old Scranton Transit Co. in downtown Scranton the other day, and we spent a few pleasant minutes talking about those less hectic days of a few decades ago, when people had time to get to know their bus drivers and the bus drivers were pleasant enough to want to know and be friendly with their customers.

The driver I met used to drive the old Dunmore-Jessup run, and, as a resident of Jessup, I got to know him quite well. In fact, after awhile, all regular riders pretty much got to know all of the drivers on particular routes.

In that era, people were a bit friendlier than they are now—or maybe it just seems so to me. In any case, a good driver, who knew his route, knew more than the roadway—he knew the people he served.

This made for an informality that the Public Utility Commission and even the old Scranton Transit Co. management probably would have fought against if they had known about it. For instance, on a rainy day, a driver would often stop the bus right at your home if you happened to live along the route—or he would take you to the closest location, regardless of whether it was an official stopping place or not.

And it was not unknown for a bus driver to stretch the fare zones a bit to give you a longer ride than you had paid for—to save you an extra 8 cents, which was the zone fare in those days. Later, even after the fares crept up to 12 cents, the same sort of thing would occur. And it was appreciated, too, because that was a period of tight money.

The company was always on its guard against such things, and often hired "spotters" to ride the buses to watch for such infractions. But a good driver who knew his customers could pick out such a person easily as he surveyed the faces of his passengers in his rearview mirror.

In Jessup, the bus route ended at the old St. James Church, a famous old building that is now a garment factory. But since a good part of the so-called "uptown" area was further up on the hill from this spot, many of the drivers would go up a few more blocks to round up some stray customers on cold winter mornings, or do the same thing to deposit them nearer their homes on cold winter nights.

I'm aware of one chronically late person, who often had the bus pull up to her home beyond the end of the route and have its horn blare out to get her moving a bit faster in the morning. Maybe that wasn't efficient, businesslike, or even technically within the power of the firm's franchise, but it was downright friendly, and it did help that one rider to get to work on time.

During the period I was dating the girl I later married, we sometimes would ride the evening's last bus home from a movie in Scranton, going right back to the end of the line. If the driver had some time to spare within his schedule, he might wait for me to walk my girl to the door and then to get back to the bus stop to ride free to my own home at the other end of town. Again, it wasn't technically correct, but I sure appreciated it.

On a slow day, when you found yourself alone or virtually alone on the bus, the driver might beckon you to sit right behind him to engage in conversation.

Often, you swapped stories about persons on the route that you both knew primarily from riding the bus, and it was all done under the "Do Not Talk to Operator" sign.

A driver who knew his customers knew where and what time they usually boarded, so if he got there and someone was not at the bus stop, he might slow down or stop to look up a side street to see if he could spot the person running down the sidewalk. Likewise, if a person dozed off, the driver might stop the bus and wake him to tell him that this was his stop.

The age of the automobile lessened the tendency of people to ride the buses, but now the world's shortage of petroleum may force them back again. Already, we in Lackawanna County have a public transit system and a fleet of new buses. But somehow, I feel we will never be able to recapture the informality and friendliness that once made bus drivers not just public servants, but friends—even at the risk of losing their jobs.

OLD MR. CLARK
SPREAD SUNSHINE WITH APPLES

Right around this time of year, Mr. Clark would make his rounds with his recently picked apples.

Mr. Clark was a tall, thin, elderly farmer who also sold his own products as a part-time huckster. But usually he restricted his business to his own specialties—apples and eggs.

He had been making his rounds for years and got to know his customers quite well. He could make a pretty good guess at what customers might buy, taking what he thought they would want to their doors and usually being correct in his judgment. To do this, of course, he had to know the size of families and the size of pocketbooks. And his customers knew him, too, and knew that whatever he sold was exactly as he represented it. There was no need for any consumer protection service to intervene in such transactions in those days.

There are several things I remember about Mr. Clark. One is that he always wore a cap and that he had old-fashioned manners that caused him to tip it every time he saw a lady and to remove it whenever he entered a home.

I also recall that he always had a leather pouch suspended by a chain around his neck. This well-worn bag was filled with bills and coins, and his fingers could plunge into its interior and fish out a shiny copper penny for a child who happened to be in the kitchen when the sale was taking place. But more often than that, he passed out big red apples to children.

"Clarkey," the name we used to describe him when he wasn't present, made his rounds in a rickety Ford truck—possibly a Model T. From time to time he might sell other products than apples and eggs. For instance, in the fall he made a special run with the truck loaded with cider.

Mr. Clark, who often quoted the Bible, sold nothing but sweet cider. However, with a bit of a smile he would pass on to a customer all that needed to be known about letting the cider age into something a little harder.

In our house, however, the mildly fermented apple juice was so delicious in its sweet cider stage that it never got a chance to move to a more potent stage. The cider was a rare treat for children who in those days got few soft drinks.

When Mr. Clark made his rounds at this time of the year, he had apples for every use—big sweet ones for eating, tart ones for making pies, huge ones that cried out to be smothered in brown sugar and baked, and ones that didn't look very pretty and were rather bitter, but which made delicious applesauce or even apple jelly.

Wooden baskets must have been cheap and plentiful in those days, because Mr. Clark gave them out with the apples and they would later be used for holding ashes and for other tasks around the home.

I don't recall what the apples cost, but they must have been cheap, because otherwise we couldn't have been buying them.

Mr. Clark also had eggs that he probably harvested in his henhouse that very morning. They varied in size and color, being sold in the same variety as they were laid. Occasionally, that meant opening one that had a double yolk. And often one would find tiny feathers stuck to the shells, because the eggs were sold just the same way they were found in the hen racks.

The eggs were sold loose, with the customers supplying their own containers. Mr. Clark carried the eggs to the home in a galvanized pail, and lifted them out three or four at a time with his huge, bony hands that never seemed to drop one or even crack a shell. Again, like the apples, the eggs must have been inexpensive for us to buy them in such quantity.

I have to assume that Mr. Clark is dead now, because this was more than 30 years ago that he made his rounds of the valley, including our home in Jessup, and he was elderly then.

But come to think of it, he probably didn't make a lot of money. He spent a lot of time on the job just chatting with his customers, bringing some sunshine into their days. He wasn't really a huckster, after all, but more like a friend of the family.

DOG'S LOVE
EARNS FAMILY MEMBERSHIP

Our Candy is so ugly she's absolutely beautiful.

If that sounds like a contradiction, it really isn't. It simply means that our family dog defies all the rules that apply to canine beauty, and yet she remains beautiful to us. Remember, beauty is in the eye of the beholder.

No doubt a person looking at Candy for the first time would regard her as something far from pretty. She's too fat, for one thing, and this makes her head appear to be too small for her body. She has unlady-like grey eyebrows and beard which don't go well with her black fur. Her hair is too unkempt, even by today's standards of casualness. And her underside droops more than it should.

But despite such shortcomings, Candy looks fine to us. She's a member of our family and such membership is not predicated upon looks. It's based upon love.

True, Candy is inclined to be lazy, particularly in these later years. She'd much rather be curled up on the floor near a warm radiator in the winter than out chasing squirrels. (I just have to assume that in her long naps, she dreams of great hunting expeditions. It's one explanation for the grunts and groans she makes while she is sound asleep.)

Candy has been made terribly soft by civilization. She prefers to stay in the house when the weather is the least bit inclement. At night, before she goes to bed, Candy is asked to leave the house to get herself ready for the night. But if it's raining or snowing, she often has to be scooted out under protest.

As this bedtime hour nears, Candy usually is sound asleep in the living room. Then she hears a voice: "Come on, Candy, it's time to go out."

She may not hear—or she may pretend not to hear. So the message may have to be repeated to stir her. Then she may open her eyes without moving the rest of her body. Thus, it may take another sharper command to get her to stand up and to walk to the door. This movement is done in agonizing slow motion, and much cold air sweeps into the living room before Candy finally clears the doorway.

A few minutes later, Candy arrives at our backdoor and is now (we hope) ready to spend the night on a soft chair in the basement without any accidents. If the backdoor is not opened promptly, she will paw at it or bark sharply to let us know that she is ready to come in.

There are other times, however, when Candy moves more rapidly. When some of the youngsters are going out into the neighborhood to play some kind of running game, Candy joins the crowd. On these occasions, she's as frisky as she was 10 years ago.

Then there is the vigilant watchdog who leaps to her feet—usually from a sound sleep—and barks sharply when the mailman opens our mailbox, the oilman uncaps our intake pipe, the garbagemen take lids from the garbage cans, or someone other than a family member rings the doorbell. But all she ever earns for this barking is a sharp verbal rebuke to be quiet—something I'm sure is bruising her ego.

Another time Candy comes to life is when a family car is about to move. As soon as a driver prepares to leave the house, Candy will look appealing and the question is right there on her face: "Can I come?" If the driver says, "OK, you can come," Candy immediately knows what it means and she is ready to knock anybody over who might stand between her and the car.

Candy is good at communicating with family members. When she wants to go outside, to be given water, or to be fed her supper, she can get across such messages by looking directly up at a family member, wagging her tail, and then running toward a door or her dish. And if the first pitch fails, Candy will press her cold nose against the nearest family member to demand some attention.

Yet, compared to some dogs that do all sorts of fancy tricks, Candy is quite untalented. But what she lacks in skills she makes up in love. And that's what makes her such a treasured member of our household.

October 10, 1976

"WRITE IT AS YOU TOLD IT" WAS GOOD ADVICE

When I was just starting out in this news business, I often had trouble with the final sentence of a news story.

The first sentence is always a challenge, but to a green newcomer it often was the cause of mental agony. The tradition in journalism is that this introduction to the story—called "the lead"—is supposed to summarize the contents of what is to follow. At the same time, it is supposed to grab the attention of the reader sufficiently to cause him to read more of the story. But those two goals are easier to describe than to achieve.

At the time I'm writing about, I was the newest reporter on the staff of the *Scranton Tribune* and I was working one of the night shifts that are so common on morning publications. I had been given a rather big story to handle, and now I was back in the office with a bundle of notes but without a good idea on how to start the news article.

I looked around the newsroom and spotted one of the veteran reporters—a real pro named Gordy Williams. I was timid about going to him because he was pounding out a story of his own, and I feared that he might not like this young and inexperienced reporter interrupting him. But I had a deadline problem that told me I had to get started—so I went to him and asked for help.

He stopped, looked at me, and, for a second, I wasn't sure what he would say. But Gordy, who sometimes was a gruff and hard-nosed reporter, spun his chair around and said: "OK, tell me about it in your own words and we'll see what we can do." I proceeded to detail the story to him, step by step, and he listened patiently as I worked my way through it verbally.

When I finished, I waited patiently for this old pro to suggest some complicated sentence for me to use as the lead for my story. But then he threw me a curve. "Write it just as you told it to me," he said as he swung back to his own typewriter and resumed writing his own story.

I waited a moment, thinking that Gordy might reconsider and give me more real help. But he kept pounding away on his typewriter—he was one of the fastest writers I have ever met in this business—so I walked away dejectedly and returned to my own typewriter.

So there I was, frustrated by this task of starting a complicated story. I saw no one else in the room that I felt I could ask for advice. And the clock was recording the passage of precious minutes between me and my deadline. Then a strange thing began to happen. I began to rehear the advice Gordy had given me: "Write it just as you told it to me." I said to myself: "Well, why not try it?"

Then I began to peck out the story in the same simple and conversational language that I had used to explain it to Gordy. The sentences came easy. Most were brief. And I was able to string them together in a block of short paragraphs. It turned out that the story wasn't all that complicated, after all.

The completed pages piled up and soon the story was finished. It really was almost exactly the same story I had told Gordy. And it was written in just about the same way I had described it verbally. Gone were the long and complicated sentences with the big words that I had thought were the marks of a clever writer.

I turned the story in to the city desk and a little while later an experienced man there was complimenting me on the way it was written.

But by this time, Gordy was gone for the evening, so I couldn't thank him. And I don't believe that I ever got around to it in the future. I just digested the lesson in journalism to write a story the way I would describe it verbally—sometimes even talking to myself as I go along. A few years later, I moved down the street to the *Times*, but I kept the same writing technique, which reflected Gordy's advice.

Gordy has been dead a number of years, but I still recognize the debt I owe him. So now, 27 years later, this is an attempt to repay him by honoring his memory.

ONE RIDE ON FIRE TRUCK
ENOUGH FOR A LIFETIME

I have ridden a fire truck once in my life, and that satisfies any craving that might have been born into me to do such a thing.

It was a cold, cold night back in 1949, and I was just starting in the news business. I was living in Jessup at the time and was serving the *Scranton Tribune* as a correspondent.

Now, for people outside the business, I must explain the difference between a correspondent and a reporter. The former is a person who covers hometown news, often on a part-time basis, and is paid a very modest sum for his efforts—or at least that is the way it was when I was a correspondent. A reporter, on the other hand, is a formal member of the newspaper's staff, and as such, he works regular hours and is paid more generously for his work.

But one way onto a staff job is to become a correspondent, do a good job, say a few prayers, and hope that one of the officials of the newspaper will get interested in you and will promote you to a reporter's position.

Even as a correspondent, I was green. I was eager, though, because I now had my college degree and I hungered for a job as a reporter. So I was determined to do a good job as a correspondent, to become noticed, and to win a staff assignment.

Then came the cold winter night in question. I heard the fire whistles blowing across the Lackawanna River in Peckville, so I called the fire headquarters there and was told that a combination bar and apartment house was burning.

The fire was about two miles from my home, but I set out on foot—no car being available at the moment. In the frigid weather, I double-timed it most of the way and got to the fire as it was burning furiously out of control. I went to a nearby home, introduced myself as a newsman, and asked permission to use the telephone. Permission was granted and I breathlessly phoned in an alert to the newsroom that the fire was burning and that I was right on top of the story.

I then did all the things that the book called for in covering such a story, including finding out who owned the building, how many people had lived there and their names, determining that everyone had escaped unharmed, and getting an approximate value on the loss. I had just about everything that I needed, in fact, when there was great commotion among the volunteer firemen at the scene.

I approached one and asked what was going on. He told me that a major fire had broken out in a home in uptown Jessup—about three miles away. The Jessup companies that had gone to Peckville to help fight the fire there quickly collected their gear and headed for the fire in that town.

As one of the trucks began to roll, one of the firemen said: "If you want to go, hop on." So I jumped on the back of the fire truck and held on to a metal bar as the vehicle began its trip to the scene of the second blaze.

As the truck bounced over bad pavement, I feared that I would fall off. So I wrapped my arms around the bar and held on as tightly as I could. I even chanced my hat blowing off, because I had no hands left to cling to it. But fortunately this did not happen.

The fast ride through the extremely cold air forced me to close my eyes to stop them from watering. But within minutes we arrived at the scene of the second blaze and I again began gathering facts for my mushrooming story.

By now, however, my fingers were so numb I could hardly write. Yet I managed it somehow. And a short time later I called the newsroom again to give the details on the twin fires—reporting the second one before they were even aware of it.

The next morning I was thrilled to find that the two blazes constituted the top story on page one, and there, for the first time, I saw my very own byline. By this time, I also had learned that parts of my bare wrists, which had been exposed to the freezing bar on the fire truck, were actually frostbitten. So I had to treat them for days as one would treat real burns.

But it was worth the effort. I clearly recall the fires, the frigid air, the fire truck ride, the byline, and the frostbite. And within a few months, I was elevated to a regular reporting job. Yet I no longer have the slightest desire to ride a fire truck.

EVERYONE SHOULD HAVE ONE "BEST" CHRISTMAS

Everyone should have a "best" Christmas.

I realize, of course, that most Christmases are happy occasions, so one is tempted to think of most of them as nice. In fact, reaching back through one's memory to the Christmases of childhood, I find they have a tendency to run together, like so many pleasant dreams.

But in everyone's life, there must be one Christmas that really and truly stands out as the "best" of all Yule holidays.

There is no contest in picking out that "best" Christmas of mine. It occurred just seven years ago—but I know I would remember it just as clearly if it were many decades ago.

In order to explain this special Christmas, I have to give a little background first, starting with the fact that my wife and I were blessed with twin sons on July 12, 1966. And for more than three years, Tim and Tom were blessed with good health.

In December of 1969, however, Tommy—then approaching his fourth Christmas season—began to complain of stomach pains and to run a low temperature. Since we now have six children and we had a lot of experience with routine sicknesses, this was not alarming. We simply treated him for what we thought was a mild virus attack.

But instead of it going away, the condition hung on for many more days. He still got occasional stomach cramps. His appetite fell off. And the low fever continued.

In the course of this ailment, we consulted with Dr. Steve Pascucci, our trusted pediatrician, and he counseled us on what steps to take and to keep him informed of any changes in Tommy's status. After several days of this, however, he insisted that we bring him to a local hospital where he could have some tests done—"just to be safe."

Since there was no sign of any major health problem at this point, we still were not awfully concerned. That is why it came as a shock to us a few hours later when we learned that the diagnosis was appendicitis—something rather rare in three-year-olds. At this point, Dr. Herb

McDonald came into the case and scheduled surgery immediately. Our scared little boy was sobbing as he was wheeled away from his room, and my wife and I had lumps in our throats, tears in our eyes, and fear in our hearts as we kissed him goodbye. We then went to the cafeteria and forced a few things down our throats, this being suppertime. Then we went to the hospital chapel where we did some real hard praying. Later, we returned to Tommy's room to await his return.

A couple of hours later, the surgery was over and Tommy came back, now with a tube in his nose pumping wastes from his stomach, and several other tubes attached to his thin arms to give him nourishment. At first he was drugged and fought little against the tubes, but as he awakened, he did his best to remove them. So his hands had to be tied down to keep him immobile.

It was only now that we learned Tom's appendix had actually ruptured, and that he was one of the youngest persons this has happened to in this area in quite a while. It was then that we also learned that if he had not been operated on when he was, he might have died.

Taking turns, my wife and I spent the next several days and nights with Tom as he regained his health. Soon the tube through his nose was removed. Then, when he started to eat, the needles in his arms came out, too. First, he began to eat. And then he began to play with the teddy bears and the other toys that had been given to him.

All this was taking place as Christmas neared, and each day saw Tom grow stronger. Then, finally, the day came when he was recovered enough to go home. We carried him out in his pajamas, wrapped in blankets, and he was mobbed by his brothers and sisters when he arrived.

The day he came home was Christmas Eve. He still had some recovering to do, of course. But this little three-year-old who might have died without the care and skills of two physicians and many wonderful nurses was now back home.

And this is why that 1970 Christmas was the "best" of my life.

KITCHEN'S COAL STOVE
CENTER OF FAMILY LIFE

This is the sort of winter that conjures up memories.

The very cold and snowy weather which we have been having lately is the kind that can make a person nostalgic about very simple things —for instance, putting one's feet into the warm oven of a big coal stove. But since these relics of the past are in few kitchens anymore, all we have left are our memories of the roles they played during severe winters.

In an era when the kitchen was the warmest room in the house, a person—particularly a child—coming in out of the cold knew that the quickest way of getting warm was to pop his feet into the oven.

There was a right way and a wrong way of doing this, of course. First of all, you didn't dare put your feet into the oven while still wearing boots or rubbers. It was too hot for that.

One had to put the feet into the oven with the shoes on, taking care to keep rubber heels from touching anything too hot. It was also too hot for bare feet or stocking-covered feet, and a careless move without shoes could cause a pesky burn.

Sitting in front of the stove (ours was a Pittston Stove Co. grey model with a black top and gleaming nickel trim), one carefully put his feet into the oven. Within a few minutes, you could feel the heat seeping though the frozen shoes and reaching the equally frigid feet. Soon the feet were warm as toast. And as if by magic, the warmth quickly radiated upward in the body until the entire winter chill was chased out of you.

There were times when the oven might be in use for the baking of bread or some other purpose, and it was not available for thawing out feet. When this happened, one could sit in the same spot in front of the stove and put the soles of your shoes right on the oven door. Since this could cause scratching of the glazed surface, this involved a risk of being yelled at. But sometimes you got away with it.

If there was too much danger of getting caught with the shoes on the hot oven door, then you could prop your feet up on the nickel trim around the stove—venturing as close to the firebox as you dared until the heat seeped through the cold leather. There was a danger here, of course, of searing the leather and producing a strong odor in the house—but that did not seem a high price for the comforts produced.

Just as there was a danger of leather shoe soles being burned, there also was a danger of leather in gloves being dried out too fast when put on the open, but still hot, oven door.

After several hours of outdoor fun, kids would always return with gloves that were saturated with water and often frozen stiff. Since this was a time when there weren't "extra" pairs of gloves around the house, there was a need to dry them quickly for the next use. That's why the oven door was risked. The trick was to remember to remove them within a short time to keep them from being baked. But when they were forgotten and they became stiff as boards, it sometimes became necessary to revitalize them by rubbing Vaseline into their pores.

(Wet shoes left to dry too long in an oven could be turned into something akin to cardboard, which didn't make them very comfortable to wear. So one had to be careful of this type of speed drying, too.)

Actually, the kitchen stove did provide a good place to thaw out and dry gloves, shoes, scarves, and hats without any danger of hurting them. That was the top shelf, where it was warm but not hot. But if there was a need for speed, then the oven door was used—at a certain risk.

All through the winters, the kitchen stove was the center of most family life. It was the place to stand near in the morning after fleeing from frigid bedrooms. It was the place to stand near after coming in from outdoors. And it was the place to warm cold feet and dry out wet clothing.

Now, of course, we have warmer homes and the dirty old coal stove is just a memory. But it still lives there. And if I try really hard, I can still remember the smell of leather being gently burned, and the delicious feeling of frozen toes being warmed.

September 18, 1977

DAILY NEWS
LENSMAN JOINS THE CELEBRATION

It was a rainy and overcast day in New York City, but at least one section of that metropolis, Brooklyn, was happy.

The Dodgers still were a Brooklyn-based baseball team and in an afternoon game that day in Boston, they had beaten the then Boston Braves to win the National League pennant.

The *New York News*, where I then was working as an office boy, wanted to add local color to its story of the Dodgers' success, so it dispatched several photographers to Brooklyn to get some pictures of celebrating fans.

Since this occurred 28 years ago, I'm not sure how many photographers were involved, but three is a fair guess, and each had an office boy assigned to him to help carry his equipment.

It was just about this time of the year, and the fog and mist were getting worse as the afternoon wore on. My photographer and I crossed the Brooklyn Bridge in a *News* car, but when we arrived we found the streets virtually deserted. Even Dodger fans, apparently, were not crazy enough to do their celebrating in rain and fog.

So my photographer, being a resourceful fellow, headed for the nearest bar. As soon as we entered, his theory was proven: A rainy day is good for bar business. Thus, here at last were Dodger fans to photograph.

My man, using expense money furnished to him in advance by the city desk, told the bartender that we were from the *News* and that we wanted to get some pictures of Dodger fans celebrating. He told the bartender to draw beers for the house and he happily complied. After all, a picture in the *News* would be great advertising for the bar—and bartender.

In a loud and clear voice, the bartender made the announcement that a photographer from the *News* wanted to get some pictures of Dodger fans celebrating. The cameraman then suggested that everyone raise his glass in a victory salute to the victorious Dodgers. After a little bit of elbowing for good positions in the front row, the patrons did as the photographer suggested.

While all this was going on, my man was having a few beers himself. And when he finished, he ordered another round for the house and he took part in that, too. But as for me, his young and inexperienced assistant, he frowned on me drinking, and kept me from temptation by having me carry his expensive equipment several blocks to put it in the truck.

Soon we left this place and drove to another neighborhood where the scene was repeated. And then we went to another bar—and then to another—and then to one more.

By the time my man had taken 50 pictures or so—all basically the same—he also had taken on enough beer to put him in a mood to celebrate, too. And I began to get treated like a nagging wife, because I started warning him that it was getting late and the *News* was going to need our pictures soon if they were going to make the early edition that evening.

I never did learn what my man spent on this assignment, but I'd guess it could have been $25 or so in those days of 10-cent beers.

When we finally arrived back at the newspaper, my photographer was wobbly but still navigating. Fortunately for him, he did not have to develop his own pictures because the paper had darkroom assistants who did that. And I had the caption cards with information on the various pictures, so he was spared that work, too. So my man retired quietly to a room where photographers hung around waiting for assignments. And my guess is that he slept the rest of his shift.

Meanwhile, the pictures of Dodger fans taken by the other photographers were all processed and the whole batch then went to the picture editor for a decision on what to use.

That night when the first edition came out, there was only one photo in it showing Brooklyn fans celebrating in a barroom. But, alas, it was not one taken by my man.

Thus, as far as I was concerned, our day was a total loss. But I suppose that my photographer—wherever he is today—would not agree with me. He had a good time celebrating the Dodger victory himself. Or then again, he may have been a New York Giants fan intent upon drowning his sorrows in beer.

BOTH PARTIES ENGAGED
IN RING-UPS LONG AGO

Elections certainly have changed.

In last Tuesday's balloting in Lackawanna County, there were so many watchers and overseers at the polls that it was often difficult to wade through them. And as for the possibility of doing anything dishonest, well, it seemed impossible.

But there was a time in my life, when I was just coming of age in Jessup, when I thought that a person was *not* allowed to go behind the curtain of a voting machine alone.

Back in those days, a Democratic party worker stood at the machine and when friendly people arrived, he went with them into the booth and he did the voting.

That being Jessup, a solid Democratic town, the voting invariably included pulling the straight-party lever for the entire Democratic ticket.

I suppose that my memory may be faulty on all the details, because common sense tells me that there were some Republicans around, even in Jessup, and there must have been certain times when "assistance" was not commonplace. Elections in the 1930s and 1940s certainly were a lot different from what they are today.

Ticket-splitting in those days was regarded as something akin to being disloyal to one's country. And the mere idea of a Republican carrying Jessup, which has happened in recent elections, was unthinkable in those days.

Democrats, of course, did not have a monopoly on this type of Election Day conduct. In many other parts of the county, where the Republicans were in control, they did the same things.

In that era, too, it was commonplace for husbands to go into booths with their wives to do their voting for them. And fathers often did the same things with their of-age offspring. No one, of course, objected to these things, because they were regarded as family matters unrelated to the election.

In a solid Democratic town such as Jessup, the Republican election board members had very limited goals. There were only a few Republican voters anyway, so the party workers were happy when they could report to party leaders in Scranton that they got out all or most of their votes.

In order to do that, it might involve ringing up votes for those Republicans who hadn't bothered to vote. The trouble, of course, was that this could not be done without Democratic permission, because they were in the majority and were running things.

There was a way, however: the Republican worker could look the other way while the Democrats rang up votes for their people who had not gone to the polls. In return, the Democrats turned their backs to permit the Republicans to do the same thing. Then workers from both sides could tell party leaders in Scranton that it was a good day for the party in that district.

This bit of chicanery would occur just before the polls closed, lest some persons might cause trouble over being illegally voted. So the ring-up was delayed as long as possible.

Such elections often made it appear that just about every eligible voter, even the sick, the lame, and the aged, was vitally concerned with the political processes because they always voted. This devotion sometimes went to the extreme of producing more votes than the registration indicated was possible, but the real pros tried to avoid that sort of embarrassing situation.

Straight party voting occurred in those days on a scale that today's sophisticated ticket-splitter could not even imagine. The Democrats put together a "cosmopolitan ticket" that included all the major nationalities and party members were supposed to respond to this by supporting such a ticket to give all ethnic groups balanced representation in government.

If an unusually heavy number of Republican voters showed up in a Democratic district, as might happen when a strong candidate was on the GOP ticket, the Democratic party leaders were generally suspicious that party workers were simply not doing their jobs. And there were those who might even suspect that some Republicans must have voted twice to produce such strange results.

Times indeed have changed. Party labels mean little anymore. And, I have to believe, elections today are pretty honest—despite all the stories one hears on the days after the elections about certain dark deeds.

But, some old-timers might argue, people were more civic-minded in those days. After all, how else could you explain them going to the extreme of voting even after they had died and were buried?

FRANK O'HARA
GUIDED GI STUDENTS IN STRIDE

It was in July of 1946 when I entered the University of Scranton and first saw Frank J. O'Hara.

Those were the hectic days in the old main building on Wyoming Avenue, which has long since been removed.

I was not an ex-GI myself, but I was swallowed up in a horde of those ex-soldiers, ex-sailors, and ex-Marines who were going to take advantage of the GI Bill of Rights to get themselves an education. The only trouble was that this school was never designed to hold such a mob.

There was mass confusion in the halls—or so it seemed—as we freshman entered the school at this odd time of the year. To accelerate the education of eager veterans plus some recent high school graduates, the school had already started working 12 months a year. Thus, the unusual July start.

During the first few days of that semester, many of us had schedule problems. I was trying to work out my own schedule when I first encountered Mr. O'Hara, the school's registrar. In a few moments, he moved around several of my conflicting classes and he had me straightened out —showing amazing knowledge of the overall schedule of classes. He called me by my first name, shook my hand, said he was glad I had decided to study at the school, and told me that if I ever needed any other help, not to hesitate to come to him.

Despite his kind words, however, I did not feel like a buddy of this person. Maybe I was too fresh out of high school to be able to shed that mixture of fear and respect that I had for school officials. And I could sense that Mr. O'Hara was a key official here.

In the days ahead, as battle-scarred veterans waited patiently in long lines to get their schedules straightened out, Mr. O'Hara was everywhere. I can remember him working in his shirtsleeves, with his pipe constantly in his mouth and a batch of papers in his hands. The heat of those summer days added to everyone's discomfort, but somehow or other Mr. O'Hara put it all together almost single-handedly.

While he had been registrar of the school since 1925, Mr. O'Hara had never faced the problem he encountered in 1946. This was the biggest influx of students in the school's history. As a result, the institution was bursting at the seams. In addition to the main building, the science building, and LaSalle Hall, the school was using borrowed and leased classrooms in the Scranton Preparatory School, then at the corner of Wyoming Avenue and Mulberry Street; at the old Franklin School on Franklin Ave., and in the old Powell Business School in the Scranton Tribune Building on N. Washington Avenue. In addition, it was pushing the construction of converted barracks for extra classrooms on the site of the present campus near the Scranton estate.

Every student had to be booked into classes built around his course of study. Given the limited space of the school and the patchwork staff that was being put together, this was a problem akin to keeping the New York subway system in operation. And my recollection is that Mr. O'Hara was there from very early in the morning until very late at night.

Somehow, with Mr. O'Hara's skills and possibly with a miracle or two from the Jesuits, a system was put together and we received a good solid education related to the school's motto of religion, morality, and culture.

Eventually, those July 1946 freshmen received their degrees, some in 1949, when I got mine, and some in 1950, for those who were not in a great rush. Then we went out into the world to earn our daily bread.

For those who stayed in this area, there was that constant reminder that Mr.' O'Hara was still at the U. of S. and was still working in its behalf. Time after time his name would pop up in news stories relating to the school. And for all the graduates, there was a periodic letter from him reminding us that we owed a debt to our school, and that we could help repay it with a periodic donation.

I was lucky enough to become quite friendly with Mr. O'Hara in the course of my work as a reporter. And I remember how satisfying it was to learn from him that he often read this column of mine. Coming from this person I once held in fearful regard, this was a mighty big compliment.

Mr. O'Hara has now left us. But I'm sure that in his new abode, he still is working among U. of S. graduates for the spiritual advantage of our alma mater. And even in heaven, I'll bet he will do a hell of a job.

SLEEPING HOBO PROVES
A FASCINATING "FRIEND"

It was just about this time of the year. In fact, it might even have been Memorial Day, or as it was known then, Decoration Day.

The weather was May at its finest. It was about ten in the morning and it was already warm and sunny. So with about three playmates, I went to a nearby vacant field to bat and catch a baseball.

As we arrived, however, we saw what looked like a body near the large rock that we usually used for third base.

At first we could not be sure if it was a body, but as we tiptoed closer we found that it was, indeed, a man lying on the ground, partially covered by an old coat and with a cap pulled over his eyes. And we could see his chest rising and falling rhythmically, so we knew he was simply asleep and not dead.

We retired a respectful distance and sat on a nearby hillside to consider our next move. Should we start playing with our ball and bat and chance waking him? That didn't take long to reject. Actually, we were a bit afraid of this stranger even though we were within sight of our homes.

What if he were some kind of crook . . . or even a killer, our childish imaginations wondered. Given such concerns, we decided the prudent thing to do was to wait at a safe distance until he awakened.

As we sat there, we were able to observe many things about this stranger. First of all, we could see a bundle of belongings beside him and that told us he probably was a hobo—not an uncommon character in America during the Depression period of the late 1930s.

Then there was a crutch lying beside him that told us he had some kind of a walking impediment. That encouraged us that if we had to run away later, we had an advantage.

His unkempt gray hair and beard, and old and wrinkled clothes told us that it had been a long time since he had visited a barbershop or clothing store.

Suddenly we became aware that he was awakening. He rolled over on his back and uncovered his eyes. Then he sat up. He stretched. He scratched his head and glanced around. Obviously he was surveying this spot, which he had made into his bedroom after dark the previous night.

Then he spotted us and he waved. We meekly waved back. Then he beckoned us to come closer. So, sticking close together, we walked slowly to his "bedside." And we made sure we had our bat with us, just in case.

But within seconds his manner put us at ease. He wanted to know the name of the town where he was. But Jessup meant nothing to him. He dug through the bundle of his possessions and pulled out a map and studied it. As he did so he told us a bit about himself. He said he was from Ohio, but that he had been a drifter for years.

Most of the time, he said, he traveled by railroad freight cars. He claimed that he was looking for a place where a man with a bad leg might find a job and settle down.

The stranger told us that he had been wounded in the leg in France in World War I. To back up the story he dug into his bag of possessions and pulled out a well-worn paper that showed that he had been honorably discharged from the army. And he also showed us a Purple Heart medal, which was still in its case—obviously one of his most treasured possessions.

Fishing further in his pack, he found a handkerchief that held a few crumpled bills and a few coins. He untied the knot and counted it out. Then he asked where the business section was because he wanted to go there to get something to eat and also try to find a job.

We timidly asked him if we could get him some food, and without any hesitation, he said that would be fine with him. So we ran to my home, only a few doors away, and managed to scrounge up the makings for a couple of sandwiches, a hunk of cake, and a huge glass of lemonade. We then ran back with the food and watched him as he gobbled it down. And, in between bites, he spun us stories about life on the road, fighting in France, and even the life he lived as a child on a farm in Ohio.

Only God knows if the stories were true, but we never doubted one word.

Soon he got to his feet, put his pack on his back, put his crutch under his armpit, and shook hands with us all. Then he hobbled off down the road, heading for the business district of town.

Of course we never saw him again, nor did we ever hear anything about him.

But now, 35 or 40 years later, I wonder what ever happened to this homeless drifter. I'm still happy that we treated him well, and that, for a few minutes at least, we were friends. But it is sad to contemplate the lonely life that seemed to be his future.

This, then, is a true story of a lovely May day when a group of boys found adventure that was more fascinating than baseball.

GOLD RUSH
FIGURE A DISAPPOINTMENT

I don't know when I first became conscious of John Mahady, my great-uncle.

But it had to be when I was a very young child. In fact, that's how I learned that there was such a place as California. I learned that as I heard stories about my great-uncle who lived there.

That was just the start of the story of this man who had become a legendary figure in my young mind. I had heard many tales of how he turned his back on the coal mines of this area and headed west to seek his fortune.

Even as a child I had trouble getting the story straight. There were tales that I didn't know whether to believe. For instance, I had heard that when he went west, part of the journey was on stagecoach. I wasn't sure if that were true. But I accepted, as fact, the story that Great-uncle John had gone to California in search of gold and that he found it.

I remember bragging to my friends—maybe when I was in third or fourth grade—that I had a great-uncle in California and that he struck it rich by discovering gold there. All kids had seen enough western movies to know that there was gold in California, and that lucky persons often found it in streams or in underground veins. So none of them, I'm sure, had any trouble visualizing the kind of a relative I was claiming.

Given this situation, it is easy to imagine the thrill I felt when I heard that Great-uncle John was heading east to visit relatives. I could hardly wait to see this man who probably had more gold in the cuffs of his pants than we poor relatives ever expected to see in our lives.

In this period of the Great Depression, a person of wealth took on almost mystical qualities, particularly among kids. The only time we ever saw rich people was on the movie screens. And even we kids knew that they weren't real. Thus, the prospect of seeing one in the flesh was a cause of much excitement.

Great-uncle John was a brother of my deceased maternal grandmother. He also had another sister in Jessup and one in New York's

Bronx. And when he came east, he went to his sister's home in Jessup, and his sister from New York also came to visit. This arrival of two out-of-towners caused a great deal of visiting.

As the time came for me to meet my great-uncle, I dreamed that he might reach into his pockets and pull out some gold nuggets and give them to me. After all, that sometimes happened in the movies. And looking back on it, I suppose that might be the reason why my sister decided to go with me to meet him.

When we got there we saw a tiny old man in a rumpled black suit with no external signs of wealth. He was friendly enough after he was told that we were the children of his niece, Clare Reap. But there were no gold nuggets exchanged in the handshake.

Yet, hope dies very slowly in the young, and my heartbeat quickened as Great-uncle John said that he wanted to take my sister Clare and I to the store to buy us something. Maybe this was when we would see some of his gold, I thought.

We walked several blocks to a store and he bought us a 5-cent Baby Ruth candy bar. I was never more disappointed in my life.

Soon Great-uncle John left Jessup and returned to the West Coast. A few years after that, I remember hearing that he died there. And if we needed any proof, it was confirmed that he had no gold or anything else, for that matter, to constitute an estate.

Yet, legends die hard. Not long after the visit I was told by some adult relative that Great-uncle John really had been a rich man who had discovered gold in California. But the new version went: he got in a big poker game on the train heading east and got skinned out. Thus, I was lucky that I even got the Baby Ruth candy bar.

I tried hard to believe this new tale, but I couldn't do it. Unfortunately, Great-uncle John turned out to be just another poor relative.

August 6, 1978

SUNDAY DINNER
DREAMS BEGAN ON WEDNESDAY

Sunday dinner!

Ah, what a mountain of memories is locked up in those two words.

There was a time a few decades ago when there was ONE meal a week that was truly out-of-the-ordinary. I refer, of course, to the one served in most households about 12 or 1 P.M. every Sunday.

Although the meal could vary considerably according to individual family habits, in our house it generally involved a beef pot roast cooked for many hours in a black iron pot atop a coal stove.

Odors from this meat activated salivary glands long before the meal was ready, thus heightening the anticipation of the delights to come. In the cool or cold weather the odors were confined to the house, but in the summer, when the windows were open, one could tell throughout the neighborhood that there was a pot roast being prepared for a feast.

Onions, which were always cooked with the meat, added their own rich odors to the air, just as they added their own rich flavors to the meat.

Eventually, when the meat was cooked to the point where it could easily be split with a fork, it was gently lifted from the pot and put on a dish at the rear of the stove, where it would remain warm until it was sliced. Meanwhile, work would begin on making that special "Sunday dinner" gravy—a dark brown liquid that was an essential part of this special meal.

Another major ingredient was the tremendous pile of mashed potatoes, softened with a generous amount of butter and a small amount of milk. These were important because potatoes were then a key element of the American diet—a position from which they have slipped badly.

There were always vegetables, too: possibly string beans, peas, or carrots. Rarely did they come from a can. In fact, their preparation often was a job for the kids of the family. Thus, the snapping of string beans, the opening of pea pods, and the peeling and slicing of carrots was a skill that most children acquired early in life.

The meal might also have sweet potatoes or turnips, which generally were side dishes.

There were plenty of other extras on the table, too. A major one was homemade bread cut in irregular slabs. This could be made into a meal by itself, because it contained body that today's commercial imitations never seem to match.

If there was no homemade bread, there might be hot rolls made just before the meal and served right from the oven. One had to be careful while eating these not to let the melting butter drip onto the tablecloth.

Then there often was cabbage salad, a simple mix of cabbage ground up in a food chopper and mixed with mayonnaise. Another frill might include hot slaw, which was cooked cabbage flavored with vinegar and God knows what else. Its main characteristic was an odor that could travel farther and faster than even that of the pot roast.

There were other extras too, including pickles, relish, apple butter, applesauce, succotash, or olives.

We drank water with the meal, this being an era when water was still regarded as something that could be drunk and not just used for washing.

After the main course, there would be fresh-baked pie. The kind varied with the season, but apple and lemon meringue were the most frequently served.

My mother had a neat trick to make sure we kids cleaned our plates before getting pie. She required us to turn our plates over to receive the pie on their bottoms. Naturally this could not be done until every scrap of food was gone. The result: every bit of food was eaten before the pie arrived.

After this meal, the food for the rest of the week was adequate to sustain good health, but nothing very fancy. Thus, about Wednesday, one began to dream again of the next Sunday dinner.

In an age of abundance, it might seem strange to become nostalgic over a meal. But that is the way things used to be.

September 10, 1978

LIVED A RISKY LIFE
WITHOUT KNOWING IT

All the news recently about schools being declared unsafe because of fire hazards makes me wonder how I ever survived.

Now that I look back on it, I realize that in my 16 years of school—from first grade to college senior—I never spent a day in a building that would pass fire inspection today.

First there was the old "Back Road School" in Jessup where I studied for my first six years.

This all-wood building, more properly known as the Robert Morris School, probably was the most dangerous of all the learning centers that I ever attended. Even in the "modern" 1930s, it was heated with potbelly coal stoves.

The all-female faculty (there were no males in elementary schools in those days) had to tend the fires while teaching, often pausing in the middle of lessons to shovel in more coal or even take out an ash pan.

On real cold days in the winter, the fires were pushed to their limits to keep the schoolrooms barely above the livable level.

Thus there were times the stoves actually glowed red-hot. And there was no firewall around them to make them fire-safe. There was only one precaution that I could remember: a sheet of tin under the stove served to catch sparks or hot coals to prevent them from igniting the unpainted wooden floor.

In retrospect, I know that the floor was more prone to burn then than floors would be in schools today. It was common then to oil the floors to give them a uniform color, to hold down dust, and even to keep them from squeaking as they were walked upon. But apparently nobody ever worried that the oil made them more of a fire hazard.

This same school had very rudimentary light, with bare bulbs suspended from ceiling fixtures by nothing more than their electric wires. But I never remember anyone ever saying that this was dangerous, too.

This old school, which must have dated back to the 1800s, never did succumb to fire. It just died of old age and eventually was abandoned and later was razed. Now there is nothing but grass where it stood.

In my seventh year, I went to St. Patrick's School in Olyphant. And by the standards of the Jessup school, this structure was really "modern."

For instance, this structure had a steam heat furnace in the basement and it even had a fire escape from one second-floor classroom. But the furnace did not have any firewalls around it, and the fire escape provided the only entrance and exit from this one isolated room. And most of the wiring here was unsafe by today's standards. But in that era of the early 1940s, it apparently never bothered anyone.

This school was wooden, too, and it had oiled floors. But despite all its fire hazards, it never did burn down. It, too, died of old age and its grave is now covered by a grassy lawn.

Then I went to Jessup High School, a massive three-story wooden building that had its share of fire hazards, including the oiled floors, exposed wiring, and unprotected furnace rooms.

Yet, I walked out of there with my diploma in 1945 and it was still standing. In fact, it lived another 26 years, finally succumbing to a fire one night in 1971 when no one was in it. There were rumbles then that someone might have set the blaze, which would mean that the fire hazards never did cause its demise. But I can't be sure of that.

Then I attended the University of Scranton and went to a collection of buildings that contained plenty of the same type fire hazards that existed in my previous schools.

In that period, the university was bursting at its seams with the influx of the World War II GIs. So new classrooms were created by the overnight erection of wooden former military barracks on the campus. And they were as fire prone as the school in Jessup where I had been a first grader.

Ultimately, all of the old university buildings were razed, with fire never touching one of them.

With my college degree, I left school in 1949. And since then, I have never given much thought to the grave danger I had been in during those years as a student.

But now I read about school after school being closed down because of fire hazards, I can't help but wonder if we are not overemphasizing the dangers they represent.

Obviously, as the father of six children, I don't want to invite the cremation of school children. But most of us live in wooden homes that have no fireproof stairwells, enclosed furnace rooms, fire escapes, sprinkler systems, and other such things without feeling threatened.

If schools are such incendiary threats, how did my generation and those before us ever escape with our lives?

MANY IMPORTANT PEOPLE
ALSO AMONG THE NICEST

One of the great discoveries I have made in three decades of journalism is that many of the most important people in this world are also among the nicest.

Let me illustrate the point with a personal story:

About 23 years ago, as close as I can calculate, I was a reporter with the *Scrantonian-Tribune*, spending most of my time digging up feature stories for the Sunday paper.

Expected to turn out several major features a week, I was constantly on the lookout for story ideas. One day, Patrick McGlynn, a deskman who knew my needs, happened to spot a reference in a syndicated column about Eugene F. McDonald, the president of Zenith Radio Corp.

"You might get a story out of this guy," McGlynn said to me, adding: "He used to live in Scranton."

Being desperate for a story, I checked the newspaper's reference room to see if it had much material on McDonald, but I could find nothing. I wondered if McGlynn knew what he was talking about.

That was the end of the line that day as far as a McDonald story was concerned, so I found some other subjects and spun them into features.

But I kept thinking of McDonald, the millionaire whom the column had said had just spent a fortune on a new yacht. Finally, I figured I had nothing to lose by trying; I wrote him a letter saying I would like to write a story about his recollections of his years in Scranton. And, much to my amazement, I had a letter back from a secretary in a few days promising me that I would soon be hearing from McDonald.

A few weeks went by and I had almost forgotten the request, when I received a letter personally written by McDonald. He wrote of his family moving to Scranton from Syracuse, NY, and a job he took here at the age of 16 as an automobile mechanic.

The automobile was little more than a novelty when McDonald went to work for an agency that handled Franklins, an early model vehicle that has long since passed into history. He wrote that he recalled taking cars out and road testing them around a lake that he recalled was near central city. But he could not remember its name.

McDonald, whose father came here to publish the *Catholic Light*, also filled the letter with several other remembrances of his growing-up days here before he left for Chicago, where he found fame and fortune before the age of 30. I put all this information into a story that was buttressed by data on his career, which was provided by Zenith's public relations department. And the package, complete with a Zenith-provided photograph, made an interesting feature.

Because McDonald had noted in his letter that he would like to see what I eventually wrote, I tore the story from the paper and sent him a copy. Within days I received a thank you letter that said that a more concrete form of thanks also was in the mail for me.

In a few days a small package arrived and I opened it to find a transistor radio, a relatively new product in those days, and this one being the best that Zenith made. The radio, about four inches wide, five inches high, and an inch thick, had amazing power and could not even be compared to the cheap pocket radios that later came to dominate that market.

I have used this Zenith Royal 500 for over two decades, but some months ago I found a need to have some repairs made to it. A few radio shops here told me that it was too old to fix. So I sent it to the company in Glenview, Ill. to have it serviced.

The gold printing on the front of the radio says "Made Expressly For and Stolen From Joseph X. Flannery." To explain that, I included a note that this model had been given to me by McDonald prior to his death in 1958.

The radio was quickly serviced and returned to me without charge, with a note from the public relations office that the firm was happy to do this in McDonald's memory.

Thus, I still have my radio and it serves as a living reminder that there are persons around who rise to great heights and yet remember where they came from. McDonald rose from the obscurity of being an automobile mechanic in Scranton to become one of America's major industrialists, yet he took the time to answer a letter from a young Scranton reporter who was looking for a feature story. And then he had a personalized gift sent to say thanks.

As I said at the start, some of the nicest people in the world are found at the top.

MONEY FOR A DATE?
SURE, HERE'S $1.06

Imagine a full date for $1.06.

In this era of $3.50 movie tickets, 90-cent hamburgers, 30-cent cups of coffee, and cars that burn gasoline that costs over 60 cents a gallon, it is hard for a young couple to spend an evening together without it costing the young man a full 10-dollar bill.

Having three eligible daughters who are the beneficiaries of male-financed dates, I can feel sorry for the young men who have to visit a mint before going out.

And having two boys who have yet to reach the dating years, I worry about inflation of the future. Will they need a $20 bill from good old Dad before going out on dates? Or might it be worse?

I go back to 1945, when I dated my wife and when a few coins could get us through an eventful evening.

In particular, I mentioned the $1.06 date so I should explain that one a bit further:

This was a frequent outing to travel from our hometown of Jessup to attend a record dance in Archbald. It began by us walking from her home to Ketchum Corners in Peckville, a distance of about two miles, and then waiting for a bus there. Soon it would come and I would pay fares of 8 cents each, for a total expenditure of 16 cents. That would get us to Archbald.

From the bus stop there, we would walk a few blocks to the second-story dance hall where we paid a fee of 12 cents for admission. That included the basic charge of 10 cents plus a 2-cent "war tax."

The dance was not a very fancy affair. There was a man on a stage with a pile of records, a record player, and some amplifiers, and he would play the 75-rpm records in sets of three—two slow numbers and then a fast one—all evening. Glen Miller's Orchestra predominated, but the Dorsey bands were also included, and there were a few ballads by a young singer named Frank Sinatra.

During intermission, the man with the records and his friend who was selling tickets combined to sell *Cokes* at 5 cents each. So a dime took care of that pause that refreshed the dancers for the second half of the musical program. Then, it was back to dancing.

Inevitably, the dancers would hear "Good Night, Sweetheart" being played and they knew that this was the number that always ended the dance. So we would leave the hall, walk to the bus stop, and again pay 8 cents for the ride back to Peckville. So the cost for the two was another 16 cents.

Then, after arriving in Peckville, we would walk back to Jessup and stop at a local restaurant that featured 10-cent hamburgers and 5-cent coffees. Throwing in 10 cents for the tip, the total cost of this stop was 40 cents—the biggest outlay of the evening. (And bear in mind that the hamburgers were huge and so were the cups of coffee.)

Thus, the spending for the evening ended and the tally looked like this: bus rides, 32 cents; dance admission and *Cokes*, 34 cents; and the restaurant stop, 40 cents, for a grand total of $1.06.

Yes, those were the days when pennies, nickels, and dimes were coins to be respected and could finance many dates without any paper money to accompany them.

There were opportunities, too, for more economical dates than going to a dance in another town. For instance, a trip to the movies in Jessup would cost just 24 cents—10 cents each for admission and 2 cents each in "war tax." And another 10 cents would get us two huge candy bars that might cost you 40 cents each today.

Or we could go to a local jukebox parlor where all you had to do was buy a couple of nickel *Cokes* to spend a few hours there listening to music other richer kids were playing at a nickel a record.

And on special occasions, we could sometimes go to Scranton on the bus or D&H train, go to a movie there, go to a restaurant for pie and coffee, and get by with about $2.50 or so. That was expensive, of course, but we could swing it every once in a while.

Now, in this era of "cheap" $10 dates, I pity the young men who have to finance such outings—or those that cost much more. And, more pointedly, I pity their fathers who might be the ultimate source of the dating funds. Alas, that day is coming for me.

WAS RADIATION LEVEL
MORE THAN WE KNEW?

Hardly any layman understands radiation and therein lies the reason why most of us fear it so much.

Anybody who has ever been X-rayed knows that you never feel a thing as the photograph of your innards is taken. Yet, as if by magic, *something* does pass through your skin and flesh.

Mankind's brief experience with the use of radiation has been marked with some spectacular successes and some terrible failures.

The medical X-ray is an invaluable aid to prolonging life, but its early use did not involve enough precautions. Many a doctor, dentist, nurse, or technician working around X-ray machines developed some form of cancer because safety standards were not high enough.

I think it was the atomic bombs that were dropped on Japan 34 years ago that caused a new appreciation of radiation and led, indirectly at least, to a tightening of safety rules on its medical usage.

Sometime in that pre-atom-bomb world, I recall shoe stores in downtown Scranton that had portable machines that enabled persons to examine the skeletal structure of their feet as part of the shoe-fitting process.

These were big attractions to children, because they could stand in front of such machines, insert their feet, and then look through a glass screen that showed their foot bones and an outline of the nails and other metal parts of the shoes.

When these stores weren't busy, I used to love to examine my feet in these X-ray machines. It was fun to watch the bones move under layers of leather, cloth, skin, and flesh.

There was no indication of any danger from these devices, but only God knows how much radiation I and thousands of other persons picked up by using it.

In the same period, there were numerous clocks and watches on the market with the hands and numbers covered with radium paint that glowed in the dark. We had a few such alarm clocks in our home and I had a few such watches. And again, there was no indication of any danger from their use.

It was in the same era when dentists and physicians used to take X-ray pictures without taking adequate precautions to protect themselves or the patients. In fact, the very equipment they often used was faulty because it allowed for the leakage of too many damaging rays.

But after the first bombs went off, the study of radiation was intensified. Slowly but steadily the conviction grew that radiation was much more of a hazard than had ever been realized.

Gradually, the X-ray machines quietly disappeared from the shoe stores. The clocks and the watches with the radium paint were banned. And many X-ray machines were condemned as dangerous and were replaced with new machines and new technology that were based upon a new appreciation of the dangers of these invisible rays.

But these battles are not won quickly. During the tension-filled years of the Cold War, as the United States and Russia sought to gain military advantages, there was a furious race to create bigger and better nuclear weapons.

So testing was done on a large scale, not just in lonely parts of the South Pacific and Siberia but also in New Mexico, Colorado, and Nevada. All these tests pumped radioactive material into the earth's atmosphere, and again, only God knows how many persons may have been made fatally ill from the fallout.

Both the United States and Russia always insisted that the testing was not causing dangerous levels of radiation to fall on our heads. Yet, when other nations such as France and China began testing nuclear bombs later, the United States and Russia both screamed that they were damaging the world's environment.

A few years ago, in fact, we in Pennsylvania were radiated upon with fallout from Chinese test bombs. I believe that report was factual but at the same time I find it hard to believe that the Chinese bomb could cause radiation here—halfway around the world—and not believe that bombs set off in Nevada, for instance, did not do the same.

Mankind's long-range dealing with radioactive material shows a pattern of technology being more advanced than knowledge. Thus, we often had usable machines involving radioactive material before we realized their danger.

Marie Curie, one of the pioneers in the study of radioactive materials and their adoption for medical use, became a victim as she died of leukemia.

That sort of trail can be seen throughout mankind's use of radioactivity. And it is safe to assume that deaths have occurred here as the result of faulty X-ray machines, radium paint, and, yes, even atomic bomb fall-out.

Now we are into a national agony over the history of nuclear energy as a result of the accident at Three Mile Island—just about 130 miles from here. Some power plants now supply about 12 percent of our nation's electricity, but there are those who say that they are so dangerous that they should be put out of service immediately.

It's obviously another case where our technology has exceeded our knowledge about radioactivity.

April 17, 1979

COURTHOUSE SQUARE SHELTER
BECAME A COMFORT STATION

It always amazes me how quickly a national mood can be forgotten after it has passed.

And that is particularly true of bad moods we are not necessarily proud to remember.

For instance, how clear is our collective memory of the Great Fallout Scare of the early 1960s?

That was a time when Russia and the United States were rattling their nuclear swords, and we were all being warned that doomsday might be just around the corner.

Let me tell you, fear is an awful force once it begins to run wild. And in that era, we were being told that if we wanted to survive an almost certain nuclear war, we had to stay in a shelter until the radioactive dust had settled.

While this fear was a national phenomenon, the flames were fanned even more here as Emil Legman, who had won local fame as a leader in the fight of taxpayers against expensive government, suddenly took an interest in the nuclear fallout threat.

Legman, a charismatic speaker who could scare politicians with his tax-fighting techniques, had them eating out of his hands with the fallout issue.

The political figures, relieved that Legman was finally asking for something other than the curbing of taxes, promised him the moon when it came to his new crusade.

Thus, in quick order in 1961 and 1962, he was able to get Mayor James Hanlon to decree that no building permits would be needed for fallout shelters; County Commissioner Michael F. Lawler to agree to let a model shelter be built on Courthouse Square; and School Board President Patrick Mellody to order a study for the quick movement of children into shelters if a fallout emergency occurred.

Of course, it wasn't just Legmam who was frightened of Russia. There were many persons going around those days warning that many would die of radiation if a massive shelter plan were not adopted. In fact, the fear quality of some' of those talks was so great that it would be an embarrassment today to identify some of those speakers who still live in the community today.

Business got into the act too, as many firms offered bargains on shelter construction. Some advertised 10-by-eight-foot shelters for about $250. Others offered the materials for the do-it-yourself crowd at about $150.

The Civil Defense organization went into high gear, issuing all sorts of warnings from Washington on the kind of shelters that would do the most good, on how to stock them with food, water, and other provisions, and how long to stay in them in case of attacks.

A CD information rally at the Masonic Temple in 1962 attracted 400 persons, which seems like a good turnout, but it was reported as "disappointing" to its planners. They had warned that anyone interested in staying alive should attend.

Legman, who ultimately was named a CD aide in charge of fallout shelters, was assigned a police escort to take him around the city to examine railroad tunnels, buildings, and other sites as potential mass shelters. If there seems like a bit of hysteria in that now, consider that a shelter was also being built in those days for Gov. David Lawrence in Harrisburg and the Jermyn bank was incorporating a shelter into its plans for an addition that was then being made to its building.

Ultimately, the federal government began pumping money into the CD program to save millions from radioactive fallout. A system was devised for fallout shelters to be located in basements of public and private buildings. Then the stocking of these centers was begun.

Actually this work carried into 1963 and 1964, with the centers being marked with public signs and with supplies being moved into them for a potential attack. Ironically, by this time much of the hysteria had gone out of the situation— but the momentum of the federal government is hard to stop once it starts.

Thus, by mid-1964 it was reported that the local CD had passed only its "halfway" mark in stocking its shelters. This involved 78 buildings being equipped with 187 tons of supplies valued at $146,014. This was deemed sufficient to take care of 39,786 persons for 14 days.

Ironically, I could find no further record of this stockpiling effort because right around that time the Great Fallout Scare passed into history.

One of the first signs that the scare was ending was when some sensible people agreed that the time had come to get rid of the Legman-sponsored model fallout shelter at Courthouse Square. It had become the equivalent of a public restroom for bottlers in that neighborhood, and soon became an eyesore and a health hazard.

Quietly it was dismantled, with everybody feeling a bit silly over it ever having been built in the first place.

Over the years, most of the supplies put into the shelters here have disappeared. Some of the food was given to the Nay Aug Zoo for its animals, and some went to sportsmen's clubs to feed wildlife. But things such as medical supplies, tools, and radiation meters were stolen from most shelters.

The CD today does keep up-to-date the location of shelters and the signs, but it is a very low-keyed program that involves no stockpiling.

We have survived the 15 years or so since the Great Fallout Scare ended and so far nobody has dropped any bombs.

Looking back on that period now, it becomes clear that fear quite possibly was a worse threat than radioactivity. At least one could have built a shelter to escape from the nuclear dust. But there was no escape from the fear.

THERE WERE EVENTS IN ABE'S LIFE "LINCOLN" HIM WITH AREA

As Lackawanna County Republicans dine tomorrow night at the Casey Inn in memory of Abraham Lincoln, they will be only a few blocks away from where a bootmaker once fashioned footwear for the Civil War president.

Peter Kahler, a German immigrant who ran a large boot and shoe store at Wyoming Avenue and Center Street, knew a lot about making footwear, and quite a bit about public relations, too.

When Lincoln was campaigning for the presidency, Kahler went to New York and managed to get to see him there. He asked Lincoln if he could make him a free pair of boots, and when the candidate consented, the bootmaker had him stand bare-footed on brown paper so that he could draw the outline of his feet.

Kahler then returned to Scranton and made the boots that he later sent to Lincoln. In return, he got a letter of appreciation that acknowledged the comfort of the footwear.

Soon Lincoln was in the White House, wearing Kahler's boots, and Kahler was posting a sign in his window noting that his footwear clients included the president.

In the 1870s, Kahler and his family moved to New York City where he continued in the footwear business. And, the story goes, among the things they took with them was the brown paper that showed the outline of feet for that first pair of boots that Kahler made for the president, plus the letter that Kahler received in appreciation for the gift.

There are other frills to that story which may or may not be true. Among them is that Kahler subsequently made Lincoln several other pairs of footwear, including the shoes he wore on Nov. 19, 1863, when Lincoln delivered the Gettysburg Address.

One wonders now whether that Kahler family has descendants today who still treasure those mementoes—items that certainly would have great value because of the ongoing interest in Lincoln.

This is not this region's only link with this famous historical figure. In fact, three historical figures in their own right—David Wilmot of Bradford County, Galusha Grow of Susquehanna County, and Samuel Dimmick of Wayne County—played a major roll in setting up the strategy that got Lincoln nominated in the 1860 Republican Convention in Chicago.

Horace Greeley, the owner and editor of the *New York Tribune*, owned land in Pike County and often went there to get away from the bustle of New York. He was an ardent Lincoln backer and he was busy in 1859 lining up support. Thus, while on a visit here, it was natural for him to set up a pro-Lincoln meeting to try to get Pennsylvania on the bandwagon.

The session, held at Dimmick's law office in Honesdale, also was attended by Simon Cameron, a U.S. senator from Pennsylvania, and Andrew G. Curtin, who became Pennsylvania's governor in 1861.

At that meeting, strategy was mapped out for the Pennsylvania Republican delegation to throw support to Lincoln on a second ballot. Though planned a year in advance, that is exactly how the script turned out. The Pennsylvania surge toward Lincoln on the second ballot guaranteed him the nomination on the next ballot.

Wilmot, incidentally, a famed congressman from Towanda, was temporary chairman of that famous convention.

Another famous regional Lincoln story involves J. Summerfield Staples, a Stroudsburg man who served in the Union Army as a substitute for Lincoln.

In that war, rich men could avoid the draft by paying a substitute $300 to enlist in his name. Staples entered the army in 1862 as the substitute of a Stroudsburg man, but he developed typhoid fever and was discharged in 1863.

Meanwhile, a patriotic program was started under which men with valid deferments could volunteer to get substitutes for themselves. Under this plan, Lincoln decided that he would set a good example by getting a substitute for himself even though he was president.

How Staples was picked as the man is not known, but records show that Lincoln gave him $650 to serve in the army in his name. So he went back into the service in 1864, but got sick again and was discharged in 1865. He died in 1888 in Stroudsburg.

Meanwhile, a 36-star American flag bearing the blood of Lincoln is in the Pike County Historical Society, Milford, after having been kept for a century by descendants of a man who helped to carry him from Ford's Theater after he was shot there on April 14, 1865.

The flag, believed to have been in the presidential box when Lincoln was shot, was used to help cover him as he was carried to a home across the street from the theater. Thomas Gourlay, a member of the audience who helped carry Lincoln, kept the flag. His descendants, who later settled in Pike County, donated it to the historical society.

Thus, as Republicans sit down at Lincoln Day dinners in this region, they can do it with the knowledge that Lincoln had several direct connections with this area. They involved his feet, his political fortunes, his patriotism, and his very blood.

March 18, 1980

HONEST IS BEST:
TRY THAT ON FOR "SIGHS"

Back in 1866, Russian novelist Fyodor Dostoevsky wrote *Crime and Punishment.*

It is the story of a murder and how it haunts the guilty party long before the police ever track him down.

On a much smaller scale, I recall stealing 50 cents from my mother's purse when I was quite young—maybe 10 or 12 years old.

I say I *stole* it, but I really didn't acknowledge that at the time. Some visitor to our home—maybe my Aunt Kitty—had given me the 50 cents.

But, as often happened in those Depression days, I was told that the 50 cents was too much money for a child to carry around with him. "You'll lose it," I was told as the coin was put away—allegedly to help me buy something like a new pair of shoes at some date in the far distant future.

I felt cheated. I had grand plans for spending that 50 cents. I was going to buy a lot of candy and maybe a rubber ball and some other modest toy in Zimmerman's 10-cent store. But now I was broke again. And in those harsh times, a condition like that could be permanent.

I had never read any philosophic books at that point in my life, but instinct told me that if I were to take back the 50 cents, it would not be stealing. I would be legally justified in doing it, I figured out in my childish mind.

Thus, I resolved to act. I waited until an opportunity came for me to get my hands on my mother's purse and to open it and find my 50-cent piece. And I carried out the act, exactly as planned.

At this point, I was happy but frightened, too. I could hear my heart beat and feel my hands sweat—not unlike the central figure in Dostoevsky's classic. Yet, I was determined to make this a perfect crime.

I hid the 50-cent piece under a section of a rug which could only be reached by moving a piece of furniture. And I had made up my mind to deny any knowledge of this theft if questioned about it. Again, my justification was that this money was really mine and I was not doing anything wrong in reclaiming it by extraordinary means.

The weakness in my position, however, was that I had been trained from early childhood that it was wrong to steal, lie, or be disrespectful to a parent. Under our Catholic rulebook, the Baltimore Catechism, these were sins—pure and simple—and sins could send you straight to hell.

In the days that followed, I worried constantly that the disappearance of the 50-cent piece would be discovered. Every time I entered the house after being out for a time, I was certain that I was about to be confronted with some evidence of my crime. And at night, I remained awake long after my normal sleeping time, because this is when my mind raced with notions that I would soon be caught.

Not unlike Dostoevsky's murderer, I took to imagining certain things. Maybe, I thought, I had dreamed the whole thing. But a careful check showed that the coin remained exactly where I had hidden it.

Well, maybe everyone knew that I was the guilty party, but they were just waiting to see how long it would take for me to break under the pressure. I couldn't check that one out, but I hoped that it was not true.

During this whole period, I kept in constant touch with God. I prayed that he would remember that the money was mine in the first place and thus I had not stolen it. But I couldn't get a clear message back from God to make me absolutely sure that he understood my position. "Wouldn't it be awful if I were wrong?" I frequently asked myself.

Finally, after four or five days of this mental anguish, I decided that nothing was worth what I was enduring. So I resolved to undo my act.

Thus, I rescued the coin from under the rug and returned it to my mother's purse, being careful to put it back in the tiny change purse from whence it came. And with that done, I smiled a lot and breathed many sighs.

Over the decades, I can still remember my experience with crime and punishment. And I can understand the suffering that Dostoevsky's character endured.

I escaped, however—never admitting the crime until making this public confession.

And why do I bring it up now?

I do it to make the point that religious concepts of right and wrong are the best way to keep people honest.

If there were more internal controls stopping persons from stealing, lying, cheating, killing, and other such things, our crime rates would nosedive. But if people don't have that little voice inside them, telling them what's right and what's wrong, then civilization will not survive.

The rule will then become: Do anything you can get away with.

And there will be no punishment for crime—unless you get caught.

April 6, 1980

A MIRANDA WARNING
CAN BE FRIGHTENING

I had my Miranda warning given to me recently—and I didn't like it a bit.

That's the warning that law enforcement officials give a person when he is in danger of being charged with a criminal offense.

As laid down by the U.S. Supreme Court in a case involving a man named Miranda, a person about to be charged with a crime is given a warning that (1) he has a right to remain silent, and (2) he also has a right to be represented by a lawyer.

As a reporter who has covered court cases for years, I am well aware of the Miranda warning and what it generally means. Thus, as my rights were being recited to me, I was frightened.

Yet, I know myself well enough to know that I have never committed a crime—aside from a bit of jay-walking or parking overtime at a meter. But as the words were being recited to me, I was not unaware that there are times that cops make mistakes and charge the wrong persons with offenses.

The episode began one day recently in the newsroom when two men dressed in business suits asked a receptionist if I was in. She steered them to my desk and one immediately began by asking if there was some place private where we could talk.

It is not often that a person coming into a newsroom asks for privacy, but since there was a possibility that some major story was about to be dumped in my lap, I invited them into a private office that happened to be empty at the moment.

As soon as we entered the room, the two identified themselves as agents of the U.S. Internal Revenue Service. Then one began giving me the Miranda warning while the other took out a pad and pen as though to take notes.

I must admit I only half listened to the warning. Part of my mind was examining my past income tax returns to determine if I had made any

117

claim that I shouldn't have made. But I could honestly say my conscience was clear.

Finally, the warning was given and I was given the opportunity to ask what the gentlemen wanted to inquire about. (I must concede that the agents were gentlemen in every way, being quite polite about the way they spoke and the way they acted—up to this point, at least.)

I then was told that the IRS had information that in 1977 I had been paid $10,080 by a New York publishing company and that my tax return for that year did not reflect such a payment.

I involuntarily smiled at this point. So that was it: a $10,080 payment —an odd figure to begin with—that wasn't reported. I knew immediately that I was in the clear. It was all a mistake.

Yes, I said, I had done work for the publishing house in question. But while I couldn't be positive then of the year, I was positive that the fee I was paid was $1,000—not $10,080. And I had listed that on a tax return.

Did I have proof of that?

Well, yes, as a matter of fact, I had all my records at home and would be happy to produce them.

That day, as soon as I arrived home from work, I went through my files and came up with my 1977 records. And there, much to my gratification, I found all the proof I would possibly need to verify that my payment was $1,000. I had a letter from the publishing house mentioning the fee, a voucher that arrived with the check listing the amount, and a year-end statement from the company attesting to that being my earnings for the year.

The next day I was able to contact the same two agents and they came back to see me. I immediately showed them the records and they accepted them without further question. In fact, they seemed to be just as happy as I was that I could back up my story of the prior day.

The culprit in all this turned out not to be the IRS but a computer in the publishing house that printed out incorrect information that was sent out along to the IRS. Sure enough, it said that I had been paid $10,080—not $1,000.

I have no idea why the error occurred. But more than half jesting, I suggested to the IRS agents that they check out that company to make sure that somebody there had not creamed off some money and then attributed it to my account.

The story had a happy ending. But I cannot help but wonder what would have happened if I did not keep my records and if there was no way of proving that the computer data was incorrect.

It's a thought frightening enough to cause me to throw in a few extra bucks in my 1979 taxes that have to be paid by April 15—just to be sure Uncle Sam has enough and will not come back to read me my Miranda warning again.

JEWISH GIRL
BOOSTER OF PAGAN BABY DRIVE

I have no idea where Blanche is today, but I still remember her.

Back in the days when I was a student at St. Patrick's School in Olyphant, every collection that ever was taken up to raise funds to convert the pagan babies of the world was heavily influenced by Blanche's donation.

To understand the implication of that, it is necessary to know that Blanche was Jewish, so contributing to Catholic causes was not her obligation.

But Blanche not only gave money freely, she gave dollars in an era when many of the other kids were having trouble coming up with nickels and dimes.

These collections for pagan babies usually involved competition among the various classes. And each group was exhorted to give up candy bars and soft drinks so that the money saved could help a class catch up to and surpass the one leading the race.

However, it was always hard to beat Blanche's class, because she made big donations that usually devastated our puny efforts.

I have no idea whether Blanche's parents knew exactly where it was that her dollars were going. They had freely chosen to send her to the school and pay tuition there because they believed—and it probably was true—that St. Pat's then was a better school than the public school system of that era.

As far as I can recall, Blanche was the only Jewish child in this sea of Catholicism. She was exempted from religious classes but was a regular student of the school in every other respect.

Blanche, who came from a neighboring town, was quite bright and was quite a favorite with the nuns. Her generous parents often sent gifts for the teachers at holiday times. And given the vow of poverty that the nuns kept in those days, any gift larger or more valuable than a bruised apple must have seemed as though it had come from heaven.

The religious background of Blanche was respected, not only by her being exempted from religious classes, but also by her not being required to go to Mass, confessions, Stations of the Cross, or other Catholic rites in St. Patrick's Church. And as far as the other students were concerned, we were a bit envious that Blanche got excused from church services.

Blanche is one of the reasons that I first concluded that prejudices are learned, not inherited. In looking back over the years when Blanche was at St. Pat's, I can never recall a student thinking anything about her being Jewish—aside from envying the perquisites that went with her unique status.

I always had the idea that Blanche was rich because she always seemed to have money—including big donations for pagan babies. But maybe that wasn't really the case. Her family store eventually went out of business, which might have indicated that they were not really better off than many of us. Indeed, maybe her parents were simply more generous.

The money for pagan babies was always a big thing in parochial schools. The pennies, nickels, and dimes—plus Blanche's bills—were earmarked for missionary work. Thus, we were told that we were helping salvage the souls of babies in far-off corners of Asia and Africa.

The competition used to get pretty keen among the classes, with prizes being awarded to individuals and teams. However, if Blanche had her purse with her, it was akin to inserting Mike Schmidt as a clean-up hitter in a Little League game. We modest donors could get blown out of the ballpark when the returns came in from Blanche's class.

Blanche also was generous with her friends, seeming always to have candy or gum to pass out in an era when such treats were far from commonplace. It helped, of course, that her father's store was a 5-and-10 where such things were available to her without charge.

The same source also gave her plenty of new pencils, tablets, erasers, and other such items that were nice to have as long as there was no escape from schoolwork. That was true no matter what school one attended.

But buying up the souls of pagan babies was unique in parochial school. It was worked out mathematically how much each soul cost to convert. So a class could say with mathematical certainty that it had subsidized the conversion of a specific number of such children and put them on the path to salvation.

Catholics still give to their missions, of course. But we play down the concept of "saving pagan babies" shortly after they are born. It just is not realistic.

Yet I have to concede that it did dramatize the business of winning new converts. It made for great competition among classes to line up more pagan babies than anyone else. And even Blanche got swept up in the excitement.

April 23, 1981

DESPITE WOES,
SALVATION ARMY WAS SAVED

On Oct. 11, 1885—almost 96 years ago—there appeared a story in a local newspaper under the headline, "Salvationism vs. Housekeeping."

This was the text of the story:

"Thomas Thomas lives on Swetland Street on the West Side and his wife is an enthusiastic Salvation Army follower. She can sing and yell and go through the tactics of meeting and march like an old stager."

"On Tuesday, Thomas filed an objection to his wife's Salvation Army proclivities, because she substituted prayer and song for her household duties and thus compelled him to do more than his fair share of fasting. The way he 'filed his objection' was by beating and threatening to kill his wife, so Officer Devers had to come to the rescue by arresting the objecting Thomas and placing him 'hors combat for the nonce.'"

Well, the language is a bit stiff but the meaning is there. Mrs. Thomas was caught up too much with the spirit of the Salvation Army and her husband was not a bit happy about it.

That was not an unusual situation in Scranton in 1885—the year that the Salvation Army "invaded" the city.

Christians living here at the time, Catholics, Protestants, and Orthodox, were used to worship services that were quiet and sedate. Thus, many of them were shocked by the drums, tambourines, and parades of the Salvation Army.

Earlier that year, Mayor F. A. Beamish had issued an order to the religious group to hold down the noise on Sunday. That meant no singing.

However, the Salvation Army marched again the next Sunday, so the police chief and 13 of his officers went to the West Scranton building where the organization held its meetings. When they arrived, according to a newspaper, "the meeting was in full blast and the ringing notes of melody from the hall came re-echoing through the corridors to the ears of the waiting squad."

One of the officers went inside and, in the midst of a hymn, he called out to the person who was conducting the service that he was wanted outside. The leader obeyed the command and went out, where the police arrested him for violating the mayor's edict against singing in the Sunday parade.

On the way to the police station, the Salvation Army officer tried to get the officers to repent for their sins and to join the organization. He met with failure.

Meanwhile, a higher officer of the religious group and several of his men came to the station to bail out their colleague. A newspaper account did not describe their arrival in kind terms. It said: "They grew saucy and they persisted in their right to parade. As a result, they were soon in the cold hands of the law. When taken before the mayor they were released when they promised to refrain from making any noisy demonstration on the streets."

That afternoon the Salvation Army paraded again in West Side but this time there was no noise. Later, the leader who had been arrested was released and he was given a warm welcome by other members of the group at the meeting hall.

After this incident, a local newspaper commented, "It is believed the Army will hereafter bear in mind the suggestion of the mayor regarding order and give no further trouble."

Despite trouble of its own from husbands, the mayor, and the police, the Salvation Army survived and prospered here. And it did so without favorable publicity from the local press.

For instance, the very first story about the Army coming here on March 11, 1885, described it in less than glowing terms:

"The invaders are 14 in number and all are young men, none of them appearing to be over 25 years of age. Each wore a red jacket, across the breast of which was worked in picturesque letters, 'Salvation Army.' Some of them had letters worked in the back of their jackets, announcing that they had been saved by the Lord and like expressions. The majority of them wore peculiar shaped caps that did not improve their appearance but served to make them look more grotesque."

Yet by June 30 the movement had enough local support—reported at about a hundred men, women, and children—that it drew a visit from William Booth, the English founder of the Salvation Army. From that point on, there was little doubt that the organization was here to stay.

As for the fate of the Thomas couple, that is lost in history. And maybe that's just as well.

WEINBERG THRIVES
IN HAWAII REAL ESTATE

Don't look now, but Harry Weinberg is still making millions!

Weinberg, who made several million dollars in Scranton in the 1950s and 1960s, is now 72 and living in Hawaii—but he wouldn't know the meaning of the word "retirement."

According to a recent business magazine story, Weinberg's stock in the Dillingham Corp. recently appreciated about $13 million, largely because of his harassment of the firm's boards.

Dillingham is a $1.4 billion-a-year Honolulu conglomerate that owns much valuable real estate in Hawaii. Weinberg, who now holds 11 percent of the firm's stock, was once on its board, but he was eased off in 1967 by an offer to permit him to buy some of the firm's choice real estate holdings.

Last year, however, Weinberg decided he wanted to rejoin the board. He said he didn't like the way the firm was being run and he wanted to have more say in its control. However, the Hawaiian establishment that controls the firm short-circuited him by cutting the board from 15 to three members.

That kept him off the board but it failed to quiet him. He continued to hotly maintain that the Dillingham firm, has announced plans for the formation of a limited partnership comprising Dillingham shareholders that will take over much of the real estate, leaving the parent firm time to concentrate on its main activities of construction, shipping, and energy.

News of the plan caused the Dillingham stock to soar from about $24 to $32 a share. That jump meant an increase of $13 million in the value of Weinberg's holding.

And Corneulle grudgingly admitted what caused the development. He said: "Harry Weinberg accelerated our efforts to solve a long-standing problem."

The victory was just one in a long series of success stories for the former businessman from Baltimore who became a millionaire while operating here and who is now the richest individual property owner in Hawaii.

A rough, tough brawler, he is used to being looked down upon as an uncouth lout by the more suave and sophisticated businessmen he deals with. But with his money, he had no reason to be shy or reticent. For instance, he once told the head of the Dillingham firm: "Personally, you are a very fine gentleman. But as head cheese you have made too many mistakes."

In his wheeling and dealing in this area, Weinberg showed the same gruff exterior. But it never hurt his ability to make money.

Born in Austria, Weinberg came to America with his family when he was only 4. He grew up in Baltimore, where he made his first business successes in tire recapping and brick manufacturing. In time, he began buying and selling land. He also bought up bonds of the Baltimore Transit Co., getting into a field that would eventually attract him to Scranton and other cities.

While Weinberg became rich in Baltimore, his appetite for money was barely whetted there. He took a giant step forward by buying up bonds of the old Scranton Transit Co. at about a quarter of their face value. And by 1956 he had enough of the bonds to take control of the firm.

Weinberg's purchase was an excellent investment. He had spent a couple hundred thousand dollars and he wound up owning a firm with land and equipment worth over $1 million. He operated it for years, holding down costs and skimming off profits, but it finally went out of business in 1971. Only he knows how much he made by cleaning out its assets and selling off its land. But it had to be substantial. For instance, he sold off the firm's former garage to the city for $340,000—more than he put into the firm in the first place.

This was an economically distressed area and many persons were moving away because of that circumstance, but Weinberg found gold on our streets. He bought and sold real estate, always at a profit. And he did the same with several area companies.

Working from here, Weinberg extended his investments to New York, to Dallas, Texas, and to Honolulu. And eventually, he moved to Hawaii.

Now he is many times richer than when he was living here. Again, only he knows how much money he has. But after a business magazine once estimated his personal wealth at half a billion dollars, he pretended to be upset.

"They've ruined my credit at the bank," he chuckled.

HARD-WORKING MOM
RETAINED FEMININITY

There is no doubt about it. Mom was the boss in our house.

In many ethnic cultures, fathers try to maintain a macho image—at least in their own homes. But in Irish homes a generation ago, their chances of leadership roles were slim.

As we mark this Mother's Day, one would think that my memory of my mother might start dimming now that 29 years have passed since her death. But such is not the case.

My mother, born Clare Martina Reap, knew hard times most of her life. The oldest in a family of eight children, she had to leave school and go to work when her father died of miner's asthma. In the years ahead, she worked in a mill and then rented herself out as a seamstress to families that needed days—or even weeks—of sewing.

Back in those days there was no such thing as welfare, so a family that lost its wage earner had to support itself. Much of this burden fell first upon my mother because she was the oldest. Later, several of the other children went to work, too, but she continued to have a leadership position in her family.

Later, after she got married and had five children of her own, she remained a dominant figure. That was not a bit unusual in Irish homes. My dad was the nominal head of the family—as our religion required—but it was my mom who controlled the purse strings and made the big family decisions.

Consider, for instance, how she solved the problem of getting coal into our coal bin.

For years, our coal had to be dumped on the ground in front of our home because there was no way for a truck to climb the hill upon which the house was built. After pestering my father for years, she got him to scratch out a narrow driveway for coal deliveries. But that did not satisfy her. She wanted the job done right.

Mom finally ran out of patience. So she hired a contractor to come with a small power shovel to move hundreds of tons of dirt. The day the shovel arrived, my father disappeared. He didn't want to have anything to

127

do with the project. So my mom went out and told the workmen exactly what they were to do. And within hours, she had the digging completed. From that point on she had the driveway she wanted.

Despite such determination, however, my Mom was always a fine and upright lady. She deplored off-color language. She was deeply religious. She hated idle gossip. She was devoid of prejudice. And she loved Claudette Colbert movies.

One of the reasons why my mother was bossy was her clear perception of her duties to her family. She enforced curfews on her children because she had the notion that nothing good was going to come of being out late at night. And she was almost as strict with her mate.

The economic woes of the Depression complicated family life. Thus, my mom's duties multiplied rapidly as the need arose to save money. She used her skills at the sewing machine to make most garments needed by her brood. She could do an adequate job of cutting our hair. And she could crack lump coal if the fire needed it and there was no male around to be assigned to that job.

My mom was an amazingly creative person. With paintbrush, wallpaper, and material for drapes, she could transform the appearance of a room to match one that caught her eye in a magazine. Or she could see a dress in the same magazine, and she could copy it completely, without benefit of a pattern.

Like most housewives of that era, she was a slave to her duties. She did all our washing with a wringer machine, ironed all our clothes, baked our bread, and made our pies. When these chores were not occupying her time, she could strip a piece of furniture and refinish it, make slip covers for chairs, or even mix a batch of cement to do some bit of outside repair work.

As hard as she worked, however, she remained forever feminine. She dressed well, almost always in clothes that she had made herself. And for a holiday such as Easter, she could create a hat out of a few scraps of felt, dye a pair of slippers to match, curl her own hair, paint her fingernails, and convert herself into a marvelously attractive female.

After prosperity returned to America, my mom began to enjoy the luxury of new appliances, occasional vacations, and a few extra dollars in her purse. But then, just about the time when life appeared ready to let her enjoy many of the things she had been cheated of, she became ill. And she died—all too soon.

But on this Mother's Day, my memory of her remains strong. And I'm confident that she is the beneficiary of those rewards that God gives to all the good mothers of the world.

June 7, 1981

MURDER OF OWN CHILD
JUSTIFIED IN A DREAM

Sometimes I dream strange dreams.

For instance, there is the one where I am on the stand in court, defending myself on a murder charge.

"And now, sir, will you say if you shot one of your own children?"

"Yes, I did."

"Then, you admit it?"

"Yes, certainly."

"And will you tell the jury why you did it?"

"Of course. You see, this particular child was playing his records too loudly so I shot him."

At that point, all the members of the jury—persons of my own age —stand up or break into loud applause. The judge finally raps for order but there is no denying that he is pleased also. He looks down at me and smiles broadly.

"Your honor," the prosecutor interjects, "may I address the court?"

"Yes, go ahead."

"Your honor, not until this moment did I know the true circumstances of this shooting. But after hearing the cause of the shooting, I would like to change the charge in this case from murder in the first degree to justifiable homicide."

"What does the defense attorney have to say about that?" the judge inquires.

"Having felt the same urge to kill some of my own children, I agree with the prosecutor that this case be dropped."

"And the prosecutor? Do you have anything else?"

"Your honor, I, too, have often felt the urge to use violence to lower the noise levels in my own home. Maybe this case will serve as a warning to young people that they must begin turning down their music—or face dire consequences."

"Thank you, your honor. But I really don't know if I want to leave my quiet jail cell. After all, if I go back home and am exposed to loud music again, I can't guarantee what might happen."

"Well, with the first degree murder charge dismissed, we can't very well allow you to stay in our jail. So I'm afraid that you'll have to leave."

And on that note the jury stands up and gives me another ovation as I walk from the courtroom.

Then the dream switches to the outside where there is a big bunch of reporters, all wanting to interview me.

"Take it easy. You'll all have your chance," I say calmly. And then I start an impromptu news conference, telling the story of my act of violence.

"You see," I relate, "I had warned this child hundreds of times that it was annoying to have him playing his records too loudly. And many times I said that if the volume control was not lowered, I might kill him. Unfortunately, he never took the threat seriously. So I felt I had to act decisively once to get my other children to obey my quiet commands. That's why I did what I did."

The TV people asked me to make the same statement a few different times to make sure that they had it perfectly for the 6 o'clock news. And the newspaper photographers continued to snap away as long as I agreed to pose.

Dozens of private citizens also besieged me, asking me for my autograph. Others just wanted to shake my hand or tap me on the back and extend their congratulations.

By then my car came gliding up to the curb and I got into the back seat. Even as I closed the door, I could still hear the scattered applause of the spectators and news personnel.

Soon I was home again, surrounded by not only family members but by friendly neighbors, too. Even those closest to me said they understood what had provoked me, and instead of hating me, they admired me.

It was quite noticeable that evening that my home was unusually quiet. There was no raucous music, no screaming singers, and no pounding drums. One could hear a proverbial pin drop.

Thus, in this sedating atmosphere, I dozed off in my favorite lounge chair. And thus I slept with a big smile on my face.

My real dream that had started in the courtroom ended abruptly, however. One of my kids had put on a record and the sharp, piercing noises had crashed through my consciousness.

I jumped up, ran to the stairs, and yelled: "Turn that thing down before I kill somebody around here!" And with that, I shuddered involuntarily. What an awful thing to say to one's offspring.

THERE'S HISTORY INVOLVED IN KRESGE STORE CLOSING

A large piece of history was involved in the recent closing of the S.S. Kresge store at 415 Lackawanna Avenue.

Sebastian Kresge, who built the Kresge chain, was born in Lackawanna County and got his first taste of business in this city 95 years ago.

Kresge was one of those old-time business geniuses colorfully described by historians as "merchant princes." He built a simple idea into millions of dollars, yet never let his mind wander far from this area of his birth. He lived his latter years at Mountainhome in the Pocono Mountains, and he died at the age of 99 in a hospital in Stroudsburg 15 years ago.

The Scranton that the 20-year-old Kresge came into in 1887 was a booming town, but there was little in his first few years here that would hint that he would become one of America's most famous businessmen.

However, the newcomer who had given up on teaching because it paid so little must have noted that one of the successful downtown businesses in those days was a store that featured items for a nickel and a dime. It was run by Charles S. Woolworth, himself a newcomer to this bustling new center of anthracite coal production.

Kresge must have been in the Woolworth store often, and he must have been impressed by the way the working people of the community were buying up the cheap goods that were on display there. So maybe, many years later, that is where he got his idea for a similar store, and eventually, a chain of such stores.

Kresge was 30 when he opened his first store in Memphis, TN, in partnership with John McCrory. The year was 1897. By 1913 when he got around to opening a store in Scranton—the city where he got his first commercial jobs—he was well on the road to becoming rich.

Thus there is a strong Scranton tie to the Kresge chain, now more famous for its Kmarts than its older "ten-cent stores."

As noted, the city also had a historical link to the Woolworth chain. It was here in 1880—70 years before Kresge moved to Scranton—that one of the Woolworth brothers opened a store specializing in items selling for a nickel and a dime. That store turned out to be the second successful one in the chain eventually put together by the Woolworth family.

That Woolworth store, originally located at 125 Penn Avenue, is alive and well at 427 Lackawanna Avenue, right next door to the building that formerly housed the Kresge store and is now due to become the studios of WDAU (Channel 22).

This area seemed to have an affinity for "five-and ten-cent store" merchants. Fred Morgan Kirby, who built a string of such institutions, lived in Wilkes-Barre. In fact, C. S. Woolworth and Kirby were once partners in the operation of such a store in Wilkes-Barre. Later, they built their own chains and then they merged them all into the F. W. Woolworth chain.

Kresge, by the age of 55, felt that he had earned all the money that he could ever hope to own. He then made the vow to start giving it away through his Kresge Foundation.

Over the years, this area has done well in obtaining grants from the organization. The West Side Boys' Club was given $100,000 and Geisinger Medical Center was given $75,000 in 1975; the University of Scranton got $100,000 in 1976; the Scranton Primary Health Care Center got $140,000 in 1978; and Marywood College got $200,000 in 1981.

One of the chronic weaknesses of this area over the years has been a lack of philanthropy. Many of the persons who gained great wealth through coal and other area business enterprises moved away and promptly forgot the region. However, the Kresge Foundation reflected the wishes of the chain's founder not to forget the city that played such an important role in his early history.

Kresge, born in Ransom Twp., saw much poverty in his youth. His parents were farmers, but they were not very successful at it. He worked on the farm as a child but also studied hard and eventually became a school teacher. However, the pay was low and there was something stirring within him that urged him to move to Scranton and see what life was like in the big city.

His start was modest. He became a clerk and delivery boy for a grocer. Later, he went to work for a produce merchant. Then he became a bookkeeper for Howley Bros., a plumbing firm. Yet, the craving within him was not satisfied. So he decided to go on the road as a salesman, selling pots and pans.

The next five years were spent in a sort of on-the-job training program for becoming a merchant. He got to know people and to understand the psychology of selling. In particular, in his travels throughout the northeast, he was quite familiar with the stores that featured no items that cost more than a dime. Eventually, he had about $8,000 saved, and he and McCrory decided to go into business.

After the first store in Memphis succeeded, they opened a second one in Detroit. Later they decided to split, with McCrory keeping the Memphis store and Kresge keeping the one in Detroit. They both went from there to build their own chains. The rest, as they say, is history.

Now, however, the local Kresge store that the chain's founder quite often visited is gone. Of course there are the newer Kresge creations—the Kmart discount store—in Dickson City, Moosic, and Pittston. But with the closing of the downtown store, the personal link with the past has been severed. That chapter of local merchandising history has been closed forever.

February 11, 1982

QUINN FINDS JOY
IN QUEST OF PRIESTHOOD

I had a letter the other day from Joseph G. Quinn, the former U.S. magistrate here, who is now in the North American College in Rome studying to become a Roman Catholic priest.

But before I go into that letter, let me tell you a story from almost exactly this time last year.

I was home enjoying a day off when Quinn called and asked if I could meet him in his office. He said it was urgent.

"Could it hold until tomorrow?" I asked.

He replied that he didn't think it would.

"Is it something you could write out and I could make arrangements for someone else to pick up for me?" I asked, thinking that he had some sort of a news release.

Again, he indicated that there was an urgency about the matter and that he wanted to deal with me personally.

So I drove to town, found a parking lot near the federal building, and went up to his office on the fourth floor. En route, I had guessed what I thought he might want to talk to me about.

Four years earlier, I recalled, Quinn had discussed with me a notion that he might run for the Democratic nomination for mayor. A lot of persons were getting into the contest at the time, and Quinn, a handsome 30-year-old bachelor who oozed charm, asked me what I thought about the idea.

We talked in depth on the subject and I brought up all the points that I thought were pertinent: Could he get the endorsement? Could he raise enough money for a campaign? Did he realize the commitment he would have to make in the use of his time? Would a plunge into politics hurt the law practice he had just started to build?

I don't mean to create the impression that Quinn talked only to me. I assumed he picked the brains of a lot of persons in his deliberative process. He is bright, so it was characteristic of him that he would bounce his idea off many people before he would make a decision.

In the end, Quinn decided not to run for the mayoral nomination in 1977. But on that day of February 1981, when he asked me to come to his office, I began to suspect that he might be going to run for mayor. The more I thought about it, the more certain I became about my guess.

When I went into his office, he greeted me warmly and asked if I had any idea why he wanted to see me. I said that my guess was that he was about to take the plunge into politics that he decided against four years earlier.

"No," he said, "I'm going to study for the priesthood."

I was amazed. My news sense had failed me. But at least I could understand his insistence upon dealing with me personally. This was a delicate matter to disclose. Yet, he had to do it publicly, because he had to give formal notice to the federal judges—his bosses—that he would be trading his magistrate's robe for a cassock.

Frankly, I felt honored to be able to break that story. It was an important thing to be entrusted with, and I was pleased that Quinn was so insistent about seeing me on my day off—when I was trying to put it off until the next day. He had pressed me to do it quickly because he already had told his family, and he knew that news of his plans would soon be something less than a secret.

Well, all that happened a year ago. And now I have a fresh letter from Quinn, reacting to the decision of the *Sunday Times* to name him local religious newsmaker of 1981. He said he was "humbled" by the decision.

The letter continued: "Looking back upon 1981, I readily acknowledge that it was truly a remarkable year in my life, a turning point, so to speak. Once you have penned that very first article, I knew that life would never again be the same."

"And yet I really don't think I was ready for what then did follow. As you know, the story went out on the wire services and the 'news' traveled literally the length and breadth of our country."

"The story, of course, always read the same. The headlines, however, were something else. In Pittsburgh, for example, one paper printed it under 'Magistrate Trades Bench for Pulpit.' In Philadelphia: 'There Goes the Judge!' In the *National Law Journal*: 'Magistrate Sets His Sights Higher.' In Texas: 'Magistrate Spurns the Law.' And in Chicago: 'He Had It All, But His Life Was Empty.'"

"It was quickly obvious to me by the reactions of others that the news was, putting it mildly, a shock to most people. And yet to those who know me in the fullest sense of the word, the act of acceding to what I had long perceived to be a standing invitation to serve God as a priest came as no real surprise. The unexpected aspect was the timing of my response to that invitation."

"I should hasten to inform you that my circumstances are not all that unique. Among the 180 seminarians here at the North American College, there are currently six lawyers. When asked why so many lawyers were turning to the priesthood, a friend remarked that there were no simple explanations, but jokingly added that next year's class probably would include a few former air traffic controllers."

"Whether the apparent change in my life's pursuits warrants the attention given, it is a determination I deem best left to others. For me, it was the resolution of at least 10 years' reflection and prayer. I had always sensed that my vocation was Christ's priesthood. Yet when presented with the alternative options along life's path, 'the other road,' whatever it was at that particular juncture in my life, loomed as the easier one to travel."

"At this admittedly early phase of my formal studies, I can say that no other path—in law, in government, in politics, in education, or in community service—as I experienced it—ever challenged or enthused me as does the goal of service to God and my fellow human beings in the capacity of a priest."

Quinn added a kind word for the people he left behind, saying that he knows of none anywhere who are as friendly, loving, and supportive as those who live in this area. He added: "'I longingly look forward to my ultimate return to work in the Diocese of Scranton in service of its people in the name of Christ."

"Until then, please extend my heartfelt thanks to all for your continued expressions of support. I can only assure you and so many countless others that I remember you all daily in thought and prayer."

I can only add that letters like that give me a lift.

February 28, 1982

FROZEN WASH STUCK
TO BACKYARD LINES

Oh, how I hated to take in the wash from the backyard line on a cold day in the winter.

The clothes often were frozen to the rigidity of plywood, and taking them off the line meant bending their stiffened corners to pry them free. This had to be done carefully, because there was always the danger that a fabric, welded by ice to the rope, would tear if it were not removed with care.

The general idea was to take the garments from the line and to crunch them up into a clothesbasket—usually a wooden one that came into the household originally as a holder of apples. Getting frozen garments into a basket was not easy, however, because they were so stiff.

One had to almost wrestle with a suit of long underwear, for instance, to get it into a container. And even when the job was done, the "legs" and "arms" of the underwear were usually sticking out in the grotesque shape of a person with many fractures.

Long underwear was a particularly tough garment to take from the line because it apparently held more water than, say, a bed sheet or a dishtowel.

Thus, shortly after it was hung out it was frozen stiff, and it remained that way until night began to fall, and getting the clothes back into the house became a family chore that had to be completed before the early winter darkness arrived. It was at such times that the general order was issued for the kids to help take in the clothes.

Sometimes a suit of long underwear was frozen so solidly that, after it was freed from the line, it could be stood straight up against a fence or the clothesline pole. Several of those in a row made a strange sight indeed.

The long underwear and all the other frozen pieces would unfreeze shortly after they were taken back into the house. They were draped over kitchen chairs, over the oven door, on the water heater behind the stove, or anyplace else where the drying process could be completed.

Depending upon the size of the wash and how quickly the clothes had frozen when they were outside, the garments were sometimes almost as wet—when they thawed out—as when they went through the last wringing process in the washer that morning.

For a time, this made the air inside of the house, especially in the kitchen, quite moist. Soon all the windows would be covered with steam, and sometimes it would freeze at the edges if the air outside was cold enough. Meanwhile, the drying garments also would give off the aroma of the strong laundry soap that had been used to get them clean. Oddly, the memory of the moist, warm air and the odor of the soap remain with me after all these years.

Despite the inevitability of garments freezing on the line on cold winter days, it was never considered not to hang them outdoors. There was a general feeling that the outside air and the sun had a cleansing quality about it, so it was necessary to "air" washed garments even on the coldest days of winter.

Wooden clothespins were used to anchor the garments to the line, but after the articles were frozen, the clothespins could be removed and the garments would continue their frozen clutch onto the rope line.

To conserve line space and clothespins, it was general practice to lap the corner of one garment over the corner of another—thus making it possible for one clothespin to do the work of two. That was fine when the clothes were being hung, but when it was time to take the frozen garments back into the house, there was the added task of disconnecting the corners of the garments. Again, if this wasn't done carefully, there was a danger of the fabric being ripped.

In our house, at least, there was a custom of washing the rag rugs in the washer after the regular clothes had been completed. The idea was to save water—much of which had to be heated on top of the coal stove, because the small water heater attached to the stove could never produce hot water in the volume that was needed. Besides, the rugs didn't have to be cleaned with the same thoroughness as, say, the long underwear.

The rag rugs, when wet, weighed a ton—or so it seemed. Thus, they were not put on the rope lines for fear they would break them. Rather, they were hung on a fence.

Naturally, these rugs froze along with everything else. When they were taken into the house at dusk they were like boards. Drying them inside the house usually involved draping them over several chairs overnight.

Today, all this is changed. New man-made fabrics don't hold water the way the older fabrics did. Automatic washers spin much more water out of the clothes than did the old wringer-type washers. Thus, if clothes are hung outside they are less apt to freeze like the waterlogged clothes of yesteryear.

However, most persons use automatic dryers anyway, making it completely unnecessary to put the garments outdoors in the dead of winter.

I'm all in favor of those changes, of course. Only a fool would want to return to the days of frozen clothes on a clothesline. Yet, automatic dryers produce nothing that is apt to be remembered by any column writer a few decades from now. I'm glad I don't have that problem.

November 4, 1982

WOULD-BE "STAR"
HITS CUTTING ROOM FLOOR

I never thought of being a movie actor until Jason Miller, the ex-Scrantonian, brought up the subject.

"Joe, I'm going to make you a star," he said to me one night last June, as I chatted with him about his movie project in his room at the Nichols Village Motel in Chinchilla.

But while his tone was jocular, he did, in fact, want me to play the role of a press photographer in his film, *That Championship Season*, which he then was preparing to film here.

My reaction at first was negative. I probably would not do it right, I thought. The only prior show business experience I had had was as the stage manager of a high school play. Besides, I would hate a movie to get panned by some smart-aleck critic because of my fumbling of lines.

But Jason insisted. "Come on, there's nothing to it," he said with the assurance of a person who was nominated for an Academy Award for the first role he had had in a film.

I wavered in my resolve.

Then he added the magic words: "And you'll get paid according to the Actors Equity scale."

"Where's the script?" I said, jutting out my chin to create an interesting profile.

Well, to make a long story short, I went through with the filming as planned.

I spent several hours one evening at the scene of a staged "accident" at the old Household store on Lackawanna Avenue, pretending that I was taking pictures for a newspaper. I got $27 for that nonspeaking role.

Then I spent a 12-hour day filming a single scene in the elephant pen at the Nay Aug Park Zoo, a grueling experience because of the 95-degree heat and the need to repeat "takes" 10, 12, and 15 times before Miller was satisfied. I spoke in this scene and was paid $298 for my labors—the basic rate for a single day of filming with dialogue.

That did not end my involvement with the movie. A few weeks after the film ended, a film crew returned here and I was told that I was needed for a few close-up shots that would be filmed in the elephant's pen. This time it took only a few minutes, but, because this was part of a "talking" scene, I was paid another $298.

At that point I was starting to feel that acting was not such a bad way to earn one's living.

I started to kid about being "an actor between movies." And I also began to look forward to seeing my film debut on the giant silver screen in the New York City premiere set for Dec. 8.

I know, of course, that I was sharing the acting in the movie with such stars as Robert Mitchum, Bruce Dern, Paul Sorvino, Stacy Keach, and Martin Sheen. But, as far as I was concerned, this was "my" movie. Besides, I'm not afraid of competition.

Well, that's the way things were until yesterday. Then I got a telephone call from Bill McAndrew, another local resident who has a much bigger role in the movie. He was calling from Hollywood, where he had gone to add some dialogue to the sound track. And he had some bad news for me.

Bill had seen the movie at a private showing in a theater in Beverly Hills, and he reported that numerous local scenes had been deleted, including my own.

"What!" I cried. "They can't do that to me! Let them cut scenes of Mitchum or Dern or Sheen. But leave mine alone!"

However, my outcries were useless. The deed was done. I was on the cutting room floor.

The movie still is in the editing process, and there is a chance that some of the deleted footage could be added again, but my instincts tell me that this is not about to happen. The movie still is running a little long at one hour and 56 minutes, and Miller still is talking of picking up its tempo with more trimming. That doesn't sound very hopeful.

I can console myself with the knowledge that there are literally hundreds of persons in this area who are on the cutting room floor with me, including a few who had talking parts. But one tends to become very selfish in show business. I wouldn't be surprised, for instance, if Paul Newman would be upset if one of his scenes were cut to make room for one involving his wife, Joanne Woodward. Yes, show business truly is a dog-eat-dog business.

Thus, I have to face the fact that my show business career may be over—my talents as an actor never to be showcased for the world to see.

Tragically, it came at a time when I was hoping for something a bit more serious in my next film—maybe, for instance, something from Shakespeare.

March 3, 1983

CURLEY REMEMBERED
FOR HIS SHENANIGANS

They called him "James Michael Curley Hisself."

That is the way the Boston Irish referred to him in his glory days.

He was a four-time mayor of Boston, a member of the U.S. House of Representatives, governor of Massachusetts, and the last of the big city political bosses.

Curley also was the main speaker at the St. Patrick's Day dinner here in 1936. He was governor then and was known to his enemies as "King James I of Massachusetts."

Curley spent two terms in jail, running for alderman during one of them, and being mayor during the other. He faced a third jail term once for keeping money belonging to the city, but when the people heard about his troubles, they came by the thousands and donated money to pay the obligation.

Curley got into many fights, both physical and otherwise. On the morning of his inauguration as governor, he settled a grievance with the outgoing governor with punches. And when he sought to become ambassador to England, France, or Italy, but was offered instead the ambassadorship to Poland, he barked at President Franklin D. Roosevelt: "Why don't you resign the presidency and take it yourself?"

Fate was indeed cruel to Curley. He was married and had nine children by his first wife. She died of cancer while some of the children were tots. In the years that followed, seven of the children died. One of the two survivors, the Rev. Francis X. Curley, S.J., of Holy Cross College, was on hand to give his father the last rites of the Catholic Church when he died in 1958.

Curley was a determined man. When the state's Democrats froze him out of the Massachusetts delegation to the 1932 Democratic National Convention because he was backing Roosevelt instead of Al Smith, he made other arrangements. When the roll was called on the presidential nomination, the chairman of the Puerto Rican delegation was "Jaime Miguel Curleo," and he proudly cast the island's six votes for Roosevelt.

Curley, the child of Irish immigrants, dropped out of school at 15 and became a deliveryman for a grocery store. But he had a quick mind and a silver tongue. Thus, he drifted into politics, first as a ward worker and next as a candidate for the Boston Common Council. He lost in his first race, but immediately went to work planning a second one.

Part of that preparation was to do favors. In one case, he took a postal examination for a friend who was trying to get a job as a mail carrier. The plot was uncovered and he was arrested. That earned him a 60-day jail term.

However, Curley was a positive thinker. While he was in jail he started his campaign for alderman. And he turned his criminal conviction to advantage by bragging that he was proud to have helped another man get a job.

In the campaign, he was often confronted by a heckler who peppered him with embarrassing questions. One night he invited the man to the platform, smiling broadly as he said: "Please make a path for the gentleman."

The man warily approached and began climbing the stairs. When he was near the top, Curly punched him, knocking him to the ground. Curley's men then carried him from the area. "I think that answered the gentleman's questions," he said.

After a few terms as a city legislator, Curley decided to run for Congress. The Good Government Association opposed him, so he formed a group with a similar name.

When his opponent put up signs that said, "Send a big man to do a big job," he had his own people paste inserts at the bottom of the signs reading, "Elect a humble man, James Michael Curley."

Curley sent workers out in the middle of the night to pound on doors and ask persons inside to vote for his opponent.

When Curley, the congressman, decided to run for mayor, the incumbent was Francis "Honey Fitz" Fitzgerald, the grandfather of President John F. Kennedy. Curley wanted him to get out of the race, but he refused. Curley knew that Fitzgerald had a female friend named Toodles Ryan. Thus, Curley put an advertisement in a newspaper that said he was preparing a speech called: "Great Lovers from Cleopatra to Toodles." Fitzgerald dropped from the race and Curley coasted to an easy victory.

Curley was a busy mayor, improving the appearance of Boston with hundreds of public projects. However, it was clear to most observers that he got cuts on all the contracts.

When he ran for a second term, his opponent, a fellow Irishman named John Murphy, loomed as a major threat. Curley had his people spread tales that Murphy ate steaks instead of fish on Fridays, and that he was about to get a divorce to marry his 16-year-old girlfriend. Curley also had a "Baptists for Murphy" group formed—for reasons too obvious to mention. He also paid a minister with links to the Ku Klux Klan to attack him, Curley, on his Catholicism, and to make sure the news of it got into newspapers. Then, when Enrico Caruso died, Murphy issued a statement expressing his grief, but Curley went to a public memorial and cried loudly in front of 25,000 mourners.

As mayor, Curley often was balked by the bankers when he sought city loans. But he could play hardball in that league. He called one banker, told him that there was a city water main right under a bank, and if the bank did not approve a city loan immediately, the pipe might spring a leak and flood its basement vaults. The loan was granted.

As governor, Curley remained unorthodox. He appointed a woman as state librarian although she owned no books and confined her reading to *True Confessions* and *Spy Stories*.

While a member of the U.S. House, Curley had the misfortune of lending his name to a company that existed to bring business firms and government procurement officers together. The company paid little heed to the law. Eventually, Curley was arrested, along with the other officers.

With that hanging over his head, he ran for mayor again and got elected. But just as his term was starting, he went to trial and was convicted. He was sent to jail for six to 18 months, but he remained as the mayor. And when he came home, a huge crowd was there to meet him.

That pretty much was Curley's "last hurrah." He ran for office a few more times but lost. Then, at 83, he died—ending a most improbable career.

MICHAEL DAVITT REMEMBERED AS CHAMPION OF IRISH FARMER

This has nothing to do with St. Patrick's Day, which will be marked Thursday, but the proximity of the Irish holiday serves as a convenient excuse for today's column.

I recently received a clipping from the *Irish Echo*, a New York City publication, with a note from Prudence Murphy, the retired Scranton School District secretary. The story told of a fundraiser being held in New York to help the town of Staide in County Mayo, Ireland, to erect a monument in honor of Michael Davitt, a one-of-a-kind Irish patriot who was born here.

In the accompanying note, Miss Murphy said that her late uncle, historian and *Times* associate editor, Thomas Murphy, had often written about Davitt, a frequent visitor to the home of his sister, the late Mary Padden, in Scranton.

Davitt, who died in 1906, still is remembered in Ireland for the role he played a century ago in opposing the eviction of Irish farmers from their soil by English landlords. In 1879, he founded the Land League, a political movement that fought for tenure guarantees for Irish farmers, for reasonable rents, and—when necessary—for fair prices in sales.

Davitt's visits to the United States occurred in the last two decades of the 1800s and the first few years of this century. Whenever he came, he tried to get to Scranton to visit his sister. On his trips to America, he also was suspected of gathering financial support and maybe even guns for those who felt the only way to free the country was through open warfare—an idea close to his own heart. Whether any such business was ever carried out in Scranton is pure conjecture, but given Davitt's radical background, such a notion is not hard to believe.

Stories in the *Times'* files noted that Davitt's nephew, James, operated a hotel at North Washington Avenue and Phelps Street for a number of years. Whether there are any kin living here now is unknown to me.

Davitt eventually became somewhat of a radical among Irish rebels. He was anticleric in the most Catholic land of the world, and he tilted toward socialism in a period when such economic doctrine was considered an invention of Satan.

Mayo, where Davitt was born, was one of the poorest counties in Ireland, and incidentally, it was the one from which many of the Irish settlers of this area came.

When Davitt was only six years old, his father, a peasant farmer reeling from the economic impact of a massive potato blight, could not pay his rent to the Englishman who owned his farm. Thus, he and his family were evicted and were forced to migrate to England, the nearest place where jobs might be available.

At the age of 10, Davitt had to go to work in a cotton mill. During one of his long work shifts, his clothing became entangled in a machine and his arm was amputated.

With poverty constantly gnawing at the family, the one-armed child was then sent to a printing shop. In the next few years, he mastered the printing craft, and might have spent the rest of his life in it if it were not for his fierce loyalty to Ireland and the cause of freeing it from English rule. Thus, at 19, he joined an underground Irish paramilitary organization in England and began working for Irish independence.

Davitt was arrested at 24, charged with sending guns into Ireland, and was given a 15-year sentence by the English court. He was paroled after seven years, and in 1879 he sailed for the United States, where his mother and the rest of his family had resettled after his father's death.

By this time in his life, Davitt was totally dedicated to the Irish cause. He went back to Ireland, joined forces with Charles Stewart Parnell, and helped persuade the latter to incorporate agrarian reform into the demands that were being pressed by Irish politicians in the British House of Commons.

However, while Parnell was a polished statesman, Davitt was a hothead. Shortly after he organized the Land League, he was rearrested because of the violence he was preaching in many of his speeches. After three years of detention, he was released again, but he resumed his anti-British attacks and soon was in custody again. This time, while in prison, he ran for a seat in the British House of Commons and won. However, he was blocked from taking the seat because of his criminal record. He was released from prison shortly thereafter.

If anything, Davitt was becoming more of a radical by the day. He began to call for Irish freedom with nationalization of the land for the peasants. Parnell, himself a landowner, broke with him on that idea.

Davitt subsequently was elected twice more to the House of Commons, but was blocked again from taking his seat, first because of his criminal record, and the second time because he was involved in a bankruptcy. Elected a fourth time, his opponents then ran out of excuses for blocking him from being seated. In the Commons he fought primarily for concessions for Ireland, but resigned in protest over British military actions against Dutch farmers in South Africa.

According to the *Times'* files, Davitt made numerous visits to this city while he was a famous Irish patriot. One story said of him: "He was pleasant and interesting and made many friends here."

Davitt is indeed from the distant past. But in his hometown in County Mayo, he still is a hero and will soon be memorialized there.

March 17, 1983

IRISH STORIES HAVE STAYING POWER

This being St. Patrick's Day, I'd like to share some Irish jokes with you.

The first four are tales the late Con McCole, the humorist and former Wilkes-Barre mayor, told me when I did a feature story on him years ago. The final one was told to me by James A. Kelly, the local lawyer, who said he'd heard it recently in Boston, and it is Tip O'Neill's favorite after-dinner joke.

I'll begin the McCole yarns with the one he told every St. Patrick's Day about Mrs. Flynn and Mrs. O'Toole watching a baseball game in Minooka, with their sons pitching shutouts against each other. Each woman was furiously thumbing her rosary under her shawl and calling upon God and/or the Blessed Virgin to tilt the match in favor of her son.

Suddenly, with two out in the bottom of the ninth inning, young Flynn came up to bat against young O'Toole, and as luck would have it, he knocked the ball out of the county, winning the game 1-0.

Mrs. O'Toole was deeply distressed, feeling that she had prayed hard enough for her son to win, and was more than a little upset that her prayers had not been answered. But being a good Catholic, she still knelt down to say her rosary before she went to bed that night.

It was then that she discovered that there was a bead missing from the third decade.

"Oh, would you look at that!" she said to herself, shaking her head in wonderment. Then she looked heavenward and added: "Now, Lord, I know why me boy lost."

Then there is the McCole joke about the Irish pastor who was in the sacristy and noticed a man out in the otherwise empty and dimly lit church, looking at the fourteenth Station of the Cross.

Staying in the shadows, the priest observed as the man moved to the thirteenth station, then to the twelfth and so on until he got to the sixth. Not only was he going the wrong way but it was obvious by his gait that he had been drinking.

Finally, the pastor could stand it no longer. He stepped out of the shadows and said: "Sir, what are you doing there?"

The man, startled by the voice and the sight of the priest, replied: "I'm making the Stations of the Cross, Father."

"But you're going around backwards!" the priest boomed.

"Backwards, is it?" the man mused. "That explains it! He was getting stronger all the time!"

Then there is the McCole joke about Maggie baking bread in her kitchen while her husband, John, was on his deathbed in the front room.

John, weak and resigned to his fate, suddenly became aware of a delicious aroma from the kitchen. In a weak voice, he called out to Maggie to come to him.

The poor woman, fearful that death might be upon him, rushed to his side. But she found him sitting up in bed. He said: "Maggie, darling, I can smell that fresh bread and I'd dearly love to have a tiny bit of it before I die."

"Oh, Johnny, I'd do anything for you and you know it, me love," Maggie replied, adding: "But I can't give you the bread."

"Why not, me darlin'?" he asked.

"Oh Johnny, me love, the bread's for your wake."

Then there is the one about Pat and Mike working on a broken waterline in front of a house of prostitution.

Suddenly, Pat said: "Mike, did you see that? The Rev. Elliot Thitterspoon just went into that terrible place! What a scandal there'd be if his good Protestant parishioners saw what we saw!" Mike agreed totally. Then they went back to their digging.

Some time later, Mike said: "Pat, that was Rabbi Solomon Silverman going in. If his good Jewish people ever saw that they'd be shamed!" Pat agreed. Then they resumed their work.

Then Pat cried out: "Oh, Mike, look at that! That's Father Clancy going in that wicked place! What do you suppose that's about?"

Mike instantly replied: "I'd say there must be someone in there who's terribly sick and in desperate need of the sacraments." Pat nodded his head in agreement and they resumed their digging.

Finally, there is the Kelly joke about English suspicions in World War II that some anti-British Irishmen might be passing military information to the Germans.

To check on the reports, the British got the Americans to drop one of their spies into Ireland to check out the reports with an undercover Irish agent named Murphy.

The American spy was told he would be parachuted into the region in civilian clothes, and that he should seek out "Murphy" at night, using a coded message to make sure he had the right person. Thus, anytime he found a "Murphy," he was to say: "The sky is clear, the moon is high, and the dawn will come."

The American was dropped from a plane at night, landed safely, hid his parachute, and started walking along a country road en route to the village he could see in the moonlight.

Just then, a horse-drawn cart came up behind him, and the driver stopped and offered him a ride. He readily accepted.

The driver, looking over the stranger's clothes and hearing his accent, immediately identified him as an American and asked what he was doing in those parts. The American faked a story that he was a visiting business-man looking for a relative named Murphy.

"Murphy, indeed!" the Irishman said, adding: "You've come to the right area. In this village you'll find Murphy the innkeeper, Murphy the school teacher, Murphy the undertaker, Murphy the priest, Murphy the tailor, and I'm Murphy the farmer."

The American, thinking that it might even be the man he was riding with that he was to meet, said softly: "The sky is clear, the moon is high and the dawn will come."

Upon hearing the words, the farmer immediately replied: "Oh, it's Murphy the spy you'd be looking for. I'll drop you at his house."

May 24, 1983

DO YOU HAVE A SECOND TO READ THIS?

We measure time in such a precise way that one might get the idea that at the moment that God finished creating the universe, he installed a clock somewhere and set both its hands at 12—all ready to start ticking.

However, time—or rather, the way we measure it—is totally a man-made system.

We created a calendar to measure time in large blocks, and sundials, and later, clocks, to measure it in smaller segments. Without them we could not record history or plan next Sunday's dinner.

The periods we measure with time have to do with daylight, darkness, and the changing seasons. What causes such things, of course, is the direction Earth faces as it makes a complete circle on its axis once a day and as it goes around the sun once a year.

But, as with most man-made systems, the one to measure time is not perfect. It has to be corrected occasionally. Centuries ago, such corrections involved large segments of time—large chunks that were dropped from the calendar to get time calculations back in synchronization with such obvious things as the change of seasons.

On one such occasion when the calendar had to be adjusted, the birthday of George Washington was shifted. The old one was Feb. 11, 1731, but the new one was Feb. 22, 1732. The change in the date of the month corrected an 11-day gap between two calendars, and the change in the year reflected a switch in New Year's Day from March 25 to Jan. 1.

If that sounds complicated, imagine how confusing it must have been for Washington's friends and relatives who had to buy him birthday presents every year.

We no longer have such big changes in our time systems. Now we are pretty much down to fine-tuning—which is what will happen on June 30 when an extra second will be added to the clocks of the world.

Few persons will notice, I suppose, that on the final day of next month there will be one minute that will contain 61 seconds. One such clock that will be adjusted immediately will be the master one at the U.S.

Naval Observatory in Washington, D.C., where the "official" time of our country is kept.

That will be part of a worldwide adjustment in time originating from Greenwich, England—the "time center" of Earth.

When our system of time was invented, the world was divided into 24 zones, with Greenwich in the middle. As one moves away from Greenwich—in either direction—there is a one-hour difference in each time zone. That's also why we have an International Date Line, where it is always one day on one side and another day on the other. (If you have trouble understanding that concept, don't feel badly, because I do too.)

To keep the rest of the world in accord with Greenwich time on June 30, identical localized adjustments will have to be made to insert the extra second into time calculations. Thus, at 7:59 p.m. Eastern Daylight Time, the 61-second minute will be observed around the globe.

This sort of fine-tuning is done whenever the international scientific community agrees that the rotations of Earth are running a little behind schedule. They recently detected such a problem, and decided that an extra second should be added to keep our 24-hour day in accord with Earth's revolutions.

The last time that an extra second had to be added to clocks of the worlds was the last day of last June, so it's getting to be a habit.

Such seconds are inserted periodically because the earth is gradually slowing down. The time it takes the earth to make a complete turn is about two hours longer than it was about 150 million years ago. But with extra seconds being added, there should be no appreciable change in our system of dividing our days into 24 hours for the next 150 million years. So I am not going to worry about it.

It takes 365 days, 6 hours, 9 minutes, and 9.5 seconds for the earth to make a complete trip around the sun. To keep that extra time beyond the 365 days from distorting our calendars, we add an extra day to February every fourth year and call it a "leap year." That simple move reduces the deviations to three days every 400 years. Then, to correct that, we interrupt the cycle of leap years by eliminating three of them every four centuries. This is done in the first year of each century. For instance, the years 1700, 1800, and 1900 were not leap years but 2000 will be. So you can go ahead and make plans for Feb. 29, 2000, that being the day added for leap year.

There are tiny variables in the speed of the earth's revolutions caused by tides, winds, and the movement of the molten mass in the center of the globe. Those changes are the reason why tiny corrections have to be made occasionally in our time system.

This sort of adjusting has been underway for centuries, with man attempting to be as accurate as humanly possible, but with the job complicated by the tools available to him at any given time. The new correction was dictated by new quartz crystal and atomic clocks that weren't available decades ago.

The job was not done nearly as well centuries ago. The Julian calendar, imposed by Julius Caesar in 46 B.C. was used in most of the world until 1582 when Pope Gregory XIII introduced the Gregorian calendar. At the start, to correct an error in time that had added up to 10 days in those 16 centuries, he decreed that the day after Oct. 4 would be Oct. 15 —a neat trick.

Though most of the western world adopted the Gregorian calendar immediately, the British held off until 1752. By then, the error in time had increased to 11 days. So it decreed in all its territories that the day after Sept. 2, 1752 would be Sept. 14.

That was the shift that mixed up George Washington's birthday.

Man's measurement of time will never again have such inaccuracies, unless, of course, the speed of Earth changes dramatically, or some other celestial occurrence upsets all the factors that now go into our system.

So when June 29 arrives and the day just seems to drag and drag, you'll know there is a good reason. It won't just seem longer than most days. It will be longer—by a whole second.

July 8, 1984

BARBERS LIKE PASQUALE LENTINI
MIX TONSORIAL SKILL WITH WIT

I went to the *Times* barber shop the other day, expecting to get my hair cut by Pasquale Lentini—more commonly known as Pat or Patsy. However, much to my shock, I learned that Pat had recently died and I had missed the obituary.

I was sad over that, because, over several decades in several city barbershops, I had been going to Pat to have him lower my ears and sharpen my wits.

Pat was one of just a few barbers I have entrusted with my hair during my lifetime. Each has had to master a stubborn "cowlick." That tends to make a few strands of my hair stand up in the back if cut too short. Still, I don't like a haircut that leaves the hair in that area too long. So an artful compromise is needed, and Pat was good at producing that result. Thus, as with the others, I stayed with Pat until he died.

However, I liked Pat not purely for his tonsorial skills. He was one of the smartest guys I knew. His accent betrayed his Sicilian origins, but he gave me more accurate information about who was going to win elections than any American-born expert. He also could give me a good slant on most public issues—local, state, or national—with a few wise words.

I swear, Pat had more political smarts than all of those guys—myself included—who write newspaper columns or have their own radio or television programs. Maybe he didn't have the language skills to put everything in perfect English, but the wisdom he spouted was clearly recognizable.

As I write this, I know that such words would probably have embarrassed Pat. He wasn't much for ego trips. His main interests were his work, his family, and the events of the day.

Pat must have been deep in his 70s, but he remained an erect, robust fellow who set a brisk pace as he walked snappily around town.

However, there was a change in Pat last fall. His wife, Angelina, died. He had anticipated that because she had been ailing for some time. But when it happened, it was easy to see that something had drained from him. He looked the same and he talked the same, yet there was a twinge of melancholy that I had never before detected.

I'm going to miss Pat when the next election nears, and I'm going to want his opinion on who will win. I'll also miss him, too, when I want his opinion on a baseball matter. In short, I'll miss him whenever I wish I could pick his brain and then use that knowledge to make myself look a bit smarter.

However, I will not despair. I know a few good barbers who have similar skills, and once they learn how to handle my cowlick, I'll be able to make a smooth transition.

In fact, I have made such transitions several times in the past due to the death of other barbers. And I always have had the good luck to find others with clipping skills interwoven with wisdom. That blend keeps me in love with barbershops.

Of course, my feelings today are conditioned by my maturity. As a tot, I never got to such a place. I always had my hair cut by my mother— a person with a dizzying array of talents, including saving money. So she held to the belief that a hand clipper with a few teeth missing was too good to throw out.

With that hand clipper, Mom would cut some hairs and pull out a few others by their roots. Overall, the experience was a dreadful one. Not only did the clipper with the broken teeth pull out hairs, but tens of thousands of chopped-off hairs slipped down inside my clothing, guaranteeing a day of itching.

When I finally graduated to professional barbershops, I found them to be extensions of heaven. First of all, they had electric clippers that cut through hair without ever pulling one from its roots. I also liked the warm shaving cream on the back of the neck; the way barbers had of keeping hair from sliding down one's neck; the lilac lotion, and the sweet talcum powder.

I loved barbershops, in fact, even when I had to suffer the indignity of sitting on a board placed across the arms of a chair. That was necessary to raise me high enough for the barber to do his work. But I was embarrassed until the barber unfurled that oversized bib that would cover me and the board, making me feel more like a grown man.

Still, it was far nicer going to a professional barbershop—even sitting on the elevated bench—than it was sitting in a kitchen chair having hairs occasionally pulled out by the clipper with the broken teeth.

In a shop, I didn't even mind waiting for my turn. As a child, I was amazed at the number of funny books that were available to read. And there were slick magazines, including some such as *Esquire* that were then considered a bit racy for a maturing boy. Sitting in a comfortable chair in a shop filled with sweet aromas and exciting reading materials was not a bad way to spend a rainy day.

Later in life, when going to a barbershop became more routine and I decided that I hated the influence of funny books on my own kids, I developed other reasons why I liked barbershops.

I began to view them as temporary refuges from the cares and worries of everyday life. Thus, even in the period when long hair was fashionable and I began wearing mine somewhat longer than I ever had in the past, I still managed to visit my barber frequently enough to avoid being called a hippie.

One reason for my loyalty to the profession in the past few decades was my appreciation of the talents and conversational skills of Pat Lentini. I'll miss him.

REUNION QUERIES HARD TO ANSWER

I had never gone to a reunion of my college class, so I really didn't know what to expect when I went with my wife to such a gathering at the University of Scranton.

I graduated in 1949 so this year was my 35th anniversary.

The U. of S. annually combines homecomings for classes having anniversaries. This year, more than 400 graduates of 10 classes dating back to 1934 were on hand for cocktails, dinner, and dancing.

I was there just a few minutes, chatting with a number of persons I know from everyday life in Scranton, when a man approached me.

He looked familiar but I couldn't come up with a name. I glanced at the sticker on his coat. Of course! It was Jim Deviney, an old friend and classmate.

"I haven't seen you since you got out of my car after our senior prom," I said.

"That's right," Jim confirmed.

"That was 35 years ago," I volunteered.

"Don't remind me," said Jim, a dorm student from Mauch Chunk who retired after 35 years with the U.S. Labor Department and now lives in Springfield, Va.

Jim and I had graduated from the school when it was literally bursting its seams with the influx of World War II veterans.

Now, as Jim and I partook of cocktails on "The Commons," which once was Linden Street, we had to admit that the school had changed greatly since we left it.

The reunion program—presided over by attorney Henry Burke, a 1969 graduate and now president of the alumni—involved the presentation of awards to several old grads.

John Malone, a 1934 graduate from Carbondale who is now retired as assistant director of the FBI—one of the top jobs in that agency—received the award for public service.

Judge John D. Butzner, Jr., of the 1939 class, a Scranton native and now senior member of the U.S. 4th Circuit Court in Virginia, was given the law award.

Gene Gibbons, of the 1964 class and now the radio voice of UPI from the White House, received the award for arts and letters. (That made me feel old because I covered his father, Gene, when he was serving on the Scranton School Board.)

Dr. Frank X. J. Homer, also of the 1964 class and now a history teacher there, was given the university's service award.

William J. Murray, another member of my 1949 class and now the science curriculum specialist with the Northeast Educational Intermediate Unit, won the science award.

Dr. Robert Wright, of the 1959 class and now director of medicine at Mercy Hospital, was given the award for medicine.

Cyril P. O'Hora, of the 1939 class, who is chairman of the math department at Scranton Prep, and Francis P. Long, of my 1949 class, now chairman of the U. of S. classical languages department, shared the education award. (O'Hora probably does not remember this but he taught me math in summer school at the university in 1947.)

James Kinney, a Scranton native who was in the 1964 class and who now is vice president of Atlantic Financial Federal Corp., one of the 50 largest savings and loan associations in the nation, won the management award.

There was a common strain in the conversation throughout the evening. "You certainly look great," was a line that frequently was used—and misused. Few of the old grads had lost weight. Most, in fact, had put it on. And many had either lost their hair or had it turn gray. (Some were coloring it, too.)

"What do you do now?" was a common question. The graduate asked that might explain that he is an attorney.

"I thought you were in the business course," the reply might be.

"No, I was never in business," the attorney might insist.

"Oh, I must have mixed you up with someone else," would conclude that conversation.

Another common line started:

"What ever became of ...?"

Sometimes there was a ready answer. "He's a doctor in Philadelphia now," someone might say. But at other times no one knew the answer.

Still another common line started:

"Do you remember the time we ...?"

There were sad moments. Many persons had died—prematurely, from the standpoint of the classmates of approximately the same age.

There were surprises in learning that some graduates who had been given little chance of success had done extremely well in life. And there were surprises that some who seemed destined for glory had fallen by the wayside.

The hardest question I was asked all night was one from a fellow member of the '49 class.

"Joe, where did those 35 years go?"

I couldn't think of anything funny to say in reply.

FRONT PORCHES, ONCE ESSENTIAL, ARE HARDLY EVER USED ANYMORE

In strolling through residential neighborhoods these summer evenings, I have made a startling discovery. Hardly anyone uses front porches anymore.

Walking by home after home one can see big porches lavishly outfitted for the summer with swings, chairs, plants, and rugs.

However, missing most of the time are the people. They are generally inside gazing at TV.

I really can't understand this. I have a lovely home, but its one big imperfection is that it does not have a front porch. Having grown up in a home where the porch was the focal point of our summer lives, I miss not having one. I am envious of the owners of those homes with majestic porches, but irked with them when they don't use them.

Years ago—before TV—sitting on the front porch was the way most persons spent every warm summer evening. It was a great forum for family conversations. It invited neighborhood visiting. It provided a marvelous view of the stars. It was also a good theater for watching faraway lightning. It was a perfect place for a nap. And it was perfect for just doing nothing.

The creak of the swing blended with the mating songs of the nighttime insects. The rhythm of the rockers matched the croaks of the frogs. Lemonade was the perfect refreshment for such relaxation.

Then along came the architects who decided that homes did not always need porches. And many of them—mine included—were built without them. That was a sad day for civilization.

In the heyday of porches, there once was no such thing as home air-conditioning, and window fans had not been invented. On hot summer nights, upstairs bedrooms were very uncomfortable. So the children who would ordinarily have been banished to their beds were given a reprieve and were allowed to spend nighttime hours on the porch, too.

That was a big deal for tots. Getting lemonade—and maybe some cookies a few hours earlier—was a distinct bonus. And being allowed to go off the porch in pursuit of fireflies—more commonly known then as lightning bugs—was great fun.

In those days, hardly anyone believed that smoking would really injure one's health. Thus, porch-sitters—mainly the males—smoked a lot as they talked. Smoking made it easy to determine if a nearby porch was occupied. The occasional flare of a wooden match was a giveaway that there was a smoker ready to light a cigarette, cigar, or pipe. And from that point on, it was easy to watch the glow of the burning tobacco growing suddenly bright whenever a puff was taken in the dark.

Sitting on the porch on a summer's evening was so institutionalized that, even if company arrived, that's where everyone remained deep into the evening. It was hard to keep track of time in the dark, so it was usually a late whistle from a factory or borough building that warned everyone that it was getting late.

Of course, there was one big hazard for porch-sitting. Mosquitoes could have a picnic of their own with all those humans available. But, as annoying as mosquito bites could be, I never remember the threat diminishing porch-sitting.

I had an aunt and uncle who moved to New York City and lived in a nice, brick apartment house in Queens. They were both natives of this area and came back to visit as often as his work would permit. Almost invariably, on every summertime visit, my aunt would decide to stay an extra week or two beyond what she had planned. So my uncle would return to New York alone and pick her up at the end of her extended stay.

And what was the big attraction that kept her here? It was the front porch. In New York, she had only a concrete stoop where virtually everyone in the six-family apartment buildings sat on hot evenings. It was a poor substitute for a big, wooden porch. So when she came to our home to visit, she spent most of her time with my mom on the porch.

Storytelling was a great porch activity. Spooky yarns were very effective when one was sitting in the darkness, with the only illumination coming from a distant streetlamp. And if a bat was flying an erratic course around the light, that added to the atmosphere. And so did the noises of the night, including the rustle of leaves, the whistle of a distant train, the howl of a dog, or the hoot of an owl.

Even during a summertime rainstorm, porches were nice places to sit. As long as the wind was not blowing the drops sideways, it was pleasant to sit there and watch nature water its plants. Of course, if there was thunder and lightning, everyone was ordered inside. People had a good healthy respect for lightning in those days.

One of the first jobs homeowners had in the spring was to get the porch ready for summer. It was important that the furniture was taken out of storage and was positioned for summertime use by the time the first unseasonably hot weather came in May. And the furnishings were kept on the porch until mid-September to make sure that not a single warm night of porch-sitting was missed. (Besides, it was psychologically depressing to strip the porch of furniture, so the task was put off as long as possible.)

As great as nighttime porch-sitting was, not too much of it was done during weekdays. Leisure time hadn't been invented yet. That didn't come until work-saving machines became commonplace in the home.

But that is all ancient history now. Most porches that do exist are furnished for the warm weather. But then they are hardly ever used.

Damn that TV!

November 6, 1984

ELEANOR VISITED AREA FOUR TIMES

The 100th anniversary of the birth of Mrs. Eleanor Roosevelt reminded me and anyone else age 40 or older of this remarkable First Lady.

Born an aristocrat, she had the common touch and was a tremendous asset to her husband, President Franklin Delano Roosevelt.

Mrs. Roosevelt came here on four occasions, three as First Lady and once as the widow of the president. On each visit, her desire to seek out and touch people was apparent. On her last visit 28 years ago, when she was 72, she said she never wanted to be a recluse. "I hate the idea I might lose touch with people," she said.

Stories of her local visits tell much about Mrs. Roosevelt and the tremendous changes that have occurred in the lives of First Ladies.

For instances, on April 27, 1937, on her first visit to Scranton, she drove her car from Avon, CT, where she had visited a relative.

Being the wife of the man in his second term as president, she would have received a police escort, but she never let anyone know when she would be here. It was about 11:40 a.m. when she pulled up to the Hotel Casey in her coupe, accompanied by her secretary, Malvina Scheider. A news story said she looked "tired and worn" from her seven-hour drive through heavy rain over winding roads.

Mrs. Roosevelt came to participate in a workshop for teachers at the Masonic Temple, accepting a fee for the visit, but turning it over to charity. She gave two talks.

She also met with a host of local politicians, including Scranton School Board President John F. Padden who surprised her with a gift. It was an old bread knife that contained a coat of arms on its handle, much like the Roosevelt family's coat of arms from Holland. He had been given the knife by a traveling tradesman, who passed through this area regularly, sharpening utensils of barbers.

Mrs. Roosevelt, obviously pleased, gave Padden a penny in return, reciting a belief that to accept a pointed instrument without making a token payment would break a friendship.

That evening, Mrs. Roosevelt telephoned her husband at the White House from her room at the Casey. She then went to the Lackawanna Railroad Station and got a train for Washington, leaving it up to her secretary to drive her car home.

She came back on Sept. 23, 1940 to observe W.P.A. education and recreation projects, which her husband's administration had sponsored.

Just as she had done on her first visit, Mrs. Roosevelt drove here in her own coupe, this time from the family home at Hyde Park, NY. She arrived in front of the Hotel Casey at 11:45 A.M., again accompanied by her secretary.

In the course of that day, Mrs. Roosevelt visited Callista (Tootsie) Smith, 1402 Cedar Ave., a child whose spinal column had been severed in a sleigh-riding accident just two years before, and who was then being rehabilitated through a W.P.A. program for homebound youths.

When Mrs. Roosevelt arrived, Miss Smith was lying in bed, practicing typing on a specially constructed table. Mrs. Roosevelt marveled at the abilities of the child who later became the bookkeeper for a restaurant still operated at that address by her family. She did that work until her death in 1978.

Mrs. Roosevelt posed for pictures with the child and chatted about their mutual skills in knitting.

Mrs. Roosevelt, after her four-hour W.P.A. tour here, drove back to Hyde Park.

On April 19, 1941, Mrs. Roosevelt made her final visit as First Lady, going to Wilkes-Barre to speak at a program sponsored by a Methodist Bible group. She traveled there by train from Buffalo, NY, sending word ahead that she did not want uniformed police in any escort she might be given. Wilkes-Barre officials compromised by assigning her plainclothes officers.

In that visit, she bemoaned the fact that federal studies were showing that parents were not doing enough to correct the eyes and teeth of their children—problems first pinpointed in draft examinations for World War I, but never taken seriously by parents.

She said that much of the problem was in rural areas, particularly of the South. But she said the health of our youth was a national concern, because men would be wanted from every corner of the land if a draft were needed again.

Mrs. Roosevelt's final visit here came on Dec. 3, 1956, 11 years after her husband's death. She arrived by commercial airplane at the relatively new Scranton-Wilkes-Barre Airport, and again said she did not want police protection.

She spoke the next day at a Chanukah dinner for Israel in the Hotel Casey. She said that Israel's recent invasion of Egypt was "a good legal case of self-defense."

Though 72 then, Mrs. Roosevelt remained active for several more years. Tomorrow marks the 22nd anniversary of her death.

May 5, 1985

REAL 'AMERICAN TRAGEDY' KILLER WAS ELECTROCUTED 50 YEARS AGO

Theodore Dreiser, an author who was distinguished by his realistic novels of tragic lives, wrote a book about an ambitious young man who murdered his girlfriend by beating her with a camera in a rowboat, causing her to fall overboard and drown in a mythical lake near Utica, NY. The act was motivated by his desire to marry a richer and more socially acceptable girl, rather than the pregnant one who was pressing him.

The book, an *American Tragedy*, was published in 1925 and became a classic of American literature.

Then, on July 31, 1934, 21-year-old Robert "Bobby" Edwards, a mine surveyor from Edwardsville, Luzerne County, took his childhood girlfriend, Freda McKenzie, to Harvey's Lake for an evening swim.

Freda, who was five years older than Bobby, told him the day before that she was five months pregnant. There was no doubt that the baby was his. Bobby told her he would marry her on Aug. 1 and they would go to Virginia to start new lives. Freda, who worked as a telephone operator, was deliriously happy.

What Freda did not know was that Bobby, while attending Mansfield College two years earlier, had met and fallen in love with Margaret Crain, a student from East Aurora, NY. Their romance blossomed and was kept alive by letters and occasional visits. Finally, Bobby, a Mansfield dropout, and Margaret, a Mansfield graduate who had become a music teacher in Endicott, NY, agreed to get married on Nov. 1.

At the lake, Bobby pondered his plight. He sat on the dock and watched Freda—the girl carrying his baby—frolicking in the water. He also thought of Margaret, a girl of better education and more social standing to whom he wrote periodic letters of torrid love.

What happened after that became the subject for the jury to decide. Did Freda die of natural causes in the water and did Bobby—fearful that her pregnancy would make him responsible for the death—fake a fall from a boat by striking her on the head with a blackjack? Or did Bobby beat Freda to death in the boat to get rid of her to clear his path to marry Margaret—just as happened in Dreiser's an *American Tragedy*?

Because the case followed the plot of the popular novel, it made national headlines as the "American Tragedy" murder case, even though, ironically, Bobby said he had never read the book.

Dreiser, at the peak of his career, was sent to cover the trial by the *New York Post* and *Mystery Magazine*. Jimmy Kilgallen, the Pittston native who had become a famous columnist, covered it for the Hearst papers. And the *New York Times* sent F. Raymond Daniell, one of its best, to write the story that it carried on its front page. In the flowery style of that day, Daniell wrote that the slender, handsome Bobby had "hair as black as the anthracite his family had mined for generations."

Margaret, shocked by Bobby's arrest, sent him a Bible but refused to go to the trial even though she made available to the prosecution Bobby's love letters. She also said she would not marry Bobby—no matter how the case turned out.

In the end, the jury chose not to believe the story Bobby told from the witness stand. Instead, it saw him as a man who preferred Margaret to Freda and who decided murder was the only means to achieve his goal after Freda became pregnant. The panel convicted him of first-degree murder and recommended death. The judge followed the recommendation.

Despite over 1,000 letters asking for clemency—including one from Dreiser—the execution was scheduled. Thus, on May 6, 1935—50 years ago tomorrow—Bobby was strapped into the electric chair at Rockview Prison, Bellefonte, and at 1:33 A.M. he was put to death.

Among the witnesses of the execution was Edward J. Donohoe, then a reporter with the *Wilkes-Barre Times-Leader* and later the managing editor of the *Scranton Times*.

Donohoe, who was a look-alike to the defendant, developed a friendship with him during the trial and became a witness at the execution at his request.

Paul Beers, associate editor of the *Harrisburg Patriot-News* and author of six books, wrote about the Bobby Edwards case in a book called *The Pennsylvania Sampler*. In that story he made a reference to Donohoe's story about the Edwards' execution, calling it "one of the gems of Pennsylvania journalism."

Donohoe, now retired, started his career in journalism as a paperboy at the age of 8. By the time he was 27, he had—as a reporter who specialized in criminal cases—witnessed eight executions.

Of the Edwards' execution, Donohoe wrote in part:

"Silent, somber—his agony betrayed only by cheeks that blanched as he neared the threshold of eternity—Edwards strode firmly to the electric chair at 1:30 this morning and cancelled his debt to society for the slaying of Freda McKenzie."

"His lips parted in what seemed to be a final prayer as the gargoyle-like leather mask was placed over his face."

"Three minutes and five seconds later—so will state the death house records—Robert Allen Edwards was dead."

"Thus was written the finis of Wyoming Valley's *An American Tragedy*, a real-life drama far more gripping than the Dreiser novel it paralleled."

June 6, 1985

TO SHED LIGHT ON WAR DEAD

As the United States wound down its involvement in Vietnam in 1972, I was depressed that the antiwar feelings generated by the conflict would cause those who died in the war to be honored less than those who had died in other wars.

So I put those thoughts into a column, forming a prayer that those who fought and died in Vietnam would not be forgotten.

I was not proposing anything at that time—merely noting that the dead of the Vietnam War should be held in high esteem.

A few days later, much to my surprise, I received a letter from the late Mrs. Kitty Collins, a local resident and mother of Broadway playwright Jean Collins Kerr. She enclosed a $25 check and said it should be used to start a fund for the Vietnam War dead.

No proponent of the war—she called it immoral, obscure, futile, and unnecessary—she nonetheless agreed that those "brave boys" who died in it should not go "unhonored and unsung."

I read and reread Mrs. Collins' letter and concluded that a monument was a great idea. I did research and found that not a single major monument had been erected to honor the 300 county residents who had died in World War I, the 1,500 who had died in World War II, the 150 who had died in the Korean War, and the 50 who died in the Vietnam War.

"If a monument is to be built, why not dedicate it to the memory of those 2,000 county residents who died in the four U.S. wars of this century—not just Vietnam?" I asked myself. That would truly make the Vietnam War dead equal to those of other wars, I reasoned.

I knew from the start that to have a monument erected on Courthouse Square, I would need allies. While I was pondering how to do this, attorney James A. Kelly, an old friend, a World War II Army Air Corps tail-gunner, and a member of the American Legion became donor number 2. He sent his check for $100 and said he would do anything else I wanted.

I asked if he would agree to serve as treasurer, a job I wanted to avoid because I knew it would involve running to the bank and keeping records. He said he would.

In addition to doing all those jobs, Kelly also donated his services as a lawyer, getting Internal Revenue Service approval of the project to make donations tax deductible and filing annual reports.

It was in that time period, too, that I received pledges of help from two other ardent backers. Gino Merli, an old friend, a World War II combat hero, and the country's only living holder of the Congressional Medal of Honor, said he would be happy to serve as chairman. Dr. Almo Sebastionelli, a former major in the Army Air Corps in World War II, undertook the critical task of getting veterans groups, including his own American Legion, to back the project.

At the start, when the Vietnam War was fresh in the minds of most persons, the donations mounted. But later, they almost stopped. The low point was when the committee hired the Bob Crosby band to perform at the Masonic Temple and there seemed to be more persons in the band than in the audience.

However, the bright side was the backing that the project got from the veterans' organizations. The American Legion alone gave thousands of dollars, usually with prodding from Sebastionelli and another ally and World War II veteran, Bill Kays.

The committee first had visualized a monument that would have cost about $30,000. But after four years of meetings and fundraising, the budget was cut in half and a $15,000 monument was installed at Courthouse Square. It was dedicated on May 19, 1977—five years after the project began.

After all the bills were paid, a modest balance remained in the fund and the committee thought it would be a good idea to illuminate the monument. Again, it proved difficult to carry out the idea because we didn't have sufficient funds.

A major breakthrough occurred recently, however, when the county commissioners illuminated the exterior of the courthouse. I learned that they were so pleased with the project they were thinking of expanding it to include other things, including a courthouse wing and statues.

Sebastionelli, Merli, Kelly, and I turned over to the county the $643.41 remaining in our treasury to help finance the illuminating of the 20th Century War Dead Monument.

The formal turning-on of the lights will take place at 8 P.M., Thursday, June 13. Merli will deliver the Pledge of Allegiance. Kelly will be the master of ceremonies. Sebastionelli will introduce the guest speaker, State Auditor General Don Bailey, a highly decorated veteran of the Vietnam War.

I'm hoping a big crowd will be on hand, including relatives of all the persons who died in the four wars. Lighting the monument should be a patriotic moment of local history to remember.

GEORGE M. COHAN PREVIEWED HIS SHOWS HERE, DESPITE CRITIC

One of my favorite local books is *If You Can Play Scranton*, which was put out in 1981 by Nancy McDonald, a Dunmore resident who teaches at West Scranton High School.

The book is the best thing ever written about Scranton's long association with show business, particularly the era of vaudeville, when it was common for shows to be tried out here before being moved to New York.

I had reason to reread parts of the book recently after I watched James Cagney in the 1940s movie, *Yankee Doodle Dandy*, which was about the life and career of George M. Cohan, the legendary songwriter, playwright, singer, dancer, actor, producer, and theater owner.

In the film, Cohan had just written the play, *Little Johnnie Jones*, and it became the biggest hit of the 1904 Broadway season. Among its songs were "I'm a Yankee Doodle Dandy" and "Give My Regards to Broadway," which are perennial songs in most sing-alongs.

As I watched the movie, I recalled that there was something in Miss McDonald's book about that play being tried out in Scranton before it went to New York. I looked it up and found it.

Here is the story, as told by Miss McDonald:

"In 1903, the *Scranton Tribune* had a young reporter who genuinely loved the theater. By pestering the city editor, he managed to wangle a theatrical assignment. Eventually, he was given a column, 'On and Off the Stage,' which he wrote for the Saturday edition under the pseudonym, 'The Man in Front.'"

"In 1904, George M. Cohan came to premiere *Little Johnnie Jones*. The cub reporter sailed into Cohan with the force of a cavalry trooper charging against the enemy. He sneered at the 'preposterous mélange of 'ten-twen-thirt' melodrama and cheap vaudeville that couldn't be dignified as musical comedy.' As for the songs, 'I'm a Yankee Doodle Dandy' and 'Give My Regards to Broadway,' he felt 'the less said the better.'"

Well, nobody's perfect. *Little Johnnie Jones* naturally became the biggest hit of the season and established Cohan as a theatrical force. This didn't stop the cub. He continued to flail Cohan until somebody called the journalistic assassination to Cohan's attention. At this point Cohan began to insert items into his weekly news columns such as "A guy on the *Scranton Tribune* doesn't like me; that's liable to hurt my business in Wichita," or "I started a new song the other night, but I tore it up. I knew that *Scranton Tribune* guy wouldn't care for it."

The barbs continued until the cub worked up enough courage to call on Cohan in New York. After a kind reception, he promptly became "a worshipper at the throne."

The then unknown reporter was John Peter Toohey, who later became the chief drama critic for the *New York Herald-Tribune*.

Miss McDonald's 129-page paperback book was privately published and about 400 copies were sold. Unfortunately, it no longer is available for purchase. However, copies are available at the Scranton Public Library, in Marywood's library, and at the Lackawanna Historical Society.

Miss McDonald, who began researching Scranton's links with big-time show business in a college thesis and later expanded it into a book, lists scores of famous show business personalities who appeared on the stages of Scranton theaters.

Cohan, who was born into a show business family on the Fourth of July in 1878, was typical of the stars who ranked Scranton as a key testing ground for material.

He performed as a violinist at the age of 9 and became a child star at 11, playing the lead in *Peck's Bad Boy*—the show that gave rise to that cliché description of a precocious youth.

Cohan later worked in vaudeville with his parents and sister, billing themselves as "The Four Cohans." But Cohan yearned for more. Miss McDonald referred to him as "a struggling song and dance man" who had written a play, *Running for Office*, that played in Scranton in 1903.

She said the show did well on the road but was not produced in New York.

That was the situation when he created *Little Johnnie Jones* and tried it out here. Miss McDonald wrote: "Everybody in town was hailing Cohan as a genius. Within a week, *Little Johnnie Jones* was a Broadway sensation."

Cohan, incidentally, played Scranton for the final time in 1935. He had come out of retirement to act in Eugene O'Neill's play, *Ah,*

Wilderness, which included a performance at the Masonic Temple on its agenda.

Before I wrote the column, I asked Miss McDonald if I could retell her story about the local critic who hated Cohan's famous hit. In our talk, I said that her book is much too valuable to slip into oblivion. It details a piece of local history that should never be forgotten.

December 19, 1985

'GRAVITY' ENDED 100 YEARS AGO

With a little imagination, one can almost hear the "whish" of the cars speeding quietly over the rails.

It was 100 years ago yesterday—Dec. 18, 1885—when the last run was made on the "Gravity," the common name applied to the Pennsylvania Coal Company Railroad.

The cars sped along the strips of iron atop the wooden rails. Every four miles there were axle-activated greasing devices that would splash oil on each wheel as it sped past. That made them run faster.

The three-crew members on that last trip were bundled up against the fierce windchill factor.

The ride began near the Bunker Hill section of Dunmore. A stationary steam engine pulled the cars up an incline. Five full cars at a time was a normal hoisting load. That made a lot of noise as the engine strained to do its job.

At the summit, where several blocks of five cars were linked together, hauling ropes were discarded. The cars—carrying up to five tons of coal apiece—were then cut loose. They drifted down the graded right-of-way, quickly picking up speed. Crewmen often tapped the brakes to keep the cars from going beyond the safe speed of 10 to 15 mph.

That last ride started from "No. 6" at Dunmore, which was the sixth of 12 lifting stations on the Port Griffith-to-Hawley line. At each plane, the procedure of pulling the cars up a grade had to be repeated—with the work being done by steam or water-powered hoists.

The first car in that last train probably had stiff brooms in front of it. When the cars were speeding downhill, the brooms cleared snow from the rails.

Michael Loughney, as the headman on that last Gravity train, was on the rear coal car. Eddie Higgins and John Farley, as the assistants, divided duties between the front and the middle of the train.

The crew's assignment was to take the train to Hawley on the heavy-duty line used for the empties. Rather, they were told to come back in the caboose of a steam train on the Erie and Wyoming Valley Railroad, which began running between Dunmore and Hawley earlier that year.

When the last train reached Hawley, the Gravity was history—a victim of progress.

Pennsylvania Coal Co., which had begun operations in the Pittston area in 1839, had shipped its coal by barges to Harrisburg and other towns along the Susquehanna River. After a decade, it hungered for bigger markets. Its answer was to open a 47-mile-long gravity railroad to Hawley in 1850.

The first train consisted of twelve cars that took 6½ hours to travel from Dunmore—a common assembly point—to Hawley. The arrival of the train was cause of great excitement in Hawley. The three-man crew was wined and dined and then treated to a dogfight and a boxing fight. A new era had begun.

Millions of tons of anthracite were shipped over that line in the years that followed. It was all loaded aboard boats that carried it 108 miles over the Delaware and Hudson Canal to the Hudson River and thence to New York City and other markets.

The Gravity operated about 10 months of the year, being forced to shut down when the D&H Canal froze in midwinter.

While built to haul coal, the Gravity line later added passenger service between Dunmore and Hawley. The fare was $1 for the ride that usually took up to two hours.

For 35 years—a period embracing the Civil War and the post-war industrial boom—the system worked well, operating daily from 6 A.M. to sunset. Sometimes crews parked their trains near their homes if they couldn't complete a journey before darkness. Since nothing else was running at night, they simply stopped the train on an incline, chained it in that position, and left for home, rather than chance riding through the blackness.

In time, steam railroads began crisscrossing the nation. Staying modern, the Pennsylvania Coal Co. decided to ship its coal to market over the new Erie and Wyoming Valley Railroad. The Gravity line fell into disuse.

However, the executives—in a rare show of sentiment for that period—decided there should be one "last" journey even though some torn-up rails had to be replaced to make it possible.

Loughney, who had the honor of piloting that last train, had a way of getting into history. After the Gravity died, he went to work for the Erie and Wyoming Railroad. Later, the Erie bought out that firm and made it its Wyoming Division. In 1932, as a brakeman, he made the last run of a steam passenger train from Dunmore to Hawley.

Loughney, incidentally, was the great-uncle of Mary Theresa "T. C." Connolly, a schoolteacher from Dunmore who published the book, *The Gravity*, in 1972. It is she who called to my attention the 100th anniversary of that railroad's end.

April 13, 1986

COMMENT ON WENZEL'S INJURIES
DRAWS CRITICISM AND A RESPONSE

I know I shouldn't let it upset me, but I do when I am unjustly accused of being nasty.

I got such a letter a few days ago from a person who saw me on *Sunday Morning with Charles Kuralt* on CBS-TV last Sunday.

The segment was about David Wenzel and the way he fought back from Vietnam War injuries to become mayor of Scranton.

The writer accused me of taking "a cheap shot" at Wenzel for saying he was not wounded in combat, but as a result of stepping on a mine.

What I said was accurate. My source was the mayor himself.

In fact, a column I wrote about the mayor in 1985 describing how he lost two legs, an arm, and part of the vision in one eye was what caused Brett Alexander, a producer of the CBS-TV show, to call me. He said my column—which told of Wenzel refusing to remain a hopeless cripple —was one of the factors that went into the decision to do the piece on Wenzel.

My critic accused me of being biased against Wenzel because he is a Republican. Faulting me for saying that Wenzel was not hurt in combat, the critic wrote: "He was still in the war."

Then he added without the slightest regard for logic: "If it happened to a son of yours, would you feel that way?"

The critic still was not finished. He said I was "a baptized Democratic reporter who hits below the belt" in my writings.

Worked up into a full lather, he added: "Please, because a veteran is a Republican, don't hurt him. We fought for you. I do hope God forgives you for what you said."

In conclusion, the writer said he was quitting the paper. His sign-off was: "I still can't believe it!"

Well, neither can I. I was tried and convicted—bang, bang, bang. And the only charge I can see in the letter is that I told the truth as the mayor told it to me.

Wenzel and the city got terrific national publicity on the CBS show and I was proud to be a part of it.

But, to keep the record straight on what I said and where I got my information, I thought I would reprint a pertinent part of my 1985 column. It follows:

"The pivotal point of Wenzel's life occurred in Vietnam on Jan. 26, 1971. He was a first lieutenant leading 15 men on a mission, hoping he would get them all back to their firebase—an artillery compound where they were stationed—without any of them being hurt. 'All we wanted to do at that point was to put our time in and get home safely,' he said. Ironically, he became the only casualty."

"'We went a mile and a half from the firebase to set up mortars on a hilltop,' he said. 'Most of the terrain was flat and covered with high grass, running along a river.'"

"'It was a passing-through area,' said Wenzel, referring to enemy troops on their way to other destinations. Wenzel said his unit was directed to fire rounds across the river 'just to let the Viet Cong know we were there.'"

"Wenzel was walking along a path, seeking a spot to set up a mortar, when the path narrowed. Ever fearful of mines, he began to walk in the tall grass. It was then that a land mine exploded. 'I could have tripped on a wire or maybe I set it off by percussion,' he said."

"Diverting a bit, Wenzel added: 'I have often wondered if it could have been a shell from the Chamberlain Plant in Scranton. The Cong sometimes got our shells and rigged them as mines. I'll never know what it was or where it came from. War is very impersonal.'"

When the CBS program staff was planning the Wenzel piece, Alexander called me to pick my brain on what I knew about the mayor—a person whose political career I had written more about than any other local reporter. In fact, I wrote the original stories saying Wenzel would be a good mayoral candidate.

Alexander said he had read my column but wanted more on the campaign and public perceptions of Wenzel. As we neared the end of the conversation, he asked if I would agree to a supporting interview for the show. I said I would.

A month or so later, Alexander called again and said the crew was coming. He said he would come to my office or home to do my interview. I opted to do it in the Hilton, where the crew was going to stay.

The evening the crew came to town, I spoke to the camera and said I admired Wenzel's pluck. I said he was walking along a trail, not even in combat, when the mine blew up. That was not only accurate, but was said to emphasize the anguish of Wenzel of being wounded on an assignment that seemed routine and relatively safe.

I said in the interview that Wenzel could have come home on a stretcher and said to the government, "Take care of me." However, I said, he was determined to rebuild his life, and has done a remarkable job of doing that.

I concluded by saying if the all-Democratic city council says "no" to Wenzel, I'm sure he will not accept such defeats with resignation. I said he would fight back—much as he did from his injuries.

Alexander, incidentally, asked me for suggestions on other local figures who might participate in the segment. I suggested ex-Governor William W. Scranton, a Wenzel supporter, and City Council President William Gerrity. In fact, I gave Alexander the home telephone numbers of both. He got Gerrity but he couldn't reach Scranton.

I hope this sets the record straight.

May 22, 1986

NOT MUDVILLE THIS TIME UP

Three times prior to Tuesday, I had covered Bob Casey as a candidate for the Democratic nomination for governor.

Each time, I went to a hotel room to feel the atmosphere of what was to have been a victory.

The first was May 17, 1966. Casey, then a state senator, was in a room in the Hotel Casey. He had campaigned for two years, first to win the party's endorsement, and then to win a majority of the voters.

Milton Shapp, a Philadelphia industrialist, said Casey was "the machine's candidate" and that he would oppose him.

Shapp was one of the first I knew who foresaw the importance of television advertising in politics. Using his personal fortune, he filled the airwaves with commercials including a slick half hour documentary on himself.

Twenty years later, I recall the segment that showed World War II Gen. Mark Clark leading the American troops northward in the Italian campaign. Shapp was portrayed as a brave soldier in that army. Shapp and Clark were woven so cleverly together that a casual viewer could easily have concluded that they were the key liberators of Italy.

Casey was the favorite. But about midnight, Shapp went ahead. The news got worse after that. Casey, who does not smoke now, chain-smoked that long night.

By 3:15 A.M., Casey and his wife, Ellen, went home to where their seven children were sleeping. Shapp was the Democratic candidate in the fall and was defeated.

My next vigil was kept on the night of May 19, 1970, at what was then known as the Casey Inn. Casey was then the state auditor general—an office he had won in 1968. Now he was running against Shapp again for the gubernatorial nomination.

Shapp jumped off to an early lead but then Casey went ahead. By 10 or so, Shapp was back in the lead. It was déjà vu time for Casey and his wife, but they remained composed. However, some of their older children who had come to celebrate went off to quiet corners and cried.

Just before midnight, Casey told reporters his only hope hinged on uncounted paper ballots in Allegheny County. By 1 A.M. that hope began to melt. At 2 A.M. Casey went to the ballroom and conceded. By then, all but one child, Margie, had gone home. After the concession, the three left the hotel. Shapp became the nominee and went on to become governor.

Two years later, Casey was re-elected auditor general by a landslide. But with Shapp, a Democrat, in the governor's office, he made no effort to run for office in 1974. Shapp was re-elected.

My third vigil was on May 16, 1978. It was 9:20 P.M. when Casey arrived at the Sheraton Motor Inn with his wife and now his eight children. Casey, who seemed at the height of his popularity, was running against Pittsburgh Mayor Pete Flaherty and Lt. Gov. Ernest Kline.

The family group watched the TV in a bedroom and grew frustrated by the lack of returns. Efforts were made to locate a radio to supplement the TV but none could be found. Someone went home to get one.

About 10 P.M. it was clear Kline was losing. Casey went to the ballroom and told the news media the fight was between him and Flaherty. Casey was then ahead by 10,000 votes. His margin soared to 30,000 by 10:40 P.M.

However, the picture was being distorted by the slowness of the returns from western Pennsylvania. Kline conceded he was beaten and forecast Flaherty as the winner. That TV segment was met by silence in the Casey room.

When Casey went to the ballroom at 11 P.M. he had telephone information from the western area that things looked bad, but he clung to the hope of winning by a narrow margin. By midnight, the lead was down to 23,000. A half hour later, he returned to the ballroom and said he still thought he would win.

Back in the hotel room, Casey saw the lead dwindle. By 1:11 A.M. Flaherty went ahead. By 1:30 A.M. it was clearly over. Casey said there was no point in the family staying any longer in the hotel. He escorted his wife and children out a rear entrance and drove home. Eventually, Flaherty won the nomination but lost the fall election.

I made arrangements to be allowed into the Casey room at the Hilton at Lackawanna Station on Tuesday night. When I arrived, I was told he was still at home. So I went there and found the family preparing to go to the hotel.

As had happened so many times in the past, Casey was trailing again, but he had reports from workers in the field that insisted that he would win. He was sure it was going to be another long night.

But the climax came like a bolt of lightning. Edward Rendell, his opponent from Philadelphia, looked at his vote from that city and decided he could not win. So he called Casey and conceded. Casey coasted to an easy victory.

Election night drama is hard to beat.

September 7, 1986

BRITISH SOLDIERS BOARDING BUS AROUSE FEAR IN TOUR OF IRELAND

One of the depressing moments I had on a recent visit to Ireland was when two British soldiers boarded our bus—one with a rifle.

There were 37 tourists on the bus and we were crossing the border from the Irish Republic into the British province of Northern Ireland.

Most of the tiny roads linking the republic and Northern Ireland have been sealed by the British to keep members of the Irish Republican Army from infiltrating. They can still walk across miles of unguarded border, but not drive.

I knew some of that going to Ireland, but the reality of what it meant did not come to me until I saw the soldier with the gun at the front of the bus.

Suddenly, I realized that this was not something that you just read about. That was a real gun the soldier was carrying and it had real bullets.

On the trip from Sligo, which is in the republic, to Enniskillen, in County Fermanagh, Northern Ireland, our driver/tour guide said there is a reciprocal agreement between the two governments that allow tourists to cross the border without a passport check.

However, he also warned that vehicles must stop at the border for an inspection and that photographs are not allowed. He said soldiers sometimes confiscate cameras, or, at other times, open cameras and expose the film.

At the actual border, there was no stop required.

The checkpoint was located a few miles inside Northern Ireland on one of the few highways kept open to link the republic and British territory.

I don't know what I expected to happen after we crossed into Northern Ireland, but the road was the same, the cottages were the same, and the people at least looked the same.

Then the vehicle slowed to cross speed bumps designed to prevent vehicles from roaring past the military checkpoint.

The bus stopped at the wooden gate that was across the roadway, adjacent to a cinderblock and concrete bunker that was about two stories high.

The bunker had no windows—only gun slits like they have on armored bank cars. While I didn't see it myself, some of the other passengers said there was a machine gun on the roof.

Two soldiers approached the bus, one with a rifle and the other with a pistol in a holster on his hip. The one with the rifle stayed in the front of the bus with the rifle held casually by both hands.

The other soldier was jolly. "Everyone seems in good humor here," he joked as he began walking down the aisle, glancing at each of us.

No one was searched. No papers were inspected. No baggage was opened.

The soldier spent only about two minutes walking up and down the aisle. He then turned to the people and said, "OK, cheers, mates."

Then the two left the bus and we ended our self-imposed silence. Everyone began to chatter.

I spoke later to the bus driver and he said that on a similar stop sometime in the past, a soldier dropped his rifle, it went off and the bus driver was killed. There were apologies and a civil settlement with the man's family, but the incident made all remaining bus drivers treat these border crossings as no time for joking.

I couldn't understand the purpose of the bus check. We could have been carrying all sorts of illicit things in our baggage. The tourists included residents of the republic who could have been IRA members. But no one was bothered.

My guess is that the British do it for psychological reasons to make the IRA aware that the borders are being watched.

After the border stop, our bus traveled unimpeded to Enniskillen, a fair-sized city. My pockets were filled with currency of the republic, but when I offered a five-pound Irish note to buy film, the shopkeeper said curtly: "That is not legal tender here."

Since we had been to England before going to Ireland, I still had some English money and with that I got the film.

On the main street in Enniskillen, there was a roadblock manned by provincial police known as Royal Ulster Constabulary. They were checking cars coming into the city.

I wanted the film to take a picture of that roadblock. Recalling the warning we had received from the bus driver about the border check point, I feared getting too close to the RUC roadblock. However, from a distance of about a half block, I did snap a picture before going into a restaurant for tea and scones.

After a few hours of wandering the streets of Enniskillen, we boarded the bus again and headed back to the republic. The driver said the guards sometimes stop vehicles headed outward, too. He also reminded us that no photographs are permitted in that area.

However, when we reached the checkpoint and slowed down, the soldier on duty raised the gate and waved us through. As we moved past the guard station, one of the more playful soldiers wiggled his fancy at us —in full uniform, of course.

I was in the back seat with my camera on my lap and as we gathered speed, I felt secure enough to snap a picture. A Canadian passenger did the same thing.

Even then I felt a twinge of fear because we were still in Northern Ireland and presumably could be stopped before we would reach the border. It didn't happen, of course. But fear is never far away in that troubled area.

RETIRED TEACHER RECALLS CONFLICT

Fifty years ago, there was a civil war raging in Spain and many Americans—fearing the rise of fascism in Europe—were alarmed enough to go there to fight.

U.S. veterans of that war—a group of 2,600 that has shrunk to about 300—are marking the 50th anniversary of that struggle, some by going to Spain and walking the battlefields, and others just remembering the frustration of losing.

Theodore R. Cogswell, 68, a retired English teacher of Keystone Junior College, said it is hard to describe now what motivated him and others to go to Spain to try to keep democracy alive.

Fascism was on the rise in Europe and Cogswell was "personally alarmed."

Spain had been ruled for seven years by a dictator and for another year by a king. Finally, a republic was proclaimed in 1931 and it secularized education—an act deemed anticlerical in Catholic Spain.

The republic reeled from year to year, beset by groups from the far right to the far left. A coalition of Republicans, Socialists, Communists, and others, under the name of the Popular Front, won a national election in February 1936. The victory alarmed the rightists, including the monarchists, the antisocialists, the anticommunists, and the fascists.

Army officers under Francisco Franco revolted in July, taking much of the regular army with them and touching off the three-year civil war.

Germany, under Adolf Hitler, and Italy, under Benito Mussolini, rushed aid to Franco. Russia, under Joseph Stalin, gave more modest help to the republic.

Cogswell, then 19, was in Cleveland, Ohio, working in a factory and attending night school. He recalls that the harshness of the economic depression in the United States had made him and many others of his generation concerned over issues of social justice. "Many of us felt that fascism was spreading across Europe and it had to be stopped," he recalled.

A friend in night school suggested in 1937—the year after the civil war began—that they join the Lincoln Brigade, being recruited to fight for the Spanish democracy.

Cogswell recalled: "I said, 'Why not?' It was an adventure, a chance to travel, and a chance to support a noble cause. So I agreed."

Cogswell—now one of about 10 surviving Pennsylvania veterans of that war—said while the Lincoln Brigade is often portrayed as a communist legion, it include persons of diverse philosophies united by goals of preserving democracy and fighting fascism.

At first, Cogswell was made a machine-gunner in the American unit that was used extensively because it was better trained and armed than the government units.

However, after a battle in which many Americans volunteers were killed—including some very young ones—the U.S. State Department complained to the Spanish government. Cogswell was then made an ambulance driver.

About 1,000 Americans died in what Cogswell called "a nasty war." He said Germany supplied the bulk of the air power and artillery for the Franco forces. "The German artillery was accurate," he said, adding that the artillery of the republican troops was World War I vintage. Russia supplied some weapons for the republic but Cogswell said they were "inferior."

Cogswell, who resides in Chinchilla, recalls that the Spanish fascists were harsh opponents, often lining up prisoners and machine-gunning them. He said the Italians—who put more soldiers into Spain than did the Germans—treated prisoners well.

Franco won the war, and in the wake of the victory, many Spanish civilians who were deemed enemies were executed in bullrings, Cogswell recalled.

Franco ruled Spain for 36 years—with his leadership becoming more and more benign after his enemies were crushed. He eventually picked Prince Juan Carlos to become his successor. Thus, when Franco died in 1975, Spain became a monarchy again. Juan Carlos ordered free elections in 1977, and Spain was once again a democracy.

Cogswell, who came home from Spain and shortly thereafter volunteered and became captain in the U.S. Army Air Corps, said that the Spanish war fueled the growth of fascism and led to World War II.

Cogswell, who not only became a college teacher but one of the best science fiction writers in America, said the effort to save democracy in Spain was a worthy undertaking even though it failed.

While many of Cogswell's colleagues in arms were communists, he avoided that trap. He said a growing awareness of "what was really going on in Russia—the gap between the picture and reality" convinced him communism was evil.

Cogswell is happy that Spain is a democracy today but has no desire to return there—even in this anniversary year. "It was an interesting part of my life but it's over and I have no desire to relive it," he explained.

ELLEN CASEY TRYING TO GET USED TO HAVING A HOUSE STAFF OF 14

Ellen Casey, while showing several persons the Governor's Home in Harrisburg last Wednesday, said, "It's going to take a while to get used to this."

On the previous day, Mrs. Casey's husband, Robert P., had become governor. At that moment, she inherited dominion over the home the state completed in 1968 for its governors.

On the second floor of the three-story mansion, which is where the governor and his family reside, Mrs. Casey saw a laundry chute that leads to the basement.

"We have a laundry chute in our house, too, but I was on the receiving end of that one," she said.

Outside the master bedroom, which has a picture window providing a view of the Susquehanna River and the rolling hills beyond, Mrs. Casey was almost embarrassed to note she has her own dressing room.

A maid was busy there, unpacking a suitcase.

There was just one garment of Mrs. Casey's in the closet but more were there to be hung.

"This is a lot different than home," she said, leading the visitors to another dressing room. "This is where Bob will dress," she said, again almost guiltily.

On the first floor, where there are a number of public rooms open to tourists, Mrs. Casey saw vases and other decorative—but fragile—antique pieces. "I better keep the grandchildren out of here!" she said.

Mrs. Casey had been up late the night before, having attended the inaugural ball. That morning, she and her husband had to leave the Hotel Hershey to go to the mansion to meet press photographers.

Pictures were taken of Casey and his wife carrying in suitcases. However, while Mrs. Casey came to stay, the governor was there only long enough to have the pictures taken. He left to go to the Monongahela Valley in western Pennsylvania, an economically depressed area he had promised to visit his first day as governor. Thus, the relatives who came to call later were seeing the mansion before the governor had become a true resident.

The home is impressive. It has about 20 rooms on three floors. Many of them are decorated with original paintings done by Pennsylvania artists and furnished with Pennsylvania-made furniture—much of it old and beautiful.

The flood that wrecked Wilkes-Barre in 1972 also hit Harrisburg. The four-year-old mansion had water up to the ceilings of the first floor. Mrs. Casey showed off a first-floor sitting room, which has a continuous hand-painted mural covering all four walls. The mural, done on strips of canvas, was under water, but when the waters receded, workmen recovered the strips. They were then redone by artists.

"Didn't they do an amazing job?" Mrs. Casey asked.

Gov. Raymond Shafer was the first governor to live in the mansion. Gov. Milton Shapp, who succeeded Shafer, didn't like the mansion. First, he considered living in his home near Philadelphia and flying daily to Harrisburg in a helicopter. He got bad publicity on that plan so he reluctantly agreed to use the mansion.

Then the 1972 flood hit, and the Shapps moved into a rented home in the Harrisburg suburb of Wormleysburg. While it took a couple of years to restore the mansion and its furnishings—many of them valuable pieces on loan from private owners—the Shapps chose not to move back. Thus, it was not until Dick Thornburgh became governor in January 1979 that the mansion became a residence again.

Mrs. Casey, who has lived in an eight-room stucco home at 2002 N. Washington Ave. most of her married life, admits the mansion is bigger than anything she ever dreamed she would live in. It has a staff of 14 persons plus a 'round-the-clock' state police staff that has its office on the first floor.

The property is surrounded by a 10-foot iron fence and it is the state police who operate the buttons to open the gates for people to get in and out.

Among the persons making the tour of the mansion was Mrs. Casey's mother, 90-year-old Mrs. Ray Harding, who now lives at the Casey home here.

Mrs. Harding had been at the ball the night before, comfortable in a wheelchair provided even though she still walks pretty well. About midnight she was asked if she wanted to leave and she said with a hurt voice: "It's not over yet. I want to stay to the end." And she did, getting to bed about 1:30 A.M. Still, she got up the next day and headed for the mansion.

After seeing the residence, Mrs. Harding said: "It looks OK to me."

Mrs. Casey has a dilemma, figuring out how to run the executive mansion and keep her own home operating here. Her mother, her son Matt, 15, a sophomore at Scranton Preparatory School, and daughter Erin, 24, live there now, and she and the governor are in Harrisburg. How the family will be rearranged in the future, she is still deciding.

Meanwhile, Mrs. Casey confessed she has to get used to having staff members at her beck and call. For instance, as her tour of the mansion was ending, her daughter, Margi Casey McGrath, said her daughter Casey needed a bottle warmed.

Jeanne Schmedlen, Mrs. Casey's chief in-house assistant, anticipated the need and had a warm bottle ready.

"I won't have a thing to do if this keeps up," said Mrs. Casey as a number of her early visitors were leaving.

July 17, 1987

DID JOE THROW? WE'LL NEVER KNOW

Did Josephus Jefferson Jackson—more commonly known as "Shoeless Joe"—try to throw the 1919 World Series?

That's a question I would have loved to have asked Eddie Murphy who died at his home on Green Ridge Street in Dunmore on Feb. 20, 1969.

Mr. Murphy, whose nickname was "Honest Ed" was a teammate of Shoeless Joe on the White Sox team that allegedly let the Cincinnati Reds win the World Series in 1919.

The question about Shoeless Joe's involvement in the so-called "Black Sox Scandal" is being raised again by Ted Williams, one of the best players in baseball history. He wants baseball commissioner Bud Selig to exonerate Shoeless Joe.

And how could Mr. Williams make a judgment about something that happened 80 years ago?

Simply because of the statistics of Shoeless Joe in that series.

Eight players of the White Sox—including Shoeless Joe—were charged with conspiring to let Cincinnati win the nine game series in eight games.

However, if Shoeless Joe was trying to hand victories to Cincinnati, he did it in a weird way.

He had no errors, batted .375, had a record 12 hits, drove in six runs, hit three doubles, and hit the only homer of the series.

Eight players, including Shoeless Joe, were indicted for allegedly taking money from gamblers to fix the series. A jury found the players innocent.

However, that did not stop baseball commissioner Kenesaw Mountain Landis from banning all eight players from baseball.

I recently chatted with Edward Murphy of Dunmore, the son of the late ballplayer, who was a teammate of Shoeless Joe.

I asked if his dad had ever said Shoeless Joe was in the conspiracy.

"No," he said. "But he certainly felt sorry for him."

Mr. Murphy, a retired teacher, regrets that he never put the question of Shoeless Joe's guilt directly to his father, who was playing ball with Villanova College when a Connie Mack scout signed him with the Philadelphia Athletics for the 1912 season.

After winning two American League pennants, Mr. Mack began selling off his players. As the 1915 season neared its end, Mr. Murphy was traded to the White Sox midway through a double-header, playing the two games in two uniforms.

Mr. Murphy, who was born on Hancock, NY, had an 11-year batting average of .287 and—when he wasn't being played regularly—was the best pinch hitter in baseball.

Mr. Murphy left baseball after a stint with the Pittsburgh Pirates in 1926. He settled in Dunmore and had various jobs. During the 1930s he was a supervisor of recreation under the federal SPA, and during World War II he worked for the USE.

His son, a retired schoolteacher, said his father didn't talk much about the 1919 scandal, but he liked Shoeless Joe.

"My father felt sorry for him because he only went to school a few years and was a virtual illiterate," the retired teacher said. "Dad said he could have been easily led by the gamblers." However, he added, his father had no pity for the others.

After being booted out of baseball, Shoeless Joe allegedly played ball under various names. Later, he returned to his native South Carolina and opened a bar. Mr. Murphy said his father and a few other players went to see him at the bar. Shoeless Joe was busy so they waited until he came to them. Mr. Murphy said his father shook hands with him and said kind words. Shoeless Joe said he was afraid he was going to ignore him.

Shoeless Joe was one of eight children in a poor farming area. He was taken out of school to pick cotton. More often than not, he was shoeless, thus his nickname. Later, he made $1.25 for a 12-hour day in a cotton mill.

As a teenager, he began playing semipro ball. Connie Mack signed him to a contract in 1908 but en route to Philadelphia on a train, he turned around and went back home. Mr. Mack got him back. In his first two years in the majors, he batted .408 and .395.

Mr. Murphy did tell his son that there were several cliques among the Chicago players and Shoeless Joe was a member of the one that involved most of the players charged in the scandal.

Mr. Murphy's closest friend and roommate on the White Sox team was Eddie Collins, who had a 25-year batting average of .333 and was admitted to the Hall of Fame in 1939.

Mr. Murphy's son said one of his memories is visiting the Hall of Fame with his father and having him point out the Hall of Famers he knew.

One story he told was about Babe Ruth, then a rookie pitcher for Baltimore in the International League. The Philadelphia Athletics played a spring exhibition game with Baltimore, and he, as the leadoff hitter for the As, became the first major leaguer to bat against the Babe.

I asked Mr. Murphy how his father fared in that at-bat.

"You know, I never asked him that," he said sheepishly.

SLOVIK SEEMED TROUBLE-PRONE

Pvt. Eddie Slovik was a born loser and he remained that way to the end.

Slovik, the son of poor immigrants, grew up in the Polish enclave of Hamtramck, near Detroit. He became a juvenile delinquent, and at 24, became the only American soldier since the Civil War to be executed for desertion.

He was buried in France in 1945 and only last month was his body returned to the United States. However, the casket was mistakenly sent to San Francisco. It was tracked down and returned to Detroit where it was reburied.

Slovik had a habit of getting lost when he was alive, too. Doing it once too often in combat produced the desertion charge that led to his death.

The story of Slovik is intertwined with Scranton's 109th Regiment. The 109th, with 1,800 men, was called into federal service on Feb. 17, 1941, for what was to have been one year of training.

The Pearl Harbor bombing changed all that. The training intensified. However, the unit did not taste combat until 1944. Then it made up for lost time.

The 109th landed in France on June 26, 1944, 21 days after D-Day. From that night to the end of the war, the unit saw plenty of action and its ranks of local soldiers were depleted.

In time, the 109th became a hodgepodge of local vets, plus draftees from all parts of the country.

Slovik had been arrested at 12 for burglary. Later, he was convicted for embezzlement of a pharmacy and was sent to a reform school. Paroled in six moths, he met a girl and fell in love. At last, it seemed, he had a reason to straighten out his life.

The war was raging in Europe but Slovik was told he would not be drafted because of his arrests. On the day he and his new wife moved into an apartment, his draft notice arrived. The military needed men, so even men with criminal records were taken.

Despite chronic leg pains, Slovik passed the physical and began basic training. His commanding officer decided he was not combat material. He hated guns and asked for a transfer to a noncombat unit. The commander agreed and forwarded the request to his superiors. But men were needed for combat and he was shipped to Europe and assigned to Company G of the 109th.

Slovik's timing was bad. The 109th was in heavy combat when he arrived on Aug. 25, 1944. Intentionally or otherwise, he got lost that night and hooked up with a Canadian unit. It was Oct. 8 before he found the 109th and rejoined it at a time there was no fighting. When he arrived, he was told he was going into combat whether he liked it or not. Among those who tried to reason with him was Scrantonian John McDonald, now a retired general. However, Slovik left his rifle in his commander's tent and walked away. He returned the next day and was charged with desertion.

That was a fairly common happening. About 40,000 GI's fled from combat in World War II, but charges against them were generally reduced or dropped. Only 49 were convicted and sentenced to be "shot to death with musketry." Of those, only Slovik died.

Slovik's trial lasted an hour and 40 minutes. He refused to testify. The military panel sentenced him to death. Even the judges knew that such sentences were never carried out.

But as desertions increased during the Battle of the Bulge in December, the military felt it had to set an example. Slovik's case was perfect. Gen. Dwight D. Eisenhower approved his execution. Eisenhower ordered that the execution be carried out by the 109th. On Jan. 25, 1945, Slovik was transported from Paris, where he had been jailed, to St. Maire aux Mines. It was there that he met the Rev. Carl P. Cummings, a Catholic priest from Scranton who was the regiment's chaplain. The priest heard his confession and told him he would be with him as long as he wanted prior to the execution.

The next morning Slovik was executed by a 12-man firing squad that included Oscar Kittle, a farmworker from the La Plume area. Father Cummings said: "Slovik was the bravest man in the garden that morning."

Although executed as an example to others, the army apparently changed its mind about making the act public. Slovik's body was buried in a cemetery reserved for soldiers who had been executed for murders, rapes, and other capital crimes. His wife was told only that he died under dishonorable circumstances that prevented her from getting benefits. It was years later that a writer, doing a book, told her what had happened.

Finally, the hapless soldier and his wife have been reunited in a Michigan grave.

September 24, 1987

HOW DOES ONE DEFINE BRAVERY?

Joan Golden is a brave lady. She is facing extraordinarily complex surgery and she can talk about it without cringing. It's not that she doesn't know the risks. "Sure I'm scared," she admits with a weak smile. However, she prefers not to dwell on the negatives.

I've known Joan for decades as the wife of Walter Golden, a colleague at the *Times* who died last Nov. 1. But I never saw the qualities of bravery that came through as we chatted about leaving here Saturday for Methodist Hospital in Houston, Texas.

Joan has an aneurysm on her aorta. An aneurysm is a swelling in an artery—like a bubble on an automobile tire. If an aneurysm bursts, death can quickly follow.

Medical science has made it possible to fix such damaged arteries with tubing. Such operations have become routine.

In Joan's case, however, the aneurysm runs from chest to abdomen. Its size is unusual. Dr. Stanley Crawford of Houston is a world famous specialist. Dr. Lear Von Koch, who is head of the Mercy Hospital team that has been treating Joan, recommended Crawford.

Koch should know. For nine years, when he was associated with famed heart specialists Michael DeBakey and Denton Cooley in Houston, he got to know Crawford's work.

Joan's operation will probably take place Tuesday. Observers will include Koch, who has been practicing here for eight years but is a physician who believes the learning process never ends.

He will go to Houston with other members of his cardiac-vascular-thoracic team, including Dr. Robert Jama; James P. Yi, a certified clinical perfusionist, and Dino Sacchitti, a certified physicians' assistant.

Koch, a Palmerton native who is a graduate of Baylor College of Medicine in Houston, has gone back to Houston before. He took nurses from the Mercy Hospital to the heart center there to observe operating room procedures.

Joan said Koch is the one who recommended Crawford as tops in his field. "I guess my case is really different," she said.

Actually, it is somewhat of a miracle that Joan is here to tell her story. In January, 1986, she and her husband went to the wake of Gene Coleman, another *Times* colleague. On the way home—close to 4 P.M.—she felt a severe pain. They got to their car and started home. En route, she said she should go to the hospital. Walter thought she was kidding. But she wasn't. He took her to Mercy Hospital.

Three doctors examined her. The CAT scan crew who run the computer axial tomography machine had gone home but was called back. By 9 P.M. she was in intensive care.

Joan's problem was diagnosed right from the start. It was anyone's guess as to how long she had the aneurysm. Maybe it was there all her life. Maybe it had recently developed. Whatever its history, it was viewed as a ticking bomb that demanded immediate care.

However, Joan ruled out surgery. Walter had been operated on for cancer. From what she was told after that operation, she knew it was only a matter of time until his cancer would return. She decided it was not time for her to have surgery.

Joan was told to severely restrict physical activities and was given a lot of medication to minimize pressure of the blood on the walls of the artery. She then did her best to forget her problem.

Just two years earlier, Joan and Walter had envisioned a bright future. They had been married 41 years and had raised their family, so they retired, he as a newswriter, and she as a school secretary. They took a trip to Ireland and England, they went to the Jersey shore, and they went to the Poconos with a group of friends. Then Walter became sick and had the first in a series of operations.

Through her husband's illness, Joan ignored her aneurysm. Luck protected her. She remained with Walter until his death.

Joan recently made up her mind that it was time to take Dr. Koch's advice and have the operation. She is tired of the restrictions the aneurysm places upon her. Surgery is the only way she will be able to live a normal life.

Joan knows full well the dangers she faces and she has done what has to be done, including saying her prayers. She won't be alone. Her support team includes four children and six grandchildren. Someone will be with her at all times in Houston.

Despite the dangers, Joan's hopes are high. In fact, she has her return ticket to fly home 10 to 12 days after surgery.

Who said woman are the weaker sex?

A CHURCH ISSUE TO THE FOREFRONT

The most serious punishment the Roman Catholic Church can impose is an excommunication—cutting a person off from the body of the Church.

The most celebrated use of the power occurred in the Scranton Catholic Diocese on Sept. 29, 1898, when Bishop Michael J. Hoban, co-adjutor of the diocese, issued a decree of excommunication against Father Francis Hodur, founder of the Polish National Catholic Church.

After almost 90 years, that decree is moving centerstage once again. At the conclusion of the seventh in a series of meetings between PNCC and Roman Catholic officials, the PNCC delegation put the excommunication on the agenda for future sessions.

Relations have never been better between the churches. Both sides go out of their way to be friendly. That contrasts sharply with the years when members threw names—and sometimes stones—at each other.

Officials of the PNCC and the Roman Catholic Church have been meeting to explore what they hold in common as opposed to what separates them. The last such session was held recently at a PNCC edifice in Carnegie, near Pittsburgh. Among the participants were Bishop James C. Timlin of the Scranton Catholic Diocese and PNCC Bishops Anthony Rysz of Scranton, Francis C. Rowinski of Buffalo-Pittsburgh, and Stanley F. Brozena, Ogdensburg, NY. It was at that session that the excommunication was introduced.

A faction within Sacred Hearts of Jesus and Mary Church in South Scranton resented not being able to govern parish affairs. Father Hodur, a newly ordained priest serving in Nanticoke, was sympathetic to their views. They left their parish and, under his leadership, built St. Stanislaus Church. He became pastor.

The Scranton Diocese at the time was headed by Bishop William O'Hara, but his health was failing, and Bishop Hoban had been assigned to help him. In time, Bishop Hoban was running the diocese.

On Sept. 8, 1898, Bishop Hoban sent Father Hodur a letter, warning him to submit to his authority or face excommunication. The priest responded that he would submit if the bishop would recognize the right of the people he was representing.

That set the stage for the formal excommunication—a decree that Father Hodur tore up, burned, and dumped in a creek.

At the same time Bishop Hoban penned a letter to Polish Catholics, explaining the reason for the decree.

The letter begins with biblical quotations including St. Peter's warning, "There shall be among you lying teachers who shall bring in sects of perdition," and St. Paul's warning, "I know that after my departure ravening wolves will enter in among you, not sparing the flock."

Bishop Hoban charged that Father Hudor, before his ordination, had sworn to serve the diocese of Scranton but he "broke that solemn promise" by "cowardly" abandoning his Nanticoke parish to head a church "built through mistaken zeal. . . ."

Bishop Hoban wrote that Father Hodur had been forbidden to perform his priestly powers but he failed to obey. He added: "Wishing to spread his poison, he has tried to organize schismatic churches and has invited other suspended vagabonds to help him divide the Church of Christ and to tempt Poles to abandon the faith of their fathers."

The bishop claimed that Father Hudor was appealing to "bigotry and prejudice of narrow-minded people by raising the issue of nationalities." He added "the bishops of the United States are American are proud of their country."

Claiming that the Roman Catholic Church is the only "national church" of Poland, Bishop Hoban said anyone who "strives to separate the Poles from this, their real national church is "simply doing the work of a Russian spy. . . ." He said Father Hudor was "a traitor to the Polish cause because he was dividing rather than uniting the Polish people."

Accordingly, Bishop Hoban wrote, "we deem it our solemn duty to excommunicate and we do hereby excommunicate Francis Hodur, priest, from his rights, titles, and privileges as a member of the One, Holy, Catholic, and Apostolic Church of Christ."

The rhetoric of 1898 was severe. It is also true that the Roman Catholic Church has opened many windows during recent decades. Yet even today, the church does not let parishioners hold deeds, control their finances, or pick their pastors—which were among Father Hudor's goals. It will be interesting to see what ecumenism can do with the excommunication decree.

NEWSPAPER WORK HAS ADVANTAGES

Writing for a newspaper is not a bad way to earn a living. It keeps me in out of the rain. There is no heavy lifting, so it won't cause me back problems. And while I won't ever be rich, at least I won't starve.

Most newswriters dream of writing a book. But few ever do it—fearing, no doubt, it would not succeed. Newswriters don't like rejection. They are too used to having most of what they write appear in print within hours.

I'm no exception. I'd love to write a book about my growing-up years during the tail end days of the Great Depression. (That was the big one.) So after getting home after grinding out stuff all day on my video display terminal, I'm not in the mood to plug in my typewriter.

Over the years, I have done my share of freelance writing—op-ed page essays, magazine stories, and such things. Those pieces are relatively easy to put together, so I can get them done at home. (However, laziness has slowed my production in recent years.)

We people in the news business write a lot. There is much white space in a newspaper before a day begins—maybe the space equivalent of a good-sized novel. So we have to write many stories—and write them fast. It's a process I liken to grinding out sausage. There is a demand for it so we produce it by the yard. If I ever lose my job at the *Times*, I think I could run a sausage machine for Gutheinz Meats.

Lest I offend my fellow journalists with the reference to sausage, let me add that while news stories are carefully researched, care is needed in picking ingredients for sausage, too. News stories also must be accurate, but sausage must be blended with accuracy. News stories must be written within the framework of a formula—just as sausage must be made according to a recipe. So the analogy is fine.

About 95 percent of news stories have summary leads, which means that the first paragraph or two tells the main element of a story. The "body" of the story merely amplifies on that.

By contrast, most freelance writing involves quite a different style. Instead of putting the main message at the start of the story, magazines, books, essays, plays, and other writings bury it—maybe even at the end.

The best way to sell any written work is to know what the market wants. For years, I have leaned on an annual book called *Writer's Market* put out by Writer's Digest Books. It lists thousands of places to sell articles, books, plays, gags, poems, and a bunch of other things. And no wonder: if you run across a cute story about a cat you can look up "cat" in the index and find several publications that like cat stories.

Just recently, I acquired a copy of a new work, *The Writer's Digest Guide to Manuscript Formats*, and I have been scanning it with the idea of getting back to writing at home. The book operates on the premise that no matter how good a written work may be, if it is not properly dressed, it may not be taken seriously. There is truth in that. No publisher is going to read—let alone buy—handwritten scrawls.

Over the years, I have had my share of writing failures. In fact, I wish I had saved all my rejection slips. That would have made a great wall covering to remind me of my fallibility.

But I have had some success, too. I've had three op-ed pieces published in the *New York Times*, which I think is a record for a nonstaffer. But because of sheer laziness, I have not tried to sell it an essay in years.

One of the things you must be careful of when you make a freelance sale is paying taxes on your profits. Some years ago I sold a story to *Good Housekeeping* magazine and was paid $1,000. The following year, two Internal Revenue agents sought me out at the *Times* and asked to sit with me in a private office. When we were alone, one began reading me my Miranda warnings—meaning my right to remain silent, have a lawyer, etc.

I had a clear conscience but still was frightened. I'd seen enough movies to know what happens after one is read his rights.

After the reading of my rights, one of the agents told me the IRS had computer information from Hearst Publications that I had been paid $10,000 for a *Good Housekeeping* story. I relaxed. "I was paid $1,000 and I have a contract to prove it," I said.

The agents checked my story and one called back to say it was a computer error.

Maybe someday I'll put that in a story. Maybe someday I'll write a play. Maybe I'll get around to writing a book. Or maybe I'll just keep dreaming.

July 14, 1988

THE GOLD RUSH AND MULROONEY

Belinda Mulrooney, the coal miner's daughter from Archbald, still is famous in faraway Alaska.

Joe Quinn, a grocer and former mayor of Archbald, was recently in Alaska with his wife Nancy to visit their son Thomas, who is serving with the Air Force in Fairbanks.

While on a tour of the state, the Quinns stopped at Skagway, where they picked up a visitor's newspaper and began reading about the Klondike Gold Rush of 1897–1898.

One of the paragraphs stood out. "Belinda Mulrooney, a Pennsylvania coal miner's daughter, became one of the most successful female entrepreneurs of the gold rush. She established a lunch counter and a contracting business in Dawson City. She also managed a mining company and her employees described her as a 'holy terror' to work for. Hailed by Scribner's as 'the richest woman of the Klondike,' she soon operated Dawson's elegant Fairview Hotel."

Mrs. Quinn vaguely recalled having heard stories about a woman from Archbald becoming famous during the gold rush. They took the paper home and Vera Weatherby, Mrs. Quinn's mother, verified that the woman in the newspaper article was indeed the one from Archbald.

So Mrs. Quinn brought the paper to me, and Frank Fox, our newspaper's librarian, dug out old stories about the legendary lady in our reference room.

There was little in the clippings on Belinda's origins beyond the fact that she's from Archbald, but from a few clues I figure she must have been born about 1875. That would have made her about 22 when prospectors discovered gold in the Klondike region of the Yukon Territory.

Thousands of persons went by ship to Alaska to make the overland journey to the Klondike. Skagway and several other towns were founded and became prosperous because of these travelers.

Belinda was born with a wanderlust that a mere trip to Scranton would not satisfy. Stories about people becoming rich overnight convinced her to leave Archbald for the Yukon.

"Belinda got to the banks of the Yukon River with only one silver dollar." According to an account in a 1958 book called *The Klondike Fever* she threw that last dollar into the river as a gesture to her determination to get rich.

One version of her life said Belinda opened up an eatery for miners at Nome Creek and got rich overnight. Another is that she bought a load of hot-water bottles and floated on a raft down the river, stopping at every mining settlement to sell the hot-water bags to miners who could use them to stay warm at night.

Belinda must have had a lot of native intelligence. Within two years she owned the largest and most lavish hotel and saloon in Dawson. She also acquired ownership of much mining property, and became the only female manager of a gold mining corporation.

As soon as Belinda became wealthy, she arranged to have her sister, Margaret, leave Archbald to get an education in a boarding school in Paris. Again, the details are sparse, but Margaret eventually joined Belinda in Nome Creek, where she became cashier and secretary of Belinda's new bank.

The miners took bags of gold dust to the bank and Margaret weighed them and then credited their accounts. During the long Alaskan winters, when mining was at a standstill, the sisters loaned money at high interest rates. "It sure was easy money," Margaret recalled years later.

There is an old saying that persons lucky in business are often unlucky in love. That turned out to be true in Belinda's case. She fell head-over-heels in love with Charles Eugene Carbonneau, a champagne salesman, who claimed to be a European count. With her money, the couple often went to Paris, where they rode the Champs Elysées behind a pair of snow-white horses, with Egyptian footmen who unrolled a velvet carpet of brilliant crimson whenever they got out.

The romance soured, however, when Belinda learned that her count was an ex-waiter. (After they separated, he was arrested in Paris for selling a group of Americans and Englishmen nonexistent plantations in Cuba. What happened to him after that is unknown.)

When the gold rush fizzled, Belinda and Margaret decided to operate an apple ranch at North Yakima, Washington. Later, they moved their parents out there.

I don't suppose anyone in Archbald actually remembers the Mulrooney sisters. The 1958 book on the gold rush said Belinda was still alive and living near Seattle. But that's as far as I could track the story.

October 30, 1988

IF YOU HEAR MARTIANS ARE HERE, IT'S ONLY UPDATE OF AN OLD SHOW

Fifty years ago tonight, America was terrorized by a radio broadcast about an invasion of the planet Earth by creatures from Mars, and as far as I can remember, I slept through the whole thing.

It was our family custom to frequently visit my father's homestead in Carbondale for Sunday dinner, and that's where we were on that day. Toward evening, however, we headed home to Jessup in my Uncle George's car.

We weren't even aware of the broadcast. Besides, I fell asleep in the car.

Meanwhile, millions of Americans were at home listening to their radios. That was the custom in those days when radio was the dominant communications and home entertainment medium.

Among the programs on the air was the *Mercury Theater of the Air*, which did weekly radio dramas, often based upon classics of literature. That evening it did an updated, Americanized version of the H. G. Wells British novel, *The War of the Worlds*.

The story was reworked by Orson Welles, a 23-year-old actor who was one of the founders of *Mercury Theater*. He broke up the narration into short bites, that would normally be used on broadcasts of major news events.

Welles also played the role of a famed astronomer who gave periodic reports on how the Martians may have traveled to Earth and how they might be stopped in their bid to conquer it.

It was announced at the outset of the program, twice during the broadcast, and once at the end that the events being portrayed were fictional. However, millions of persons failed to catch those parts of the broadcast. Many assumed that creatures from outer space might soon snuff out their lives.

In this area, the broadcast was carried by WGBI, the CBS radio affiliate. The story was preceded by a few minutes of music. Then an announcer cut in with this message: "We interrupt our program of dance music to bring you a special bulletin from the Intercontinental Radio News. At 20 minutes before 8, Central Time, Professor Farrell of the Mount Jennings Observatory, Chicago, Illinois, reports observing several explosions of incandescent gas occurring at regular intervals on the planet Mars."

A short time later, an announcer cut in again to report that a large meteorite had landed at Grovers Mills, near Princeton, NJ.

Switchboards at police stations and newspapers across the nation began to light up. Police in New York City checked with the network and determined that the program was fiction. Meanwhile, the Associated Press moved a message over its wires advising newspapers that the broadcast was not the real thing. However, spreading the word to the public was not easy. the *New York Times* logged 875 calls from frightened persons.

The Newark, NJ, bureau of the Associated Press reported that thousands of persons—after hearing the Martians were using poison gas—were covering their faces with towels and fleeing from the city.

A man in Pittsburgh returned home to find his wife holding a bottle of poison and screaming, "I'd rather die this way than that." He saved her life.

What had frightened the woman—and many other persons—was the graphic description of the invasion. An announcer said that black smoke was drifting over New York City. He continued: "People in the streets see it now. They're running toward the East River, thousands of them, dropping in like rats."

Then a person who identified himself as the secretary of the Department of Interior said solemnly: "Citizens of this nation, I shall not try to conceal the gravity of the situation that confronts the country."

Scranton reported receiving hundreds of calls. In the Midvalley, a man carrying two suitcases met a neighbor who asked him where he was going. He said he was fleeing because the Martians were coming. His neighbor knew about the broadcast and finally convinced him the event was fictional. The man felt foolish as he went back into his house. Meanwhile, two women in their kimonos tried to hail a cab in Scranton. They returned to their homes after learning there was no invasion.

I've never known whether this was fact or fiction, but I grew up with the rumor that a Midvalley dentist had made preparations to put his wife and children to sleep—permanently—with injections. The story claimed he learned just in time that the story was fiction.

The radio show had a happy ending. The Martians had been able to resist all of man's weapons, but then they suddenly began to die. The cause was bacteria their systems could not fight off.

However, the shock waves from the broadcast would not end so quickly. Fifty years later, they are very much alive. I suppose I should be happy I slept through the broadcast. I was spared being frightened. But —safely removed from the event by time—I now wish I could say I had heard it.

LOCKHEED CHIEF WAS BORN HERE

Lockheed Corporation is among the largest in the nation, dealing in contracts totaling billions of dollars a year.

And who heads this massive organization?

A man named Daniel M. Tellep, who was born in Forest City.

John Guzey, a local retired businessman, told me about Tellep, a relative of his, and suggested that I write a column about him.

I must admit I was a little dubious. We had nothing in our reference department on him and I figured if a local man got to be head of a big corporation we should have had something on him. Nonetheless, I called Lockheed's public relations office at Calabasas, California, and asked if Tellep worked there. Told that he was a corporate officer, I asked for material on him.

A couple of weeks later I received a packet of information on Tellep, Lockheed's board chairman and chief executive officer.

Well, Guzey was right. Tellep's biography said he was born on Nov. 20, 1931 in Forest City.

I read all the material. It included this blurb from *Business Week*: "Daniel M. Tellep likes to pitch his easel in the California countryside and paint watercolor landscapes. He also likes to soar in his sailplane over the Sierra Nevada mountains and to run, play tennis, and go to the opera. But as new president and CEO of Lockheed Corp., Tellep may have to push those hobbies aside—at least for the next few years. Lockheed, whose sales have doubled since 1983, faces uncertain times as Pentagon budgets fall. Keeping the company healthy and growing will be a full-time challenge."

I was impressed. But I wanted more information on Tellep's local ties, so I wrote to Lockheed's public relations office again and posed some specific questions to them.

Weeks went by and I heard nothing. I figured the public relations people passed my questions on to Tellep, but he—the head of one of the biggest firms in the country—was ignoring me.

However, one afternoon my telephone rang and I answered it. The called identified himself as "Dan Tellep."

By this time, the name had slipped my mind.

"What can I do for you, Dan?" I said, playing for time.

"I called to answer the questions you sent me," he said.

Suddenly, the light went on. This guy was the head of Lockheed!

"Oh yes, Dan," I said, asking from where he was calling.

"I'm at a pay telephone at the Los Angeles Airport," he said.

I then began the interview.

Tellep told me he was born in Forest City. His father, the late John Michael Tellep, was born in Mayfield of parents who had migrated there from Russia. His mother, the former Mary Yusko, was a descendant of emigrants from Czechoslovakia.

Tellep said his father was a good baseball player in the area. He also worked in the mines.

There is little that Tellep remembers about Forest City. He said he recalls wooden sidewalks along a street. He also remembers a male choir at Christmas, and Easter services in a Russian orthodox church. But that was about it.

When World War II began, Tellep said, his parents moved to Binghamton, NY, and then to Newark, NJ in search of employment. He said he was only 8 or so at the time. His father became a machinist in the aviation industry and wound up working for Convair Corp. in San Diego, Calif.

Tellep grew up in California, one of two sons. Both his father and brother have died, but his mother lives at Pacific Beach, Calif. He went to the University of California at Berkley in an era when it cost $25 per credit. He received an engineering degree with honors in 1954 and then a master's degree.

Tellep got a job with Lockheed Missiles & Spaces Co., one of the original high tech firms in California's Silicon Valley. Over the years he played an ever-increasing role in the production of elements in our nation's missile and space programs. He received various promotions, reaching the presidency of the Lockheed Missiles & Space Co. in 1986 and the head of the whole Lockheed empire last January.

Tellep, at 57, is married, the father of six daughters, and grandfather of five children.

I had more to ask when the loudspeaker at the airport announced that Tellep's flight was loading. He said he has not been here since his parents left, but he'd love to come back someday. Then he ran to get his plane.

I thought it was nice that such a busy executive would take the time to call. That's probably how he got to the top.

IRISH LANGAN'S WORLD CONTAINED
GIDDYAPS, BUMS, STIFFS, 403s

Irish Langan's death requires me to tell some stories.

The 78-year-old Scranton native—more formally known as Thomas Martin Langan—was marked from an early age to be different.

For instance, when he was a student at St. John's Elementary School in South Side, he got into the confessional box a bit early and heard the confessions of a number of his classmates before he was found out.

"Oh, I got my knuckles rapped for that one and couldn't pick coal for a week!" he said in telling the story to me one day at lunch.

Irish, who worked much of his life for the county and the state, was in the courthouse on the day after the late Democratic County Commissioners Michael F. Lawler and William Geiger won re-election to new terms.

Irish was the building superintendent, meaning he was in charge of keeping it spic and span. Lawler decided to have some fun. He started complaining that the floors were dirty, the windows need washing, and the steps could stand a new coat of paint. But Irish took the kidding in stride. With his arms around both Lawler and Geiger, he responded: "Yea, it's dirty; but the nice thing is we have four years to clean it up."

Irish knew himself well. Once he was sitting alongside his daughter's swimming pool nattily dressed in casual sport clothes. As he talked with adults, a six-year-old child sneaked up behind him and threw a pail of water on him.

Others were horrified, but Irish kept control of himself. He said: "Leave him alone. He's just like me when I was a kid."

Sometimes it was hard to understand Irish. He colored language with so many made-up words his talk was often indecipherable.

In Irish's days as a saloonkeeper, he might have said this: "A giddyap tied a dog in my joint, so I hit him with a 403."

The translation: "A local character left an unpaid bill in my place, so I asked him to leave." [A "403" was the form used to fire persons in the old WPA (Work Projects Administration)].

214

Irish liked the sound of certain words, and used them even when they had no particular relevancy. For instance, he was once asked if he had good health insurance in his state job. He replied: "Boy, am I covered. I have Blue Cross, Red Cross, right cross, left cross, double cross, and even Stations of the Cross!"

When the Japanese bombed Pearl Harbor, Irish took it as a personal affront. He joined the Navy within days and got shipped off to Hawaii where fate played a hand in his life. He had done some boxing in his college days, so he knew much about the sport. In Hawaii, he went to a boxing show and hated everything he saw. He yelled at the boxers and everyone else.

Admiral Chester Nimitz, commander of the Pacific Fleet, was at the fights, and he summoned Irish to ask what made him such an expert. Irish, not the least bit intimidated, said the fighters were bums, the handlers were stiffs, and the referee was blind.

"Could you do better?" Nimitz asked.

"I sure can!" said Irish. From that point on, Irish was on the admiral's staff, being in charge of recreation for servicemen wherever the war took Nimitz. Befitting his assignment, he became a chief petty officer.

In Irish's opinion, the best way to beat the Japanese was to aid U.S. servicemen, no matter how many regulations might have to be bent. For instance, a legendary commander of a U. S. submarine was in port to get food and torpedoes. He told Irish he wanted a wind-up record player, explaining that he loved music, but that electronic record players made noises that enemy ships could detect. The old wind-ups didn't do that. But he couldn't find one.

Irish learned that there was a wind-up Victrola in an Australian officers' club. However, the Aussies wouldn't part with it. So Irish and the submarine commander broke into the club at night and carried off the machine. By the time the theft was discovered, it was safely in the submarine. The Aussies might have suspected Irish, but they couldn't prove a thing.

Irish was a born comedian, too, and, as such, he knew that mother-in-law jokes were crowd pleasers. One day he was standing at Courthouse Square when a friend happened along.

Irish, as usual, started in the middle of the story: "Imagine $50,000! Just like that, I blew $50,000!"

The friend bit: "What happened, Irish?"

"I had $50,000 in air travel insurance on my mother-in-law, but she just arrived safely in San Francisco," he said with a sly grin.

July 20, 1989

YES, THE BAMBINO WAS IN SCRANTON

Imagine the plight of John Hogarth, a 75-year-old retired teacher and state worker from Jermyn.

In the glory days of Babe Ruth—when every kid in America idolized him—John carried his spikes into the ballpark.

However, the last witnesses to what happened died over 40 years ago, so John—father of five children and grandfather of two—has gone through life trying to convince people he met Ruth.

"Sure, John," many say, making little effort to mask their skepticism.

John recently told me his story, and I checked the facts with old stories in our files. And sure enough, "The Bambino" was in Scranton on the day in question, Oct. 14, 1926.

Four days earlier, the St. Louis Cardinals beat the Yankees in a seven-game World Series. Ruth, the pride of the Yankees, hit .300 and hit four homers, including three in one game.

The series came down to the last inning. With two out in the ninth, Ruth was on first. He rarely stole a base, but the Yanks needed a run to tie the game, so he figured he'd try to get into scoring position.

He took off with the pitch and made a heroic—but clumsy—slide into second. He was out and that ended the game. Not only that, but the skin on his thighs and rump were brush-burned.

Back in those days, ballplayers—even Ruth—were paid modestly. So they accepted a lot of invitations to make appearances for cash. the *Scranton Times* sponsored a day of baseball at Brooks Field on Providence Road—with Ruth and some local big leaguers as guests.

John Hogarth, then about 12, loved baseball. He was thrilled when his father Tom asked him if he wanted to go to the event. Tom was a hoist operator for Neuman Clark, the project foreman who was installing a mine pumping station in Jermyn.

Tom explained to his son that Clark was taking his 8-year-old son Billy to the park, and he would like him to go along as company for the younger boy. John jumped at the chance.

217

The three went to Scranton on the Delaware and Hudson Railroad and arrived hours before the activities were to begin. Without telling the boys where he was headed, they walked to the Hotel Jermyn where he asked the number of the room of Gene Sullivan, his brother-in-law and the contractor of the pump project.

The boys went with Clark up on an elevator and then to a room where he tapped on a door.

John remembers the moment. This is how he describes it: "A man opened the door and the first thing I saw was a big man sitting in a chair who was dressed in a sweatshirt and a jock strap. When I saw his face I was dumbstruck. There was no mistaking it; it was Babe Ruth. He started to laugh and shouted, 'Come here, kids.' The next thing I knew I was seated on his left knee and Billy was on his right. He made a big fuss over both of us for about 10 minutes. Then he had to eat and put salve on a great big scab on his upper leg and rump—the result of trying to steal second and sliding without pads."

The room was Sullivan's, the contractor, and it was filled with men—mainly politicians—who wanted just as much as the kids to see Ruth.

Lunch was brought in and Ruth made sure the kids got sandwiches and soda. He also autographed baseballs for them.

Soon it was time for the Babe to go to the ballpark. He put on his baseball suit and a pair of bedroom slippers. He asked John to carry his spikes and Billy to carry his glove. Both were proud as peacocks as he steered them through a crowd in the lobby and another crowd out on the street.

Sullivan had an open car, and Ruth sat in the back seat with the boys on both sides. The route to the ballpark was lined with people, and Ruth told the boys to wave.

Police cleared a path for the car to enter the park. Then Ruth had to leave. John gave him his spikes and Billy surrendered the glove. Both boys then went to the stands where they and thousands of others watched a hitting exhibition and an amateur game in which Ruth was the player. A story in the *Times* said the day ended when a fan grabbed the last of 132 balls—most of which were hit over the fence by Ruth.

The boys never had their pictures taken with Ruth. John fingered his baseball so many times the signature wore off. Then Billy—a pilot in World War I—was killed. Thus, he became the only one who remembered the day.

But his balloon is often deflated when people don't believe him.

CHRISTY MATHEWSON SOARED FIRST WITH THE EAGLES OF HONESDALE

Sometimes I get letters from readers and I keep them because I have every intention of doing something with them. But my intentions do not always match my performance.

Back in 1985, I got a letter from David E. Gower, Factoryville postmaster.

He asked me to write a column about Christy Mathewson, arguably the best pitcher in the history of baseball, and said Lackawanna County's stadium should be named after him.

I kept Gower's letter, but just never seemed to get around to doing the column.

However, Gower was persistent. He waited four years and then wrote again with the same request.

I was a bit ashamed that I hadn't treated him well. I called to apologize. "No problem," he said, content that he finally had my attention. He said he has a lot of material on his hero and proceeded to send it to me.

Thus, I relearned that Mathewson—who was born in Factoryville in 1880—was an awesome pitcher. In 1908 he set the modern record for wins in a season with 37. He also set a record for consecutive innings without a walk with 68. He won 20 or more games 13 times, and 30 or more four times. His wins in 1903, 1904, and 1905 totaled 94. His ERA was under 3.00 13 times and under 2.00 six times. He pitched over 300 innings in 11 seasons and struck out at least 200 in five seasons. His 17-year career won-loss record was 373–188, with a career ERA of 2.13.

In the 1905 World Series, Mathewson pitched three shutout victories for the New York Giants over the Philadelphia Athletics. In four World Series, he is tops in shutouts with four and in complete games with 10.

Mathewson, who was with the five original members inducted in the Baseball Hall of Fame in 1936, also played a major role in making baseball respectable. Bright and clean-living, he became a national hero and a model for children to copy.

Mathewson was 17 when he signed to pitch for the Honesdale Eagles in 1898. the *Wayne Independent* didn't get excited. It reported on July 16, 1898: "De-Witt Clinton received his 10-day notice of release and a young man named Mathewson, who pitched for the Keystone Academy team, has been signed and is now with the team."

Mathewson was 17 at that time and experienced. At 13 he pitched for men's teams in Mill City and Factoryville, sometimes getting $1 a game. Later, he pitched for a Scranton YMCA team. He also attended Keystone Academy, now Keystone Junior College, where he played baseball and football.

Mathewson began his professional career with Honesdale. His first game was against a team at Goshen, NY. It was a wild one that Honesdale won, 16–7. A few days later the two teams met again and Mathewson posted a 2–0 win. Honesdale then played Carbondale, its archrival, and Mathewson was the winner, 7–0.

Honesdale was in the Orange County League and tied Port Jervis for the championship. When Mathewson wasn't pitching, he played the outfield. In a deciding game on Sept. 10, 1898, Mathewson pitched and won, 5–1.

Mathewson entered Bucknell University at Lewisburg that fall and became a football star and a straight-A student. (Bucknell renamed its renovated football stadium after him on Sept. 29.)

In 1889 Mathewson played again with Honesdale. In addition to pitching, he fielded and had a fielding average of .968 while batting .344. On July 18, 1899, he pitched his final game for Honesdale, a 14–6 win over Port Jervis.

Then Mathewson packed his bags and went to Taunton, MA, where a New England League team promised him $90 a month for what would be another successful pitching season. A few years later he told a reporter about the move: "There is a lot of difference between $90 a month you don't get and $20 a month that comes in regularly. At Honesdale, I worked for $20 a month and my expenses at the $2-a-day hotel. At Taunton, I worked for $90 and the most I got was $20 at a time. At the end, I got $40 for my share and went back to college in October."

In 1890, Mathewson played with Norfolk in the Virginia League for $90 a month, which he presumably did receive. He posted a 20–2 season. The New York Giants signed Mathewson late that year, beginning his 17-year career that put him in the Hall of Fame.

Tragedy overtook Mathewson. He enlisted in the Army in World War I and inhaled poisonous gas. After the war, he became a coach with the

Giants but had to go to a sanitarium with tuberculosis. He returned in 1923 to become president of the Boston Braves. Two years later, at 45, Mathewson died.

March 25, 1990

HANK'S DEED PROMPTS A REWARD; OTHER MAIL PRODUCES CHIT-CHAT

Bits from the mail. I wrote a column recently about Toni the elephant from Nay Aug Zoo who is now at the National Zoo in Washington, D.C. The item said that Toni is doing well in her new surroundings and that Hank Robinson of Archbald, who borrowed $3,500 to have her moved, had just paid off that loan.

Well, some columns get around. I received a letter from Doris Swan of Mill Creek, WA, who said she and her husband Richard moved from Scranton 40 years ago, but they still keep in touch. She said that while they were vacationing at Marco Island, FL, they saw my column and were impressed by Robinson's generosity. She sent a $50 check to help share the cost of moving Toni.

I sent the check to Hank and he said the money would help pay for his next visit to Washington to visit Toni.

A column about Scranton-made "Manor" heaters, such as the one that the local Anthracite Museum just acquired from a garage in Carbondale, brought a letter from attorney John J. McCarty, formerly of Carbondale.

McCarty, a principal in the firms of Raynes, McCarty, Binder, Ross & Mundy in Philadelphia, said he could solve the mystery of who manufactured "Manor" heaters.

However, the column still put him in a nostalgic mood. He wrote: "Growing up in Carbondale in the 1930s, I learned early on how to care for our Dickson stove before retiring in the evening. Properly stoked and banked, its coal replenished from the 'scuttle' that sat on the floor nearby, it would keep its rosy glow through the night.

"Early next morning, my Dad would shake down the grates and insure a warm kitchen in which we kids would dress.

"Were he alive today, Dad would doubtlessly recall the Manor stove and its origins."

So I still need help on that.

Local composer Richard Wargo wrote to tell me that Hugh Wolff, former director of the Northeastern Pennsylvania Philharmonic and now director of the New Jersey Symphony, is going to Ireland in July with 86 members of his orchestra, to participate in and supervise a 16-day music festival at Adare Manor in Limerick—a luxury hotel made from an eighteenth century castle.

The program will include numerous outdoor concerts involving Wolff's own orchestra and Ireland's National Symphony Orchestra, Dublin. To reciprocate, Wolff's orchestra will give a concert in Dublin. Various other Irish musical groups will participate in the festival.

Wolff is appreciated for the work he did here. However, a lot of people wonder why he never mentions Scranton when he is interviewed by big city media.

The Irish music program is the idea of investment banker Tom Kane of Summit, NJ, a board member of the New Jersey Symphony and owner of Adare Manor.

I wrote a column about the persistent rumor that the late pop artist, Andy Warhol, whose real name was "Warhola," was born in Forest City. The tale got into at least one book, and it shows up from time to time in newspaper stories. The truth is that another "Andrew Warhola" was born in Forest City, and that the author of the Warhol book found his state birth certificate and mistakenly assumed it was the artist's.

I thought that was the end of that. But recently I received a letter from Catherine Warhola of Pittsburgh, the sister of Mrs. Ann Krolikowski of Taylor, and Mrs. Mary Simms of this city. Mrs. Warhola, formerly a Lewczuk from Old Forge, is married to a Warhola who is a first cousin of the deceased artist.

Mrs. Warhola confirmed what I had written about the Forest City story being incorrect. She said that Warhol was born in Pittsburgh in 1928, and that he has two brothers, John and Paul Warhola, who still live in that area.

Mrs. Warhola added that in a few years, an Andy Warhol Museum will be opened in the Volkwin Building in downtown Pittsburgh. The museum, she said, will house Warhol paintings, films, and other memorabilia.

I had a letter recently from Palmer P. Liberatore, from Broomall, near Philadelphia, formerly of Jessup.

When I went to the University of Scranton out of Jessup High School, Palmer was among the ex-GIs in my classes. Before World War II, he had played minor league baseball. Then he served almost five years

in the Army. While at the U. of S., he served as baseball coach. He graduated in 1949, did a lot of postgraduate work and went into the insurance
business. He retired as an officer of State Farm Insurance and plans to
keep active by teaching insurance at the college level.

MOTHER CABRINI'S VISIT RECALLED

A century ago, Italian immigrants were present in many cities in America, struggling to cope with a new language, blatant prejudices, and a desperate need to earn money to survive.

In many cases, the battle to get through each day left little time for the faith that had been a big part of their lives in Italy.

Among the persons who were trying to correct the situation was a 40-year-old woman from Italy—Mother Frances Xavier Cabrini—who had come to New York City the previous year with six companion nuns from her Mission Sisters of the Sacred Heart.

The nuns had no trouble talking with the immigrants in Italian. However, to do the job that Pope Leo XIII had assigned them—to perform religious and social services—they had to master English. Mother Cabrini wrote to a friend: "I am beginning to understand English a little bit, but at first I really believed it was the language of geese."

From her early days in New York until her death in Chicago in 1917, Mother Cabrini devoted herself to being a missionary to all of America.

In 1913 she reported to Rome that the Catholic chaplain of Oregon prisons told her nuns: "You do more good in one visit to these prisons that I am able to do in a month!"

Among the 67 institutions Mother Cabrini founded was a school for the children of Italian immigrants in Scranton.

Mother Cabrini came here in the summer of 1899 at the invitation of Bishop Michael H. Hoban. She stayed at St. Cecelia's Convent near St. Peter's Cathedral, and spent much of her time visiting immigrant parishes and families in Scranton and Dunmore.

It was the practice of Mother Cabrini to build schools that charged no tuition. How such a school could be built and operated here took a bit of time to resolve. Then the Scranton School District offered for public sale an abandoned school on what was then Chestnut Street—now St. Francis Cabrini Avenue—in West Scranton. (The city erred and put the "i" in "Frances" instead of an "e.")

Bishop Hoban purchased the school and had it remodeled for a new parish he dedicated to St. Lucy. Part of the old school became the church, while part was given to Mother Cabrini's order for a convent and school.

The school was operated by Cabrini nuns for over 70 years. Eventually it closed. Then, last Friday, it was rededicated to a new purpose. The United Neighborhood Centers of Lackawanna County—through a separate nonprofit housing corporation—opened it as a secular housing complex for senior citizens and the handicapped. For historical purposes, the building will carry Mother Cabrini's name.

The project was not an easy one. As the United Neighborhood Centers nursed it through the federal, state, and city bureaucracies, it often got bogged down. During its darkest hours, there were often prayers offered for heavenly assistance. Then the project began to move again.

Maybe that's not the way things are supposed to happen in a nation that separates church and state. But I don't see why God can't lobby, too.

Besides, Mother Cabrini is a true historic figure. She helped Italian immigrants become Americans while keeping their heritage. In addition, she became the first American citizen to be canonized a saint by the Catholic Church. That process often takes centuries. In her case, it took 29 years!

The conversion of the school to an apartment complex prompted Tony Johns, 912 W. Linden St., to write to me about a visit made by Mother Cabrini to the school in 1913.

Johns wrote: "There was a big hullabaloo over Mother Cabrini coming." He recalled that when the big day came, the famous nun visited his class and spoke in Italian. "All the kids could speak Italian," he noted.

After her talk, Johns recalled, the nun walked up an aisle and stopped at each desk. He wrote: "She asked me in Italian, 'What's your name?' I said 'Antonio.' She said, 'Oh, Antonio! You know St. Antonio? He is a very big saint. Oh yes, I think he is going to watch over you. Yes, he's going to watch over you a good long time—maybe 90 years!' She put one hand on my shoulder and the other on my desk and bent down her head for half a minute. I think she said a prayer."

Johns said that if she prayed for a long life for him, it is working. He noted that he is 86, and still alive and well in Scranton.

And with her name now on the new apartment house here, the same can be said for Mother Cabrini.

October 2, 1990

PARKER CLAMBAKE PLUS FOR GOLFERS

It's funny the way things happen. One summer day in 1950, attorney Jerome E. Parker—now 78 and retired—was invited to a clambake at the old Apawana Golf Course.

The Apawana, then the only public course in the area, comprised what was left of the old Scranton Country Club course.

Before the country club moved to the Abingtons, its main entrance was off North Washington Avenue. After it moved, nine holes survived, with an entrance off the O'Neill Highway between Dunmore and Throop.

Strip mining had flawed the course, but it still attracted many golfers. But Jerry was not one of them. He grew up in Scranton's downtown in an era when it was bustling with vaudeville houses, restaurants, stores, and residences. Playing golf was not high on anyone's list of things to do. Besides, Jerry was Jewish and the Scranton Country Club did not admit Jewish members.

That day at the Apawana, Jerry and a pal got their hands on clubs and hit some balls.

Jerry was then a lawyer, having graduated from Temple Law School in 1938. He also was a new member of city council. And when the clambake ended, he was a golf lover. Jerry felt golf should be available to everyone, including those unable to pay country club dues or meet their membership rules.

Jerry learned that many municipal golf courses were making profits. He told Mayor James Hanlon and his colleagues on city council that news, but they weren't enthusiastic.

Meanwhile, in 1953, some Jewish golfers—sick of being "guests" at the Scranton Country Club and wanting to be "hosts" at their own —opened Glen Oak.

But that did not satisfy Jerry. He wanted a course that everyone could play. One day he chatted with Jimmy Calpin of the old *Scranton Tribune*, himself an avid golfer. He began supporting the idea in his columns.

Later, Jerry's quest became a subject of a newspaper story. In it he asked how many persons would pledge $100 toward a fund to develop a municipal golf course. Robert Hughes, then head of Megargee Brothers Co. and secretary-treasurer of the Scranton Country Club, made the first $100 donation.

However, all the reaction was not favorable. A letter to the editor complained about the city floating bonds for a golf course instead of patching streets.

But Jerry persisted. In 1957, a realtor told him about a 200-acre piece of farmland that was available in Mount Cobb for $20,000. Jerry viewed it from a chartered plane and liked what he saw. He and some friends chipped in $300 to secure an option on the site. He then got the Chamber of Commerce to host a public meeting on developing municipal golf courses. Experts on golf and golf courses addressed the audience. Then Jerry got up and asked for $100 donations. Before the night ended, he had $5,600 in cash and pledges.

The project picked up more momentum when Larry Tice, then president of International Textbook Co., gave a corporate gift of $1,000, saying a municipal golf course would enhance the city's image as a "more attractive place in which to live and work."

That triggered a $1,000 donation from the Globe store, $500 from the Scranton Dry Goods Co., and substantial gifts from workers at the General Electric Co. and Consolidated Molding Products Co.

However, critics remained. Another letter to the editor said the city already has "an excellent golf course—18 holes in each block."

Donations continued to come in, however. By 1958, sufficient funds were on hand to buy the land. Jerry got the support of the mayor and council to name a recreation authority to build and operate the course. The body then floated a $410,000 bond issue that the city backed. Construction began. In 1960 the course opened.

What was Jerry's payment? In 1961, he ran for re-election and he was peppered with claims the golf course would become a burden to the city. He lost by 43 votes. After that, he gave up his law practice and took a job with the U.S. Department of Housing and Urban Development in San Francisco. Later, HUD assigned him to Philadelphia, and finally, after the 1972 flood, he spent three years as HUD housing expediter in Wilkes-Barre.

In the meantime, the golf course paid off its bonds, became a source of revenue, and the city is considering more improvements. It also changed its name to the Jerry Parker Municipal Golf Course.

Ponder this: What if Jerry had not gone to that clambake?

December 18, 1990

TONY'S TOYS GET BIG PLAY

I was truly impressed when I heard that Tony Koveleski's collection of antique toys was to be auctioned off at Sotheby's, a famous auction gallery in New York City—that in the recent past sold a painting of Vincent Van Gogh for $50 million, and the everyday knickknacks of painter Andy Warhol for incredible sums.

I had known for years that Tony, a local resident who once operated a hobby shop and also manufactured miniature automobiles, had a collection of old toys.

He showed them to me in 1983 when I visited his home on Moosic Street to interview him about his song writing and ukulele playing.

During the interview, Tony took me into a side room and showed me the toys: the fruits of collecting for over a half century.

I was awed by the sheer number. Even Tony wasn't sure how many he had, but I'd guess it was close to 1,000. I thought about changing the focus of my column from music to toys.

However, Tony prevailed upon me not to mention the toys. It seems that antique toys are as hot an item among thieves as fine art. He said that if I were to write a story that he had a room filled with old toys, I might be setting him up for a burglary.

So I wrote a column about Tony's musical talents and how he often displays them under the name of "Uncle Louie."

Not long after that, a well-known antique toy dealer in Philadelphia was beaten by thieves who stole hundreds of his most valuable toys. I knew then that Tony's worries were not groundless.

I saw Tony periodically after that. Once he took me for a ride in his yellow Stutz Bearcat—a possession of incredible value that he keeps in storage.

On other occasions, he gave me tapes of new songs tied to local topics. One example: "The Old Garbage Truck Blues."

And when Tony had nothing else to promote, he often dropped by with a bottle of "Uncle Louie's Trail Mix"—his own mixture of walnuts, raisins, candy, etc.

It is now safe for me to write about Tony's toys because they are being auctioned off to collectors today at Sotheby's—a proud old firm that does not waste its time with merchandise it does not think is good quality.

As a former member and president of the Antique Toy Collectors of America, Tony was at a convention in Chicago and met an agent named Bob Shepard. He had seen photographs of Tony's toys. After learning that Tony, now in his late 70s, wanted to share his collection with others, Shepard asked if he could represent him in setting up a sale. With nothing to lose, Tony said: "Sure, go ahead."

Well, Shepard went to Sotheby's and showed them the photographs. They liked what they saw. Some of the firm's experts came here to check out the toys. They were impressed, particularly by the excellent condition of many of the rare pieces.

Eventually, a deal was struck for Sotheby's to auction off the collection, some individually and other items in groups. In all, there are 362 units to be sold.

In preparation for the sale, Sotheby's held a reception last Thursday night. Among those on hand were news media representatives, including reporters from magazines specializing in antique toys. Also present were Tony and his family: his wife Doris; his two sons, Oscar of Clarks Summit, and Ronald of Boxford, MA; and their wives and children.

Times photographer Ike Refice, who first introduced me to Tony many years ago, suggested that we go to the reception. So he got some invitations for us and our wives. We went with Russell Preston, president of the *Globe*, and his wife, Peggy, both of whom have an interest in historical curios.

Having seen the collection seven years ago, much of it in cardboard boxes and in need of a dusting, I was amazed at the transformation. Sotheby's had each piece displayed in glass cases where they gleamed like diamonds.

Tony's job was to chat with the collectors, most of whom he knows from attending conventions over the years. He also had to chat with the reporters from the specialized antique-toy publications. And it was clear he enjoyed every minute.

We won't know for a while how today's sale went. It takes days or even weeks for checks to pass through banks before sales are final.

In any case, I can breathe a little easier. I worried over Tony keeping such valuable things in his home. About the only thing that will be left now are his old songs.

January 2, 1991

ROCKWELL'S ART NOT SLICE OF LIFE

Once again during the past holidays, I had the task of carving a turkey, and once again I thought of the beautiful pictures that Norman Rockwell painted on that subject.

In Rockwell's world, the task was done at the dining room table as happy members of the family waited anxiously.

But I never carve a turkey in the dining room. When I do it, it isn't a pretty sight. I'm more of a butcher than a surgeon. My operating room is the kitchen.

I must say that this used to bother me, because I thought there was something wrong with me. But recently, lo and behold, there was an article in the *Wall Street Journal* that said, "turkey carving is another thing modern man is making a mess of," and "the kitchen is fast displacing the dinner table as the prime slicing site."

What a relief!

Males have long been given the task of carving the turkeys, it being a holdover from the day when they were also the hunters. Thus, the males became the ones who decided the size of meat chunks to give out.

There are few males among us who actually go into the woods to get a turkey—a task that would have to be followed by plucking feathers and scooping out the innards. My mother introduced me to feather plucking when I was a kid. I found it to be a hateful—and smelly—task. And as for cleaning the innards, that is not work for a gentleman.

No, it is definitely easier to go into a store and buy a turkey that is plucked, has edible organs in paper bags, and is neatly sealed in plastic.

In our home, my wife buys the turkey and makes the stuffing. I put it into the cavity and then sew up the openings. From that vantage point, I have learned that there is no uniformity in the preparation of turkeys for the market. Sometimes the openings are made with the precision of brain surgery. Other times, the birds look more like the victims of ax murderers. I shovel in the stuffing and then suture them back together. I also tie up the wings and legs to keep them from falling off during the

231

roasting. Then I put the bird on its back in the roaster. From then until my wife takes it out of the oven, I have no other chores.

However, as mealtime approaches, I get the call. The turkey has to be removed from the roaster so that the gravy can be made. I put on an apron and prepare for surgery.

I place the turkey on a wooden carving board and take down the electric carving knife that one of my children gave me several Christmases ago. (It really does a good job.)

In Rockwell's paintings this is the point at which the turkey is carried into the dining room, but I would not be able to perform surgery there the way I can in the kitchen.

My first task is to reopen the turkey to remove the dressing. That involves cutting away the stitches and getting rid of that part of the skin to prevent it from winding up on someone's plate. Rockwell would never have become famous doing paintings of a man cutting away the stitches of a turkey and scooping out the stuffing.

My next move is to take the meat off the turkey legs, thighs, and wings. Rockwell shows people eating the legs, but I always remove the meat from them. First of all, I had six children—but turkeys only have two legs. To avoid favoritism, I opted to remove the meat and put it on the platter.

Also, turkey legs have 14 wire-like tendons that get in the way of the meat. I remove the meat with a small carving knive and with my fingers. And the same is true of the meat on the wings. As for the thighs, that dark meat is thick enough to slice.

With that all done, I have bits of meat and skin all over my work area. I wash my sticky fingers and pick up the electric knife for the most serious job—slicing the white meat. That must be across the grain. But even this task gets sloppy when you get close to the bones. Hungry people are better off not seeing me picking the elusive pieces with my fingers.

I usually get sentimental when I come to the wishbone. I cut that away with a small carving knife. Wishbones should be cleaned and put away to dry. I remember the fun of making a wish with someone else and then pulling to see who would get the biggest part, which meant having the wish come true.

But now, I find, wishbones are out of date. I am told to hurry the carving because everything else is ready. Reluctantly, I drop the wishbone into a garbage bag. Rockwell definitely would not have painted that.

May 12, 1991

MOM WAS "ENGINE" FOR FAMILY
BUT SHE DIED BEFORE BEING PAID

Mother's Day is filled with bittersweet memories for me, because I never felt I had the opportunity to pay my mother back for the many things she did for me.

Clare Martina Reap Flannery was my dominant parent when I was growing up.

My father, James Aloysius Flannery, was a typical father of that era. He worked when depression conditions permitted. His jobs included selling insurance, working in a breaker, working on a railroad, working on a WPA road gang, and finally, becoming a keeper of records at the county-owned West Mountain Sanitarium. During worse periods, we were on welfare, and then he did some bootleg mining and picked coal.

But Mom was the engine that drove our family. She cooked, baked, sewed, washed clothes, did the ironing, painted, wallpapered, rocked babies, made sure we were never late for church, healed wounds, hung clothing on the line, carried frozen-stiff clothes back inside to dry on cold winter days, made sure homework was done, was in charge of discipline, took care of household finances, taught prayers, cleaned the house, got up first in the morning, got the fire going, made hot oatmeal on winter mornings, was the last to go to sleep at night, helped build a cement wall, enforced curfews, and made us aware we shouldn't sit on cold cement surfaces or stop wearing winter underwear until May 1.

Tough times were nothing new to my mother. Her father died when he was 45 and she was a teenager. There was no welfare in those days, so she had to quit school and go to work. My mother became a professional seamstress, often spending several days with a family while making garments for members of the household.

The Great Depression ruined whatever chance my mother had for an easier life after her marriage. Soaring unemployment impacted heavily upon our family. For a brief time, when my father couldn't find work, my mother was a tailor in a Scranton store. For years, we lived with a danger of losing our house, having our grocer halt our credit, and having a finance company collector catch us before we could turn off the lights and lock the door.

Somehow, we survived the hard times, paid off all our debts, and were none the worse for the experience. Indeed, I think it forever sensitized me to the fact that we—individually and as a society—can never do too much to help the poor.

Still, for me, "hard times" were not necessarily "bad times." Indeed, most of my memories about my growing-up days are good ones. I'm not sure how my mother did it, but Sunday dinners were the biggest culinary events of the week. The smell of a pot roast filled the house hours before we ate. The anticipation of eating made time drag.

Then there was Mom's homemade bread, maybe my single most favorite food. The mere memory of a piece of that bread dipped in gravy from the Sunday roast still activates my salivary glands.

And then there were other favorites, too: chicken soup, baking powder biscuits, ginger cookies, lemon meringue pie, and Christmas doughnuts freshly powdered with confectionary sugar.

Holidays were always special too. Relatives visited. Big meals were served. Someone was sent to buy ice cream. On such days there was a festive mood that transcended being poor.

Despite those fond memories of mine, cooking was not my mother's favorite activity. She always seemed happiest when she was making one of us a new garment. She could get lost in a project like that, showing great reluctance to stop to get a meal.

Just at a time when the economics of our family were dramatically improving, my mother was stricken with cancer. For a time, she kept her condition a secret. Not until the day she had to go to the hospital for an operation did we know she was seriously ailing. She underwent surgery a couple of times and those procedures did give her several more years of near-normal life. Still, she was just 63 when the cancer killed her.

By then I was married for two years, and my wife and I were making installment payments on furniture, a washer, and a car. Someday, we dreamed, we would buy a house—but that was still a long way off. We did a few things for Mom, having her down for meals, and driving her to Philadelphia to visit my sister. And, of course, we visited her and talked often on the telephone.

My regret is that we were never able to take her out to a nice restaurant, or take her to see a Broadway show, or buy her a new coat, or put money in her purse. Or even send her roses.

Today I envy persons who have their mothers for longer periods than I had mine. I hope they use that time well.

May 30, 1991

SINATRA TALE CAN BE TOLD

The recent death of Max Kearson, a show business promoter in Scranton for more than a half-century, freed me from a pledge of secrecy involving a story he once told me about Frank Sinatra.

Max knew most of the leaders of big bands of the 1930s, 1940s, and 1950s. In particular, he had a good relationship with Tommy Dorsey, a Shenandoah native who once played with the Scranton Sirens, a big band of the 1920s.

Sinatra was singing at a New Jersey roadhouse in 1939 when Harry James hired him. Dorsey went to a hotel in Chicago to hear this new crooner. He liked what he heard and wooed him away from James.

Max said it was probably 1940 when the Buddy Club, comprising himself and Karl Strohl, booked the Dorsey band, with Sinatra, to play at the Masonic Temple.

The Buddy Club booked a lot of bands in those days for dances that cost just $1.

It was customary for the bandleaders to meet Max on the day of a dance to make the rounds of local radio stations. Disc jockeys were happy to have a famous musician to interview. Sometimes during the interview, the leader would remind the audience that the band would be playing that night at the Masonic Temple.

The day Dorsey's band arrived here, its leader called Max from New York to say he had been detained on business, but would arrive in plenty of time for the dance. However, he said he wouldn't be able to do the radio interviews.

Dorsey told Max to get Sinatra at the Hotel Jermyn and tell him to make the rounds of the radio stations.

Max said he went to the hotel, got Sinatra's room number, and went up to talk to him. He knocked on the door and Sinatra answered.

"I told him that Tommy was delayed in New York and he was to make the rounds of local radio stations to help promote the dance," Max said.

Sinatra flatly refused.

236

As Max told the story, Sinatra said his job was to sing with the band, not do interviews.

So Max made the rounds of the stations on his own.

The dance was a great success. By tradition, money at the box office was counted with Max and Dorsey present. That was an institutionalized procedure that prevented cheating in making payments.

As the money was being counted, Dorsey asked Max if everything worked out earlier in the day with Sinatra.

Not wanting to cause any trouble, Max had not told Dorsey about Sinatra's refusal. But confronted by a direct question, Max said Sinatra had refused.

Dorsey, known for his short fuse, sent someone to get Sinatra. Within minutes, he came to the room where the money was being counted. Dorsey asked if Max had asked him to go to the radio stations because he had been delayed. Sinatra freely admitted he hadn't gone because, he said, that wasn't part of his job.

According to Max, Dorsey slapped Sinatra across the face.

"I'm running this band and when I give an order, I expect it to be carried out," Dorsey said.

Sinatra, stunned, left the room without saying another word, according to Max.

Max told me that story during a 1983 interview, but he said he didn't want me to use it. He was retired at the time, but I don't believe Max ever completely retired. Just in case he ever had the chance to book Sinatra, he wouldn't want him to be angry because he'd told the story about Dorsey's slap. So he made me pledge I would not use the story while he was living. I agreed.

Max had more open trouble with several performers over the years. Russ Morgan, a Scranton native who became nationally famous as a bandleader, had been sent an advance check for a 1936 booking. However, the night of the dance he demanded full payment, told the audience he was being swindled, and delayed the last half of the dance so long most persons left. Max sued and the case was settled.

In 1966, the Beach Boys began to party in their Scranton motel and decided against performing. Max sued them too, and won a settlement.

Buddy Rich, the drummer, was booked by Max to play at a city-sponsored concert at Memorial Stadium, but he quit playing halfway through the concert with the excuse that he had to keep a recording date in New York. I'm not sure how that ended.

Such cases were the exceptions and not the rule. The hundreds of other shows that Max put on involved no problems—not even secret ones such as Sinatra's slap in the face.

HEROINE SARAH TO BE HONORED

Back in 1988, I read a book called *The Revolution Remembered*.

It comprised eyewitness accounts of the Revolutionary War given by veterans and their widows to qualify for a federal pension that the Congress had approved in 1832.

Records of that war often were nonexistent so the claimants had to go to their local courthouses and tell their stories under oath to a stenographer with enough details to convince a pension board of the validity of their claims.

Sarah Osborn Benjamin of Pleasant Mount, Wayne County, who was then 81, went to the courthouse in Honesdale on Nov. 20, 1837, and told of following her late husband, Aaron Osborn, a soldier, through various campaigns. Along the way, she said, she traded quips with Gen. George Washington, witnessed the surrender of a British army at Yorktown, and dodged bullets and cannonballs.

Sarah, who died in Pleasant Mount in 1859 at the age of at least 101, is buried in Green Grove Cemetery, on Route 670, just outside the village of Pleasant Mount. She was virtually forgotten by history until the Wayne County Chapter of the Daughters of the American Revolution put a marker on her grave.

More recently, the Mount Pleasant Historical Society (the town is Mount Pleasant and the village is Pleasant Mount) undertook a campaign to have a state historical marker erected in front of the cemetery, memorializing her as representative of the many women who traveled with their soldier-husbands during the Revolutionary War—cooking, sewing, treating wounds, and carrying food and water to soldiers.

However, the first effort of the historical society was rejected by the commission that evaluates subjects for roadside markers.

I love history and was intrigued by Sarah's story. I decided to join the society's movement, compiling my own application and attaching as much historical data as I could find.

I included the sworn statement of Sarah as she applied for her pension, extracted from the book I had recently read. It included her claim that she was delivering food to soldiers at Yorktown when Washington came by. He asked if she was not afraid of the flying cannonballs. She replied: "It would not do for the men to fight and starve, too." The answer pleased Washington.

I also included extracts from an 1856 *History of Mount Pleasant* by the Rev. Samuel Whaley that said Sarah had told him she once was serving as a sentry when Washington passed by. "Who placed you here?" he asked. "Them that had a right to, sir," she replied. Whaley wrote that Washington was pleased.

In addition, I included statements of Richard O. Eldred, associate professor of history at Nyack College, Nyack, NY. A native of Honesdale, he said that Sarah performed so many military chores that she deserves to be ranked alongside of Molly Pitcher, a famous female hero of the Revolution.

I also contacted state senator Robert P. Mellow and interested him in the cause. He lent his weight to the request.

Finally, a compromise emerged. The Pennsylvania Historical and Museum Commission said it would erect a roadside plaque if the Mount Pleasant Historical Society would pay $1,250 to help defray the costs. The society readily agreed.

It took another few months for the historical society to prepare a legend for the metal sign, and to tie up whatever other red tape is involved in such a process.

Finally, a few weeks ago, George Beyer, director of the state commission, called me to say the project is ready and the commission was awaiting word from the Mount Pleasant group on an appropriate date for the ceremony.

The sign could have been installed in November but the Mount Pleasant group opted to do it around Memorial Day next year. That was agreeable to the state commission.

When the sign is erected, this is what it will say:

SARAH MARY BENJAMIN

Revolutionary War heroine. At least 101 years old at her death in 1858, she lived here after 1822 and was known for her vivid recollections of the war. Sarah traveled with her husband's New York unit, 1780–83, doing its sewing and washing and baking bread. She stood guard in his place as a sentinel at Kingbridge. At Yorktown she carried food to the soldiers in the heat of the battle.

I congratulate the good people of Pleasant Mount for remembering Sarah.

January 21, 1992

PRECIOUS RELIC STILL SURVIVES

I was working in my office on New Year's Eve when I heard the news that the Tripp House at 1011 N. Main Avenue was on fire.

I hoped the fire would not be a bad one, but four minutes later, I heard the news that a second alarm had been turned in.

"Oh, no!" I said, thinking Scranton's single most valid and authentic link to its past was about to go up in smoke.

Well, it was a serious fire—with damage totaling many thousands of dollars—but it still wasn't as bad as I feared. The fire was pretty much confined to the apartment of the caretaker on the second floor. The balance of the house had smoke and water damage.

A few days later, I toured the house with some members of the Junior League, the organization that almost single-handedly saved it from extinction.

They said that the house—which is becoming a very popular place for catered parties—expects to reopen on Feb. 14, when a wedding reception is scheduled.

There had been a New Year's Eve party scheduled at the home. However, that afternoon, the live-in caretaker, James Hopkins, a school-teacher, was making French-fried potatoes. He had a pan of hot grease on the stove. He left the kitchen for a moment, and when he returned the grease was burning, with the flames already licking at the walls. He tried to smother it with a blanket but the fire devoured that. Then he called the firemen.

They not only made a good stop of the flames, but they became heroic furniture movers, doing their best to get fragile objects out of the way of dripping water. Among the things they saved were an antique cut-glass chandelier and the ancient dining room furniture.

I've been writing about the Tripp House for years, partly because I love history and partly because I have long since been convinced that the history of the city of Scranton has always been poorly told.

The most common version is that the Slocum family started the city. Buttressing that is the fact that it was once called Slocum Hollow.

241

However, the Slocums, who set up a sawmill and other enterprises along the Roaring Brook, were grandchildren of Isaac Tripp, the first permanent white settler of present day Scranton.

Tripp was among the Connecticut residents who settled Luzerne County. Two British kings had given this area to two different groups of settlers—those in Pennsylvania and those in Connecticut. That explains why Connecticut gave land grants to 200 persons to colonize what would become Luzerne County.

In 1771, Tripp purchased land in what is now Scranton to prove this area was safe for settlement, too. He built a cabin about where the Tripp House stands today.

Tripp was an interesting character. He was the fourth generation of a British family that had settled in Rhode Island in 1635. Later, family members moved to Connecticut.

After he came to this area, he represented the settlers in the Connecticut Assembly—a task that involved riding between here and Hartford on horseback.

In 1778, during the Revolutionary War, the British encouraged their Indian allies to attack settlers in his region. That's the year when Tripp's granddaughter, Frances Slocum, was kidnapped by the Indians—and eventually became one of them. Homes of settlers—probably including the Tripp cabin here—were burned by the Indians. Finally, a united British and Indian army killed 200 or so settlers in what we know today as the Wyoming Massacre.

An American army later in 1778 swept the British and most of the Indians from the region. However, the woods of the area remained dangerous. Tripp, while visiting his kin in the Wilkes-Barre area, was slain by Indians.

The Tripp holdings here remained intact, however. Tripp's son, Isaac Tripp II, built a substantial house to replace the original cabin. It is that house—enlarged and remodeled over the decades—that the Junior League owns today.

Insurance will pay for some of the work now underway to wipe out traces of the fire. However, the Junior League will accept donations from anyone interested in preserving Scranton's most important historic relic. It will also welcome antique furniture or accessories that would be appropriate in the building. Finally, it is available for parties.

For more information, call the manager at 961–3317.

HILLARY CLINTON: SHE BAKES, TOO

I must admit that I wouldn't mind Hillary Clinton becoming the nation's First Lady.

On two occasions, I have had telephone conversations with Hillary, which was enough to prove to me that she isn't a lady who puts on airs.

Hillary, whose family roots are in Scranton, is rated among the top female lawyers in the country. Thus, she is much more than *just* the wife of Gov. Bill Clinton of Arkansas.

On Friday, Hillary made a campaign stop here on behalf of her husband's Democratic presidential campaign. En route from the airport to St. Joseph's Center—where she visited—she called me on her car telephone.

I should explain that in January, I had called Hillary in Little Rock, and wrote a column about her and her Scranton roots before much of the national press began to focus on her. In that talk, I asked her to contact me if she came to Scranton to campaign. The phone call from the car sprang from that remark.

Leaving all the heavy stuff about government and its problems to other reporters, I asked Hillary about baking cookies.

I did so because Jerry Brown, who is fighting her husband for the Democratic presidential nomination, suggested she should retire to the governor's mansion and preside at parties.

That angered her. She said she could have stayed home and baked cookies but she chose instead to develop her career.

Her remark upset many cookie-baking, stay-at-home housewives who regarded her words as a blast at their domestic careers.

Hillary, the mother of an 11-year-old daughter, Chelsea, said her remark was not a reflection on cookie-making housewives. Indeed, she said she is a good cookie-maker.

Hillary is the daughter of Hugh Rodham, a 1931 graduate of Central High School and a 1935 graduate of Penn State. He left here for Chicago, where he opened a fabric store. He and his wife settled in the suburb of

Park Ridge and raised three children: Hillary, 44; Hugh, 41, a lawyer in Miami, Fla.; and Tony, 37, who runs an investigation agency in Miami.

Like many Scrantonians who left here for economic reasons, Rodham never stopped thinking of Scranton as his hometown. That's why he and his wife brought their three children here to be baptized in Court Street Methodist Church and why the family often came for vacations, staying with the children's grandparents, Mr. and Mrs. Hugh Rodham, who lived at 1042 Diamond Avenue before their deaths.

Hillary said she and her brothers inherited a family recipe for chocolate chip cookies, and, by tradition, they baked them on Christmas Eve. "We had contests making the biggest one," she said. Asked how she did, she said: "I did well."

Sometimes, the Rodham children baked the cookies at the family's cabin at Lake Winola, which is where they spent a number of Christmases while they were growing up.

Today, Hillary is a high-powered, Yale-educated lawyer who serves on a half-dozen corporate boards and scores of public interest boards, but she said she still takes pride in the chocolate chip cookies that she bakes.

True, after her 1975 marriage to Clinton, who is also a lawyer, she used her maiden name of Rodham even after her husband became governor. However, she had professional justification for doing that. She worked under that name as a law professor, a member of the Nixon impeachment inquiry staff, and ultimately as a member of the Rose Law Firm, one of the South's most prestigious firms. It was a problem to change her name and notify thousands of people of that change. But she did make that concession to tradition.

Hillary takes motherhood seriously, too. She and her daughter were in the checkout line at a supermarket. She pointed out sensationalistic tabloids and warned her daughter that before long she could be seeing her family on the covers. "We have tried to prepare her for the mean things that people say," she said.

In addition, Hillary has taken time off to attend functions at her daughter's school, explaining: "An 11-year-old can't really understand all this."

A day after Hillary visited here, her two brothers were in town and I talked with them. Staying with the subject of cookies, I told Tony and Hugh that Hillary claimed she baked the best cookies. Neither agreed. Both claimed the honor. In addition, Hugh said he always baked the biggest chocolate chip cookies. He said his were "the size of dinner plates."

The next opportunity I get to talk to Hillary, I'll have to get her reaction to that.

June 16, 1992

SAD RENDEZVOUS IN CHICAGO

William G. McGowan, the Luzerne County genius who single-handedly broke the monopoly of American Telephone & Telegraph Co., was dropped off a week ago yesterday by his wife, Sue Lin Gin, at Georgetown Medical Center in Washington D.C. for what was to have been a routine physical therapy session.

McGowan, who built Washington-based MCI Communications Corp. into a $10 billion-a-year telephone company, went inside while Sue headed for the airport to catch a plane for Chicago, where she has business interests.

By pure chance, Monsignor Andrew McGowan, the Scrantonian who is the director of health care for the Scranton Catholic Diocese, was also in Chicago, attending a meeting of officials of the American Hospital Association.

William McGowan had undergone a heart transplant in 1987, but lately his heart had not been doing all that well. He was put on physical therapy. For a time, that seemed to be working. However, after his wife dropped him off, he began sweating. By the time he got into the exercise room, he was in bad trouble. He got medical help instantly, but there was no rescue. He died at 64.

By then, Sue was heading to Chicago by air. A company driver was sent to pick her up. En route, he was contacted on his car telephone and told McGowan had died. It fell to him to break the news.

Monsignor McGowan was contacted and learned Sue was at the airport. She had heard the news by the time he reached her by telephone. He said he was in Chicago and would be right over to get her. He rushed to the airport and met her. Together, they flew to Washington.

Monsignor McGowan also was devastated. Memories of growing up in Ashley flooded his mind. The man who died might have been one of the most famous American industrialists, but to the monsignor, he was his kid brother Bill.

McGowan's death was a surprise only because there was no warning. However, Monsignor McGowan recalled that the specialists at the

University of Pittsburgh Medical Center, where his brother had received his new heart—had said that five years was an average period for persons to live with transplants.

The five years that McGowan got was crucial for him to put MCI on a sound foundation. Proof of how well he did that was that MCI stock did not flicker when he died.

McGowan and his wife made a $1 million donation last year to the University of Pittsburgh Medical Center's Heart Institute to develop an artificial heart that could be implanted in persons who have no remaining options. Thus, McGowan's heart problems could help extend lives of persons yet unborn.

McGowan was generous. Last year, he gave $3 million to King's College, the Wilkes-Barre institution from which he graduated in 1952. Recently, H. Ross Perot, the Dallas billionaire who is running for president, went to King's College to dedicate the new William G. McGowan School of Business.

One reason Perot came was the high regard he had for McGowan. When Perot began his presidential campaign, he needed a massive telephone system to seek volunteers all over the country. He was told it would take months to install the equipment. He called and he piggybacked a Perot telephone system on an MCI system that was also being used by the Shoppers Network on cable television. Within five hours, Perot had a system in place that could handle 55,000 calls an hour.

Not surprisingly, Perot used time during an interview on NBC's *Today Show* the morning of McGowan's funeral to cite him as an example of American businessmen at their best.

MCI is a company with 28,000 workers. Its officials wanted to have him buried from massive St. Matthew's Cathedral in Washington, but his wife and family agreed he should be buried from his home church, Holy Trinity.

Monsignor McGowan wasn't sure he was up to giving the homily. His sister told him: "You know what Bill would say: 'It's your job. That's what you get paid to do.'" So, with much emotion, he did it, concluding with the words: "Goodbye, Bill, and God bless."

Later, McGowan's body was taken to Ashley for burial in the same plot where his parents lie.

When the cars arrived, several hundred persons were present—making Sue think another service was under way. When she found out these were local people who turned out to say goodbye to her husband, she said: "He's at the right place."

December 27, 1992

SNOW AND WIND FAILED TO HALT FLANNERY FAMILY REUNION IN NEW YORK

We Flannerys held our annual Christmastime reunion in New York City two weekends ago—and what a weekend we picked.

One of the worst pre-winter storms hit the Northeast with snow, rain, wind, and hail on Friday, the very day we were gathering. Nonetheless, the five of us—Tom from Baltimore, Jim from Jessup, Clare from Drexel Hill, Matt from Clarks Summit, and myself from Dunmore—arrived, four with our mates, without any damage.

Oh sure, I got a little nervous when wind-driven snow obscured the front end of my car as I was driving through the Poconos, and family members who arrived on Amtrak were soaked while trying to get a cab outside Penn Station. But by the time we were all together, we laughed over our experiences.

Before going further, I must explain that none of us are rich. We grew up in the Depression and have done well enough, but no one ever struck gold. Thus, we have worked out a way of spending a weekend in New York every pre-Christmas season without throwing ourselves into bankruptcy.

We start planning around August, but vowed to begin earlier next year to get better theater tickets. This time, we were in $50 seats in the mezzanine to see George Gershwin's *Crazy for You* and we all agreed that we should have paid more for first-floor seats.

There is an advantage to buying the tickets early. By the time we go on our December trip, the summertime purchase is long forgotten. It's as though our tickets are free.

We use the Manhattan East Suite Hotels—a chain that offers weekend specials on suites that are substantially lower in price than those of regular hotels. (With two couples in each suite, the two-night weekend cost $180 a couple.)

This time we stayed at the Eastgate Tower, on 39th Street, between Second and Third Avenues. In addition to sleeping facilities, the suites have combination living rooms and dining areas, plus kitchens. Thus, we were able to cook our own breakfasts, make sandwiches for lunch, and have our "happy hours" whenever we wanted.

We were more than 20 floors over the streets and saw blizzard-like snow showers that made it difficult to see any great distance. The Empire State Building was only a few blocks away, and sometimes we could see it and sometimes it was obscured by snow.

Luckily, however, the temperature was warm enough to melt the snow as it fell. So the snow put us in a Christmas mood, but we didn't have to contend with it on the street.

During much of the weekend, we told and retold family stories— many wrapped around Christmases of the past. As television told of the storm outside, we all recalled winter storms of our childhood that made this one seem mild. Indeed, what ever happened to five-foot snowdrifts?

A few of the more hardy souls ventured forth on Saturday to see the Christmas tree at Rockefeller Center and to visit some Fifth Avenue stores. (My wife and I bought candles and a fancy tree ornament in Saks. Since it was raining, I bought an umbrella from a sidewalk merchant for $5.)

I love the sights, sounds, and aromas of New York.

Christmas decorations are everywhere—and are particularly spectacular at night. Tourists from other countries are easily identified by their native dress. Homeless people are easy to find, too. So are the sidewalk hustlers who sell watches, scarves, gloves, etc., while looking nervously around for policemen. And the sight of ice skaters on the rink at Rockefeller Center makes me feel good.

Every now and then, the sound of Christmas music drifts from stores. Taxi horns never seem to stop, and emergency vehicles stuck in gridlocked traffic use sirens and other screeching sounds to try to escape.

Also, there are aromas of roasting chestnuts, soft pretzels, and hot dogs, among other things being cooked by street corner vendors. In fancy shops, perfume sales are stimulated by free sprays. Pizza shops and restaurants pump their own odors into the air. And Christmas trees being sold in stores provide a rich pine odor.

At times, we did different things. One couple drifted off to another Broadway show. Others—my wife and I included—went to parties to which we had been invited. Others watched the storm from their suite.

The weather Sunday was nice and we walked to church. Then we went back to the suite where we had our own breakfast. (We never mention calories on these reunions.) Finally, we checked out and went our separate ways.

En route home, we began making plans for next year.

March 6, 1993

BOMBING RECALLS NEW YORK VISIT

It always adds a dimension to a news story to be familiar with where it occurred.

That came back to me last week when a tremendous explosion shook the World Trade Center in New York City.

I've been in the parking garage of that complex three times—all tied to having Sunday brunch in the Windows on the World restaurant, 1,300 feet over lower Manhattan.

In addition, I visited the observation deck of one of the twin towers of the complex with a local group of guys on a one-day outing to New York. That was a weekday, and I got an idea how busy the building is. About 50,000 persons work there and some 80,000 visit daily.

Windows on the World is a great place to eat, because on a clear day, tremendous vistas of New York City are on display through its glass walls —Uptown, the Bronx, Brooklyn, the harbor, New Jersey, the Statue of Liberty, the bridges, etc. Meanwhile, cars on the street look like Tinkertoys, and people on the sidewalk look like ants.

Ever since the blast, I have been thinking of my visits to the center. I recalled going there once for Sunday brunch with my wife Betty, and neighborhood friends, Jerry and Ann Byron, and Joe and Theresa Smith.

To get to the restaurant, 110 floors above the street, one must ride room-size elevators that can hold, I guess, 50 or so persons. One in our group—I won't mention a name—hates elevators. However, this ride—a quarter of a mile straight up—was so fast, she got through it.

Men must wear coats at Windows on the World. On that visit, we met John Davidson, the singer and game-show host who was stopped because he was wearing a sweater. He was given a coat, and while he was putting it on, we chatted. After he learned we were from Scranton, he said we were fellow Pennsylvanians. He's from Pittsburgh.

One of the fringe benefits of the Sunday brunch is free parking below the building. On Sundays, that vast underground area—probably busy on weekdays—was near empty. There were no attendants inside to give directions, so I had to find my own parking space. (I often had fleeting thoughts about security—or lack of it—while parking.)

When I heard of the explosion, my first thought was about the vastness of that underground parking area and the ease with which a terrorist could drive in, plant a bomb, ride an elevator to the main floor, and walk onto the streets of New York without drawing any attention.

I know a few people who know that famous complex because they used to work there.

Conall Killeen of Dunmore, now employed by Blue Cross in Wilkes-Barre, was a member of the original crew that in 1981 opened the Vista Hotel, which sustained heavy damage from the blast that occurred several floors beneath it.

Killen, who is married to my niece, Deanne Loftus, was fresh out of hotel management school, and became steward over all the eating facilities in the hotel. Later, he became manager of the hotel's Greenhouse restaurant.

"I watched the pictures on television after the explosion and saw many things I recognized," said Killeen, who worked there for four years.

Jeff Gavin, a U.S. Secret Service agent, who is now on the security detail of former President Ronald Reagan, was familiar with the garage because he used to use it when he was assigned to the agency's field office in the trade center complex.

The office staffed by about 120 Secret Service agents is in a satellite building that wasn't damaged, but the agency lost a number of its 100 or so cars that were on the level where the blast occurred. Miraculously, while a few agents were in the area of the blast, none was seriously hurt.

Gavin, the son of my old friend Andy Gavin, the former saloon keeper and now a Lake Winola country squire, came to New York this week to testify at a trial, but got nowhere near the World Trade Center. However, he heard firsthand stories when he went to dinner with one of three agents who had just parked their car in the garage when the explosion occurred.

The main towers were not seriously damaged in the explosion and the Windows on the World restaurant will reopen when the buildings reopen.

I want to return there some Sunday for brunch to see if I find more garage security than used to exist.

FATHER PATRICK PEYTON'S WORK CONTINUES YEAR AFTER HIS DEATH

When the Rev. Patrick Peyton died last year, I wondered if the work he had started would continue after his death.

Well, it is not just being carried on—it is actually being escalated.

Father Pat, a native of Ireland, came to Scranton, but was too frail to work in the mines. He became a janitor at St. Peter's Cathedral and found his vocation while walking alone in the gloom of that building. From that modest start, he became a world-famous priest remembered best for his saying: "The family that prays together stays together."

Never concerned with worldly wealth, Father Pat died on June 3, 1992, in a sparsely furnished room under the watchful care of the Little Sisters of the Poor in San Pedro, Calif.

The responsibility of carrying on Father Pat's work then passed to his fellow priests in the Holy Cross order. But I wondered if such a job was transferable.

In recent times, I learned that Father Pat's projects are being carried on in a way he would approve.

The Rev. Robert J. Brennan, born and reared in the Bronx, NY, has been named Father Pat's successor.

A former pastor of Holy Cross-run parishes in Maine, Vermont, and Texas, Father Brennan said: "I'm not going to be, or even try to be, another Father Peyton. No one could do that. But I will seek to carry out his legacy and vision of serving families."

Father Pat's legacy includes Family Rosary headquartered in Albany, NY, with branches in the Philippines, Spain, Brazil, Argentina, Peru, Ecuador, and Uruguay. It was founded in 1942. Five years later, its media arm, Family Theater, Hollywood, CA, was founded.

Current undertakings of Family Rosary include creating a prayer center in Nairobi, Kenya, in East Africa. The center will seek to use mass media to evangelize East Africans in ways that blend with their culture. One means will be the use of videos in a mobile unit that will travel to villages. In time, the center will begin serving Uganda and Tanzania.

Another project of Family Rosary is the "Rosaries for Russia" campaign to collect rosaries for distribution to the former Soviet Union and its neighbors—where religion was officially banned for 70 years.

So far, 1.7 million rosaries have been collected, with most being sent to parts of the former Soviet Union. In addition, 300,000 rosaries were sent to Croatia, once part of Yugoslavia.

The campaign for rosaries is continuing. (They may be sent to Family Rosary, Executive Park Drive, Albany, NY, 12203.)

Meanwhile, Family Theater recently completed five 30-minute films that were produced by Peter Thompson, whose television credits include such shows as "Masada," "The Ann Jillian Story" and the *Quincy* and *Rockford Files* series.

The films interweave inspirational biblical and contemporary stories. The first, *The Hero*, had 231 airings over 105 television outlets. It involved two mothers contemplating the approaching deaths of their sons. One is Mary, the mother of Jesus, and the other is the mother of a boy run down by a car driven by a drunken youth.

Two other films, *The Choice* and *The Search* are being released for summer distribution. One called *The Visit*, dealing with AIDS will be released in October, which is National AIDS Awareness Month. The fifth, called *The Journey*, will be released for Christmas.

Family Theater also is planning a film highlighting the life and accomplishments of Father Pat. It will feature Bob and Delores Hope, Loretta Young, Riccardo Montalban, and the Rev. Theodore Hesburgh, former president of Notre Dame University.

The film will detail Father Pat's life, including being stricken with tuberculosis while he was at Notre Dame. After physicians gave up on him, he made a promise to the Blessed Mother to devote his life to her service—which was what got him started in the promotion of family prayer. To win the audience he needed, he asked Hollywood stars to perform on radio programs. Bing Crosby was the first to say yes. After that, he had no trouble getting others.

Father Pat was born in Attymass in Ireland's County Mayo. A move is underway now to build a complex in Attymass close to the church where he was once an altar boy. The complex, which is to include a visitors' center, a video library of his films, and a restaurant, is to be built by the Family Rosary organization in America. It is envisioned that the complex will become a stop-off point for tourists.

While Father Pat has been gone for over a year, the work he started goes on—which should be good news for his friends and supporters here.

August 26, 1993

FOR THE O'NEILLS, A CHAPTER ENDS

The death last week of Anna J. "Nan" O'Hara O'Neill of Mercersburg ended the last direct link to the famous O'Neill brothers of Minooka.

Nan, who was 93, was the widow of James Leo O'Neill, one of four brothers who played in baseball's big leagues.

Jim O'Neill died in Mercersburg on Sept. 1976. His famous brothers, Steve, Mike, and Jack preceded him in death.

With the burial of Jim's widow at St. Joseph's Cemetery last week, all four of the brothers and their wives are together again—close enough to the stadium where the Red Barons play to perpetually remind them that baseball is still alive and well in the area of their youth.

The O'Neill family came from Galway, Ireland, where Mike O'Neill and 13-year-old Mary Joyce submitted to a marriage arranged by their parents.

First in Ireland, and later in America, Mary O'Neill had 18 pregnancies, including four babies dead at birth and one who lived a few years.

In the 1880s the O'Neill's came to America, leaving Michael, a baby who was too frail for the long ocean voyage, but one of the four boys who would play in America's big leagues.

The family lived in Old Forge and Ransom before settling in Minooka. It was there that the remaining nine O'Neill children were born and where the father—a miner who was known as Squire O'Neill—became an advisor to new immigrants.

Mike, who was born in Ireland in 1877 and who was left behind in Ireland because of his age, joined the family later in Minooka. He and his older brother Jack, who was born in Ireland in 1873, fell in love with American baseball and played it in whatever free time they could get. Mike was a pitcher and Jack a catcher, and both played with many local teams.

Jack's pitching earned him scholarships to East Stroudsburg Normal School and then at Villanova. He left college in 1900 to join the Montreal Royals—using his mother's maiden name of Joyce to protect his amateur status in case he failed.

256

Mike was signed by the St. Louis Cardinals and pitched for them from 1901 through 1904.

Mike's brother Jack joined the Cardinals in 1902, and was a battery-mate of his brother through 1903. The two did not use finger signs. They merely yelled them out in Gaelic, the language of Ireland. That worked well against most batters. However, one player clubbed anything that Mike pitched. Later, he learned why. The hitter spoke Gaelic, too.

The pitching-catching team was broken up when Jack went to the Chicago Cubs in 1904. There he played with the famous "Tinkers to Evers to Chance" double-play combination. In 1906, he joined the Boston Braves.

Nearly a decade passed before the next O'Neill got into the majors. Ex-player Mike was managing Elmira in the New York State League in 1910 when his brother Steve, who was born in Minooka in 1891, came to visit. The timing couldn't have been better. Elmira's two catchers were injured, so Steve was slipped into the lineup. Later, the Philadelphia Athletics signed him and sold him to the Cleveland Indians, where he starred for 13 years. He played four years after that with three clubs and then became a manager.

In the midst of Steve's career, his brother Jim, who was born in Minooka in 1893 and who spent several years in the minors, was signed by the Washington Senators as a shortstop and played with them in 1920 and again in 1923, compiling a respectable batting average of .287. However, his big league career was curtailed by frail health caused by a lung ailment that was never identified.

Both Steve and Jim were products of the Minooka Blues, an amateur team that was as good as—or maybe better—than some professional teams. That team was managed by still another O'Neill, Patrick, who was born in Ireland and seemed to have a great future in baseball until he injured a hand in a mining accident. Though that ended his playing, he remained close to the game by making the Minooka club one of the best amateur clubs in the country.

The Delehantys of Cleveland had five boys in the big leagues. The O'Neills are the only family to have four—and might have had five if Pat wasn't hurt.

The door closed on the O'Neill brothers' era last week with the death of Jim's wife.

MISS JUDY MCGRATH OF SCRANTON IS NOW CREATIVE HEAD OF MTV

Judy McGrath, a Scranton native, was doing well in the magazine business in New York City in 1981 when she heard about a new cable television program that was to be called Music Television—or MTV for short.

Against the advice of colleagues in the magazine business, Miss McGrath decided to gamble on a new career. She applied for a job and became one of about 25 original employees of MTV.

Recently, MTV named joint presidents—Miss McGrath, 41, as president and creative director, and Sara Levinson, 43, as president and business director.

The promotions were announced by Tom Freston, chief executive officer of MTV. The women were previously executive vice presidents while the office of president was vacant.

Miss McGrath, who started writing copy at WEJL—the *Times* radio station—said she never looked back after joining MTV, which she found more exciting than being copy chief of *Glamour* magazine and her prior jobs of writing for *Mademoiselle* magazine and writing copy for National Advertising in Philadelphia.

Miss McGrath is helping to build MTV into a worldwide cable channel, visiting Marrakech in Morocco, London, and Dublin in the recent past. In countries that don't speak English, native languages are used. In addition, native music videos are mixed with the basic American MTV package.

McGrath said that MTV's European headquarters are in London, but the channel is seen through several stations on the continent. "We're in Leningrad," she said of the Russian city that recently retook its original name of St. Petersburg. In addition, MTV is in Asia, with headquarters in Japan. A station in Hong Kong is seen in the People's Republic of China. There are also stations in South America, most in Spanish, but in Portuguese in Brazil. Also, MTV is on in Australia.

On a visit to Dublin, Miss McGrath supervised a taping of a concert by U-2, an Irish rock group. "That was fun," she said.

Miss McGrath has her musical heroes. One is Paul McCartney, who gave her an autographed "To Judy" picture that is framed in her office. She also has a coffee table with a top carved in the image of Elvis Presley.

An only child of the late Charles and Ann McGrath on Orchard Street, Miss McGrath came by her love of music by taking piano lessons while in grade school and by being drenched in the recorded sounds of Duke Ellington by her father, an Ellington fan. At Central High, she was accompanist with the school chorus.

Miss McGrath said that before MTV, many groups, including the Beatles, made music videos and distributed them free to television stations—in America and Europe, where they had a chance of being aired. The idea was to increase sales of their recordings. However, Bob Pittman, who became the founder of MTV, had a better idea. He thought such videos were good enough and plentiful enough to sustain a 24-hour-a-day cable channel. It became a subsidiary of Warner Amex Satellite Entertainment Co. Today, over 200 million people around the world see MTV.

Miss McGrath, one of about five of the original staffers who still work there, said many of the others, including Pittman, went on to other things.

MTV, now a division of Viacom International Inc., operates VH-1 and Nickelodeon. In addition, it is always striving to ad to its format. For instance, Miss McGrath supervised its first ever presidential campaign coverage last year.

Maybe the most famous of all the MTV features are the "Beavis and Butthead" cartoons. Its heroes are heavy metal couch potatoes who speak in big-city street language and indulge in black humor, often of sexual or violent nature.

After a flood of complaints, MTV pulled four of the series' 35 episodes from the air. In addition, others were moved from prime time to 10 and 11 P.M. to get them away from children. Miss McGrath said that complaints have dropped off since the time of the show has been changed.

A graduate of Cedar Crest in Allentown, Miss McGrath moved to New York in 1977. She said she doesn't get back to Scranton too often since the death of her parents. Her grandparents, Tony and Frances Harding and John and Ann McGrath are also deceased.

Miss McGrath said MTV is on her TV set at corporate headquarters through her 9-to-5 workday. However, she rarely watches it at night. In fact, she said, she doesn't watch much television at her Upper East Side apartment.

She said she'd rather do a thousand other things, including listen to recordings of her favorite group, Nirvana.

February 17, 1994

THE NEW USUALLY GETS SLOW START

In the 1939–1940 World's Fair in New York's Flushing Meadows, television sets were a sensation. Millions of persons saw demonstrations of this new technology that we were assured was right around the corner. However, World War II got in the way of marketing plans. It wasn't until 1948 that television became a mass medium.

Helicopters came of age in the Korean War, and forecasts were made that personal backyard helicopters would begin to replace automobiles. Well, that never happened—not because such vehicles couldn't be made, but because they couldn't be marketed because of high price.

In the mid-1960s, I went to the Bell Telephone Laboratories at Holmdel, NJ, and saw a telephone with a television screen attached. "This," visitors were told, "will soon be in every home in America." Well, 30 years later, that technology is just starting to build a market.

I just cite these examples to indicate that when a technology is perfected in a laboratory, there is no guarantee that the public will run out and buy it.

We hear much today about a superhighway of technology that is coming to America, promising to transform how entertainment, information, and services are delivered to consumers.

Many telecommunication and media companies are preparing for this revolution with mergers. Examples are the $30 billion takeover of Tele-Communications Inc. by Bell Atlantic Corp., and the $10 billion buyout by Viacom of Paramount Corp.

The exception is that the digital information superhighway will soon reach every home and office in America—and later, most of the world. When it comes, we will be able to summon thousands of movies and television shows, tie together our telephones and television sets into one interactive unit, and yes, maybe make newspapers of the future deliverable to printers in the homes of customers.

Actually, the technology is in place to do all that. But it isn't going to happen overnight, because people aren't going to buy any service if they don't like the price. And there is reluctance in many persons—myself included—to abandon what we are used to.

Within the past year or so, new technology in our house included a CD player, two cordless telephones, and a "smart" VCR that was accompanied by a foot-long remote control that I'll have to take a week off work to learn to operate.

As for the cordless phones, I find them very convenient. No longer am I tied to a fixed position by a tangled telephone cord. I can roam around the house as I talk on these gadgets.

The new VCR is a bit more complicated. I supposed I could master it, but there is something in my subconscious which is holding me back.

Persons such as myself are not interested in a lot of technical stuff. I have a digital clock in my car that hasn't shown the right time in years. I supposed I could correct that, but it doesn't seem important to me. I have my watch to tell me the time. Only passengers in the car remark that it's four or five hours off. Actually, it's a good conversation piece.

Given that kind of hostility toward technological toys, do I want an interactive television set on which I can buy things? No. I'll probably be the last guy leaving the last store.

And what of having 500 television channels from which to choose? That's a horrible thought. I don't particularly like television. From the beginning, every time I found a show I liked, they took it off the air. That started with Wally Cox in *Mr. Peepers* being canceled. Later I got to like the *Mary Tyler Moore Show* and that ended too. Ditto for *Mash*, *Hill Street Blues*, and *Cheers*. So I don't want 500 channels that will be filled with more of the same junk that fills the channels I now get.

So I just want to issue a warning to those companies that are spending billions to get plugged into the technological superhighway of the future. I'm going to be a hard person to convince I should buy your electronic services, and I have a hunch I will have a lot of company.

A LITTLE HISTORY OF
THE WHITE HOUSE

I learned some White House history on a recent visit there, and figured the information would tie in nicely with Presidents' Day, which we will celebrate on Monday,

Every one of our presidents except George Washington lived in the White House.

However, Washington had a lot to do with the location of the capital that was first called "Federal City" but was renamed later in his honor in a district named in honor of Christopher Columbus.

In the early days of the American republic, both New York City and Philadelphia wanted to become the capital. Both built presidential mansions. However, the Congress, meeting in the temporary capital of Philadelphia, voted in 1790 to establish a new capital on land donated by Virginia and Maryland.

Washington, who became president in 1789, was given authority to pick the site for the new city. Williamsport, MD, a little town on the Potomac River, wanted to be selected. To enhance its chances, it built a main street 100 feet wide to accommodate carriages of kings and princes.

But Washington picked a patch of wilderness along the Potomac that was within a day's horse ride from his Virginia home at Mount Vernon. The little town of Williamsport now has 2,000 citizens and one of the widest main streets in America.

The site Washington picked was close to marshy Tiber Creek, which soon became the dumping ground for sewage and garbage. Flies and mosquitoes infested the area. Malaria became a health hazard. In the summers, many presidents would flee from the White House because of odors. Physicians claimed the creek gave off "deadly vapors." President Van Buren rented a home in Georgetown while Presidents Buchanan and Lincoln used a cottage at a Soldiers' Home three miles farther from the creek. President Polk died a few months after leaving office. His successor, President Taylor died after one year in office. The "deadly vapors" were blamed.

Shortly after the Civil War, Tiber Creek was covered and the street the project created became Constitution Avenue.

A Frenchman, Pierre L'Enfant, laid out the plan for the city. His intent was to have two focal points: a huge presidential home four times bigger than the one that was built, and the Capitol, with nothing between them. However, the Treasury Building erected in 1860 blocked the view.

A competition was undertaken for the design of the White House. Even Thomas Jefferson, then Washington's secretary of state, got involved. Using a pseudonym, he suggested a building that looked like a Roman temple. Many other entries looked like European palaces, courthouses, and town halls.

However, Washington liked the simplicity and democratic modesty of the design submitted by James Hoban, an Irish-born architect from South Carolina.

There was only one problem. It was too small for the cellars that had been dug. So Hoban had to enlarge its dimensions.

Formal construction began on Oct. 13, 1792. The building has no cornerstone. Rather, it has an engraved brass plate that was sealed between two foundation stones. However, its location remains a mystery because records fail to indicate it.

Washington insisted the White House be built of stone and brick, that being the European style. The sandstone that was used came from a quarry that was almost 100 years old. Fearing that the quarry would be exhausted before the Capitol could be completed, one floor was eliminated from the White House, leaving one for state affairs and two for the 54-room residence.

The White House was named pretty much by the public. Its official names included the "President's Palace and the "Executive Mansion" but its stone walls were originally whitewashed, and that gave it the name that stuck.

John Adams, who succeeded Washington as president, moved into the $232,000 White House on Nov. 1, 1800. He stayed just four months. In his bid for a second term, he was defeated by Jefferson, who had been his vice president. Thus, Jefferson got to live in the house he wasn't allowed to design.

March 19, 1994

FRIENDS' WISHES POURED IN DURING HOSPITALIZATION

Finally, a month after being struck by a car, I'm sleeping in my own bed and eating at my own table.

It took over three weeks of treatment at Community Medical Center and Allied Services Rehabilitation Hospital before I returned home.

Let me digress a moment to describe the end of what was the longest period of hospital care in my life.

My darling wife Betty picked me up and took me home. I was thrilled on the way, but an unexpected new emotion rushed over me as I entered my home. I became emotional. I suddenly realized that—but for the grace of God—I might never have seen my home again. I had trouble checking the tears.

Now I'm adapting to a new routine. I'm going to Allied Services daily for exercises for the artificial left shoulder that replaced the one crushed in the accident.

Yes, it still hurts, but experts say that nearly full movement will return. Meanwhile, I use my slightly numb right hand to write in long-hand these periodic reports to assure my readers that I intend eventually to return to work full-time.

In the meantime, I continue to be cheered by get-well cards and letters. Among the most prized is a letter from Hillary Rodham Clinton. In the midst of her "Whitewater" inquiry and her fight for national health insurance, she took time to write: "Please know that you are in our thoughts and prayers during this time of recovery." She has plenty of things on her mind these days. To get that letter meant a lot to me.

I'm happy to note a bipartisan tone to the hundreds of messages and gifts I've been receiving. One of the prettiest floral pieces I received came from ex-Governor and Mrs. William W. Scranton. He's one of my personal heroes. Those flowers buoyed my spirits.

And so did the flowers from state Sen. Robert Mellow and his wife Diane. They were the first to arrive after I woke up with my new shoulder.

Congressman Joseph M. McDade and his wife Sarah sent a delicious chocolate-covered apple and flowers; state Superior Court Judge Stephen J. M. Ewen, Jr. sent me a videotape of an inspirational film, *A Man for All Seasons*; banker-turned-educator David Tressler gave me bread he baked himself; the staff of WNEP-TV sent me flowers; and sports reporter-turned-insuranceman Jerry Griffin sent me a biography of another of my heroes, Harry Truman.

Not to be outdone, my barber, Matthew Garafolo, offered me a shave. (Gratefully, I can manage that with my left hand.)

I've also heard from many persons I don't know. For instance, Agnes Wasalinko, 407 Powell Street, Jessup, wrote that she cried when she read about my accident. "I felt so bad for you that I will light a candle for you at St. Michael's Church in Jessup," she wrote.

That was typical of scores of cards and letters from readers whom I've never met.

I also heard kind words from many clergymen, including Bishop James Clifford Timlin and Rabbi David Geffen, both of whom prayed over me. Monsignor Thomas J. Cawley, now retired, wanted to know if the car that hit me was damaged. "Is the hood mightier than the pen?" he asked. And Monsignor Anthony C. Marra, who, like myself, grew up in Jessup wrote, "I've always wanted to read a column written by a bionic author."

To all of the above—plus hundreds more who've been so kind—I can only say thanks. It's nice to have friends.

December 3, 1994

SHOPPING LIST HAS 350 NAMES

Think you have a lot of gifts to buy for Christmas? Consider Scranton's Anna Young, who is shopping for gifts for 350 or so prisoners in the Lackawanna County Jail.

Anna has been doing kind things for jailhouse residents for 17 years —and she's just as enthusiastic today as the first day she walked into the jail.

In all that time, Anna has never been treated badly by a prisoner. "When I started bringing Christmas gifts to the jail, I shook hands with each prisoner and was the first to say, *Merry Christmas*, she said. "Now they are the first to say it," she added.

Over the years, Anna said, God worked a strange transformation within her. "I went into the jail to cheer up prisoners and I gradually began to see that it made me feel good, too."

Admitting she could never do the work by herself, Anna said some churches and many individuals help her by baking the Christmas cookies, and either buying gifts or giving money for her to buy gifts to give to prisoners on Christmas Eve.

The gifts are modest ones—socks, deodorant, soap, shampoo, lotion, writing tablets, envelopes, etc. Security regulations at the prison pretty much rule out other items.

As modest as the gifts, Anna said they carry the message to every prisoner that they are not forgotten.

It's impossible to separate Anna's religious beliefs from her mission. A devout Protestant, she takes seriously Christ's counsel to serve the needy, including prisoners. In addition, she enjoys the full support of her husband Clair, who works on projects with her.

A native West Virginian who has lived in Scranton for 39 years, Anna said that the male and female prisoners have been kind to her over the years. The only disturbance occurred on her first Christmas Eve visit.

She recalled that a man in solitary confinement had his cigarettes taken away from him for some rule infraction. He yelled nonstop for a guard, saying he needed a smoke. She was distracted and asked permission to talk to him. She told him she was there to give out presents and sing a few hymns, but that he was ruining her efforts. Besides, she said, he was not going to get his cigarettes by yelling. All that was accomplishing was upsetting himself, she added.

"He quieted down and we went on with the program," she said, adding: "I also started visiting him on a regular basis and we became friends."

Anna has the unique ability to see beyond the crime that put the prisoners behind bars. She treats all the same, regardless of their offenses. "In jail, they all have the same needs," she said.

Anyone who wants to help Anna brighten Christmas Eve for prisoners can send a donation to her at 29 New York St., Scranton, 18509.

In addition to that project, Anna took on the job this year of running "Project Angel Tree," under which she hopes 239 area children of 119 prisoners—here and in other prisons—are given Christmas gifts.

The names of the children, sizes of garments, and other information are attached to Christmas trees in 14 Protestant and Catholic churches.

Members of those congregations are asked to take names from the tree and buy the suggested gifts. The items are then delivered in the days before Christmas.

Anna said that the project was about to die in this area, so she stepped in this year to run it.

Anna said that neither project she's involved in would work if other good people didn't support them. "The goodness of people still amazes me," she said of those who help.

January 29, 1995

MERLI REVISITS BELGIAN SITE OF HIS LONG, DEADLY NIGHT

Gino Merli of Peckville relived the defining night of his life on a recent visit to Belgium.

Merli earned the Congressional Medal of Honor, the nation's highest military award, on the night of Sept. 4, 1944, in a rural area near Sars-La-Bruyere, Belgium.

Recently, Merli, now 70, went back to that area and found the spot where, as a 20-year-old GI, he manned his machine gun throughout the night and into the early hours of the next day.

The German army in that sector was pulling back toward the fatherland and Merli's 18th Infantry Regiment of the First Division was trying to block it.

Merli and an assistant gunner set up a nest along a farmer's barbed wire fence to secure the area for the night. With luck, Germans wouldn't come.

However, that wasn't the case. Germans poured in. Some Americans retreated. Eight GIs were captured, but Merli and his buddy remained at their posts.

A German patrol followed the barbed wire fence and Merli opened fire. The patrol was wiped out.

However, more Germans came and the gun nest was overrun. Merli's comrade was dead. He pretended he was dead, too. The Germans nudged both with bayonets and they remained lifeless. As the Germans moved on, Merli cut them down.

The same thing occurred later. Germans overran the nest, found two apparently dead bodies and then moved on. As they left, Merli shot them down.

That was the longest night of Merli's life. Hundreds of bullets whizzed by him, but the only wound he received was a tiny sliver of steel —maybe part of a shell that exploded nearby—that imbedded itself in a finger of his left hand, where it remains a souvenir of that long night.

When daylight came, the Americans launched an attack. The Germans had lost the will to fight. They surrendered. Seven hundred were marched away.

Merli remained at his post until he saw other GIs. All together, there were 52 dead Germans nearby, including 19 directly in front of his gun.

Merli was happy to be alive but he grieved for his buddy—a replacement soldier whose name he didn't know. The next morning he went to a nearby Catholic church and prayed for the souls of his lost comrade and for the other GIs and Germans who had died during the night.

War is a nasty business and Merli thanked God his life had been spared.

Merli recently returned to that area with retired *Scranton Times* photographer Ike Refice of Elmhurst, who also saw his share of fighting Germans in that part of Europe, and Col. Peter Krenitsky of Peckville, a national guardsman who was to see combat in Korea several years later.

The visit was arranged by a group of grateful residents of Belgium and Luxembourg, some of who came to the Veterans Administration Hospital in Wilkes-Barre in 1992 for the unveiling of portraits of three regional servicemen who earned the Congressional Medal of Honor in World War II, including Merli.

In Belgium, Merli found the spot where his machine gun was located. The farm is still there and so is the barbed wire fence. Standing on that spot, he said he was speechless. "I kept getting flashbacks of that night," he said.

Merli also found the same church and went in to pray for the GIs who didn't make it home and to thank God for letting him survive the war, get married, raise a family, and reach his present age.

Merli is known best for that one night of combat, but he saw more combat than that. He landed in Europe on D-Day—June 6, 1944—and was a battle-weary veteran of almost three months when he helped stop the advance of a German unit. The following month he was injured by a phosphorous shell explosion. Two months later, during the Battle of the Bulge, he was hit in the wrist by—ironically—a machine gun bullet.

The wound resulted in him being evacuated to the United States. The following June 19, he was presented with the Medal of Honor by President Harry S. Truman at the White House.

Ever since, Merli has felt a duty to lead the recitation of the Pledge of Allegiance whenever asked. He has done that on thousands of occasions over the past 50 years.

Appropriately, when the U.S. flag was raised during a ceremony over Sars-La-Bruyere Town Hall, it was Merli, a retired government worker, who led in the recitation.

"After all those years, it's nice to know people still care what we did," he said.

April 16, 1995

SISTER ADRIAN IS BACKED
BY AN ARMY OF VOLUNTEERS

There are 2,170 families in this area eating traditional Easter meals today, thanks to the efforts of a 66-year-old nun whose main goal in life is to help the poor.

Sister Adrian Barrett and her Friends of the Poor gave out that many food baskets last week, making sure none had to forgo the tradition of celebrating the Resurrection of Christ with a special meal.

Sister Adrian started her life as a nun and schoolteacher 49 years ago. But everywhere she looked she saw people who were outside the mainstream of the good life that Americans like to think everyone shares.

As a nun in Oyster Bay, an upscale community on Long Island, she fought so forcibly for public housing that a prudent police chief assigned some undercover detectives to escort her home safely to her convent after a town meeting.

In LaPlatte, MD, her heart was broken because her own Catholic Church was segregated, with white people seated on the first floor receiving Holy Communion, and then the blacks in the gallery coming next.

"Thank God we got public housing and churches were desegregated, but we still live in an imperfect world," said Sister Adrian, after she made sure that there were chocolates and jellybeans in all the food baskets that were given out last week.

"I can't imagine a child not having candy for Easter," she said.

After a few years of teaching school, Sister Adrian became convinced her vocation was to serve the poor. In time, she convinced her superiors. Friends of the Poor is the culmination of her efforts.

The organization has few rules. Sister Adrian pretty much makes up the agenda from day to day. Feeding and clothing people are basic services. The headquarters provided by the Scranton Housing Authority are so crammed with racks of clothes that her friends and coworkers call it "Fashions by Adrian."

Some of the clothes are new and some are used, but none of it is junk. "We want to help the poor and not dehumanize them with junky clothes," she said of the rule that "Fashions by Adrian" must be quality garments.

One day recently, a man who was going out for a job interview stopped at Friends of the Poor because he had no clothes respectable enough for the meeting. He found everything he needed. As he left, Sister Adrian said a prayer that he'd get the job.

Toward the end of each month, many people come by because they are running out of food.

Where does she get the food? More often than not, it is donated by local businesses that support her work.

Sister Adrian said her organization isn't big into filling out forms. "I can tell if a person is poor by looking at them," she said. "If they pass that test, they get help."

In Sister Adrian's lexicon, "help" can mean a lot of things, including burying persons who have no families to help. On occasions, she even gets her volunteers to attend the wakes, so that the deceased will not leave this world without a decent turnout to say goodbye.

Then there are the battles Sister Adrian fights with the bureaucracies that are supposed to help the poor. Recently, a disabled man in frail health received a $25 a month cost-of-living increase in his Social Security. That cost him his welfare medical card, which was worth more to him than his $25 a month raise. That's still unresolved, but she's on the case.

Providing furniture to the poor is another part of her work. She gets some of that from stores, some from estates, and was even left furniture by a poor person she once had helped. The furniture is stored in rented sheds, and deliveries are made in a truck that was given to her organization by a friend.

In addition to the ongoing program of aiding the poor through the year, Sister Adrian conducts a summer program for children, gives out food for Thanksgiving, food and toys for Christmas, and food and candy for Easter.

Sister Adrian's overhead is minimal. Since much of her work benefits Scranton Housing Authority tenants, she pays no rent for her headquarters. In addition, the hardcore group around her is from VISTA. Finally, she has scores of other volunteer workers who do all sorts of jobs, from delivering furniture to singing at funerals.

After taking today off, Sister Adrian will be back to work tomorrow, starting her summer program, which includes uplifting the lives of children with a trip to Washington, D.C.

Sister Adrian gets most of her finances from people solicited by mail. However, after each major holiday she is just about broke—which is her condition now.

If anyone wants to help, send tax-deductible donations to Friends of the Poor, IHM Convent, 422 River Street, Scranton, PA, 18505. Every penny will go to the poor in one way or another.

May 14, 1995

CLARE MARTINA FLANNERY
FINALLY PAID THE MORTGAGE

It's been 43 years since my mother, Clare Martina Reap Flannery, left this vale of tears for a better place that God created for good humans.

Is my Mom in Heaven on this Mother's Day?

There isn't a doubt in my mind about that. In looking back on her life, I can't think of a single thing that would have even slowed her passage through the Pearly Gates.

My father, James Aloysius Flannery, was a good man who supported his family. But there was an uneven division of work in those days between men and women. The man's job was to bring in money, and the woman's job was to do just about everything else that had to be done in the home.

And my mother could do everything. She once was a professional seamstress, so she made virtually all our clothes. She made the best bread I've ever tasted. She did tons of family washes with the old wringer washer and hung the clothes on lines in summer and winter. On Wednesdays my salivary glands became active just at the thought of the pot roast we'd have the following Sunday. When she needed more cupboard space in the kitchen, she built a cupboard by herself. She also painted and hung wallpaper like a professional. And, with help from her sons, she supervised the building of an outside concrete wall.

I grew up in the Depression and very often we were destitute. There was a mortgage on our home, and it bedeviled us through the years.

In better days, my father sold insurance and did reasonably well. But in the Depression, he didn't work steadily. He had a job in a breaker but only worked an occasional shift. Not until the federal government started the Works Projects Administration (WPA) did he get back to full-time work. During gaps in his jobs we were on relief. But the pittance we received wasn't always enough to cover the mortgage. That's when a notice was posted on our house that it was going to be sold in a sheriff's sale. My mother was shamed. After they left, she pulled the sign off the house. Then she took a job as a seamstress in a Scranton store and made enough money to make a payment on the mortgage.

Poverty is not easily forgotten. I remember being sent to the grocery store with the book on which all that we bought was charged. To my chagrin, the grocer told me to tell my parents that he wouldn't give them any more food until they made a payment on their bill. I was embarrassed and tearful as I returned home without any food.

But somehow, my Mom made sure we were never hungry. She always seemed to have a few dollars tucked under a rug for such emergencies.

Mom was the first person up in the morning, getting the kitchen warm and making a pot of oatmeal for breakfast. She also was the last person up at night, ironing pants or darning socks.

It wasn't until the late 1930s that things began to brighten. My father became an official at West Mountain Sanitarium. My two older brothers, Tom and Jim, got jobs in New York, and a few years later my sister Clare got a job in Washington. All sent money home. Mom tired of paying to have coal carried to our house atop a hill. She wanted a driveway for the coal truck. My father hoped her dream would go away. But she was strong-willed. She saved some money and a steam shovel and trucks appeared. By nightfall, she had her driveway.

Over the years, my mother had little recreation time. She and a nearby cousin, Eva Mullaney, sometimes walked to a movie house, usually to see a film starring Claudette Colbert, her favorite actress and one whose hairstyle she copied. On rare occasions, she visited relatives in New York. She liked it when her sister, Kathleen Maloney, would come from New York to visit. She'd stay for weeks and the two would spend hours in conversations.

My father had a political job and he had to buy tickets for an annual political dinner at the Hotel Casey. She didn't like having to pay for the tickets, but she knew it went with having a political job. So she made the most of it. She usually made herself a new dress, put her hair up in curlers, and even polished her fingernails for that rather elegant affair.

The biggest regret I have about my mom is that by the time in her life when she had the mortgage and store bills paid off and might have been able to enjoy herself, she was stricken with cancer. It started with a pain in her shoulder and back. She thought it was a cold at first. But as it worsened, she underwent surgery that confirmed the diagnosis. She died at 63, leaving me with regrets that I was never able to take her to dinner, buy her flowers, or buy her a new dress.

Mom had given us wonderful gifts of faith, hope, and love. All I can do in return is to say: "Thanks, Mom."

July 15, 1995

AND SO IT GOES:
PIECE OF NAM COMES HOME

Linda Ellerbee, a television journalist and newspaper columnist from New York City, was recently at China Beach, outside Da Nang, in Vietnam.

A Vietnamese woman beckoned her to buy a souvenir in her shop. She held up a battered Zippo lighter.

In one of her columns, she wrote:

"Holding it in my hand, feeling its familiar heft, it felt a little like holding a piece of America that no longer exists, something from a time when cars were cars and chrome was good, a time when people smoked and ate bacon for breakfast, a time when we went to war in a small green country halfway around the world."

The lighter was engraved with the name and what Ellerbee thought was the serial number of a U.S. Marine—Michael J. Matichak.

The lighter also bore the words: "U.S. Marines, Vietnam, '68."

Ellerbee had a problem making up her mind. She didn't know if she wanted to buy this souvenir of China Beach. Maybe the lighter was stolen from a dead body. Or maybe, she thought, it was recently manufactured in Da Nang for American tourists. Indeed, she didn't even know if she wanted to buy a war souvenir.

Then she had a happier thought. Maybe, she told herself, she could bring it back to America and get it to its former owner. So she bought it.

Back in New York, Ellerbee gave the lighter to a girl in her office and asked her to see if she could track down the Marine who once owned it.

The girl had the name and a service number but no hometown. She called various veterans organizations but they couldn't help her. She finally called the Marines, and they reported back that Matichak lived in Carbondale up to 1979—which was as far as their records went. Also, the number of the lighter was not a serial number. It was a service number used before the use of Social Security numbers became common.

Ellerbee called information and learned that Matichak now lives at 6 Eastern Avenue in Carbondale.

Ellerbee got Matichak on the telephone. She learned that he joined the Marines at 17 because a buddy had joined in 1967. He was just 18 when he went to Vietnam and served two tours of duty there.

In 1968, when he owned the Zippo lighter, he was stationed at the air base in Da Nang.

He told her: "I wasn't too crazy about being there, but I realized why we were there. I'm still not sure why they pulled us out, but I wasn't too sad about that, either."

Matichak said he visited China Beach periodically to relax, but it was crisscrossed with barbed wire. He added: "It's a hard way to get a suntan, holding a rifle."

Matichak, a lifelong resident of Carbondale, said he was glad he went to Vietnam and he was glad to get back. He added he was also glad Ellerbee was sending the old lighter to him.

Someone sent me a copy of the Ellerbee column from a Houston, Texas newspaper. I called him and he confirmed that he got his lighter back. However, he has no memory of having lost it. "I had five or six of them while I was in Vietnam," he said, adding that he lost some and some were stolen.

The lighters were cheap. Matichak thought they sold for about $1.50. They were prized because they almost never failed, he added.

Matichak, who is 45 and works at Clarks Summit State Hospital, saw plenty of action in Vietnam. He recalled being in the siege of Khe Sanh, when 9,000 marines were surrounded by 40,000 to 50,000 North Vietnamese regulars. The siege lasted five months. "We took a lot of casualties," he recalled. "Then the North Vietnamese pulled out," he added.

He also served for a time as a guard at a military corrections center at Da Nang, which is when he probably lost his lighter.

He came home in 1970 when President Nixon began reducing the number of American troops in Vietnam. He remained in the Marines until 1976.

Matichak, married and the father of six children, doesn't know if the lighter works. He recently bought the home where he lives and inherited a gun cabinet with it. He has no guns so he put the lighter on display there.

The lighter isn't a thing of beauty. Matichak said it's dented, as though something ran over it or someone stepped on it.

So far, he hasn't put lighter fluid in the lighter so he doesn't know if it works. "But the igniter still throws a spark," he noted.

However, Matichak said, his doctor has been after him to quit smoking. So maybe he won't need the lighter anymore.

"But it was still nice of her to send it to me," he said.

Ellerbee ended her column with her trademark last line: "And so it goes."

I say "amen" to that.

January 4, 1996

HOLIDAY WISHES DO COME TRUE

This is a true story.

A few days before Christmas, I got a letter from a child that moved me to tears.

I don't want to identify the child or her family because I would be intruding upon their privacy. However, her letter was right out of *A Christmas Carol* and there is no way I can tell this story without quoting from it.

With some editing, this is what the girl wrote:

"I don't know exactly why I am writing to you except that I am very scared. We can't have Christmas this year, which I understand, but I need to try to help my mother. She is unhappy, but can't change the situation. Last year, my father was laid off from his job at (deleted). Then he got a job at (deleted). Then they closed. We had to leave our home and school (in Scranton) and move to (deleted).

"We don't have enough money for food and stuff so we can't have Christmas. My mother cries when she thinks we don't see her. My father got another job, but it doesn't pay much. He works on a Christmas tree farm for money and a free tree.

"I don't care for myself, but there are two things I want. You see, my little brother has been sick a lot of the year and I want him to have presents. The other thing is that every year my mother makes a big dinner and we bring my grandparents up. My grandparents are 80 and I'm afraid this may be their last visit.

"Can you help me? If I can borrow any money, I will deliver newspapers or do anything else to pay it back.

"If you can't help me, that's OK. I hope your Christmas is happy."

News people are among the most cynical in the world. I wondered if the letter was legitimate. I called and asked for more details about her family. She answered every question without hesitation. My news sense told me that her appeal was real. I said I would try to help.

The approach of Christmas had temporarily impoverished me. Yet, I had to do something.

281

Then I thought of Dr. Joseph R. Mattioli, chief executive officer of Pocono Raceway at Long Pond. I knew him to be a charitable person. I called him but got only his answering machine. I left word for him to call.

Now I was more worried than ever. I had told the girl I would do something. Then I thought of Sister Adrian Barrett, who operates Friends of the Poor. I called her and told her my problem. She said she would provide food for the holidays and toys for the children. I called the girl back and told her to get in touch with Sister Adrian.

Just after that, Dr. Mattioli called me. I read him the letter but told him that Sister Adrian had promised food and toys. However, he said he wanted to help, too. "Do you have any idea what the family needs?" he asked. I said maybe $100 or so. "I'll send $200," he said.

The girl, trying to surprise her family, had a neighbor drive her to Scranton to get the items from Sister Adrian. In the meantime, I got $200 from my credit union so that I could give her the cash while waiting for the check from Dr. Mattioli. When she came to visit me at the newspaper, I gave her two $100 bills in an envelope. When she saw them, she got teary-eyed and exclaimed: "We are going to have a Christmas after all!"

And there was more to come. Dr. Mattioli, saying he felt like Santa Claus, sent me a check for $300 instead of $200. So on the day after Christmas, I mailed the additional $100 to the family.

After the holidays, I called the girl's mother to learn how the story ended. She said the family did have a very merry Christmas. I was glad to help.

TO JOE SMITH, MY BEST FRIEND

My best friend, Joe Smith, died last Saturday after a brave fight of more than two years against cancer.

Joe, who ran Smith's Restaurant in South Scranton before he retired, will live on in my memory, in old snapshots, in vacation videos, and, finally, in my heart.

In 1958, my wife Betty and I bought a home in Dunmore. Not long after, Joe and Theresa Smith moved into a house on the other side of the street.

My wife and Theresa became friends in a short time, but I had trouble getting to know Joe. I was working nights at the old *Tribune*, and Joe went to the restaurant about dawn and came home about dusk.

As time wore on, however, we did get to know each other. We both had growing families, and our kids became like sisters and brothers. Joe would take my wife to church on Sunday while Theresa stayed with their kids and I stayed with ours. Later, I took Theresa to church while our mates did the babysitting. In time, people of our parish got very confused. Many thought I was Theresa's husband and Joe was Betty's husband.

Joe was a nice guy. If he had a vice, it was overworking at the restaurant his parents, James and Mary Smith, began as a luncheonette in their house in 1934. When I got to know Joe, he and his older twin brothers, John and James, operated the business, while their sister Callista, who was disabled by a car hitting her sled, took care of the books.

Joe was 10 when he began working before and after school in the restaurant. The eatery was in the midst of several factories. His job was to deliver coffee, milk, sandwiches, cupcakes, and other things ordered by workers in the nearby plants. Most kids used wagons to have fun. Joe used his to make his deliveries.

At the start, Mrs. Smith made the restaurant a success. She did all the cooking and baking and built up a loyal following of customers. After she died, the children took over. They expanded the operation because the business had to support a growing number of people. For them, working

16-hour shifts was commonplace. They could rest on Sundays—but only after the place was given its weekly scrubbing.

In time, Joe took over the ownership, and in recent years, his son, Kenneth became the owner. But Joe never really retired. Even after he became ill, he visited the restaurant to make sure everything was fine.

Over the years, the Flannery and Smith kids intermingled. We took their son Pat to the Baseball Hall of Fame in Cooperstown, and they took our daughter Eileen to the Long Island seashore. We stayed in adjacent cottages in Long Beach, NJ, and our kids spent the week playing together. We saw wholesome movies together—and ate popcorn—in drive-in theatres. And then there was the time I took our girls and their daughter Callista to see the Osmonds at the Allentown Fair. (Wow! Was that music loud!)

With such intermingling, Joe and Theresa became second parents to our kids and we became second parents to theirs.

Then Jerry and Ann Byron moved into the neighborhood and they became friendly with us and the Smiths. In time, we three couples began taking day trips together. Around that time, Joe started getting more time off from work. That led to our "husbands-only council meetings" in Jerry's garage in the summer and at Vito's bar and pizza establishment in the winters.

It was at one such meeting in Vito's that Joe said: "Why don't we save our money and take a trip together to Cape Cod?" I became the treasurer and travel planner. We made our trip during the annual one-week shutdown of the restaurant in July. By then, we had enough money in the kitty to pay for the condo that was big enough to accommodate the three couples.

Every year after that, we saved our money and took vacation trips together. We went to Colonial Williamsburg; San Francisco; Hawaii; Las Vegas; Ireland; Ocean City, MD; Washington, D.C.; Niagara Falls; Toronto; Cooperstown; Newport; Kennebunkport; and Boston.

Two years ago, Joe's cancer was diagnosed. He underwent surgery that we all hoped would provide a cure. Indeed, he seemed to recover well, and we were all cautiously optimistic that he'd win his fight.

His only problem seemed to be his weight. He tried to eat well but continued to slowly lose weight. Theresa plied him with diet supplements laced with plenty of ice cream, but even that didn't reverse the trend.

We thought a vacation trip to Bermuda might help. It would be relaxing and he'd get plenty to eat. So that's what we did that summer. Again, our hopes climbed. He ate pretty well and enjoyed the trip so much that he answered the call for volunteers and joined the showgirls on stage in their show-closing high-kicking dance.

However, going into the second year after Joe's surgery, he was very thin. He and Theresa went to Florida to escape the harsh winter. We and the Byrons joined them there. He had lost weight, but he hadn't lost his sense of humor. I was driving his car along an interstate highway and a seagull flew right into its path and was killed. He accused me of being a bird killer and a lousy driver.

We knew that we would again have to plan a summer vacation that wouldn't be too arduous. We went on a bus trip through New England to Quebec City and Montreal. He got through that, but we all could see his energy level was failing. Still, he was a heck of a trooper.

Since that vacation last summer, his weight loss was frightening. Nice guy that he was, he continued to put our garbage cans back in our yards. But by Christmas, he was very weak and had to go into the hospital for tests. That's when we all learned the cancer was back.

There was danger of him dying then. Sister Adrian Barrett, one of his thousands of friends, brought him a miniature Christmas tree with lights. Joe had a beautiful voice and often sang at weddings, funerals, and other events. Sister Adrian asked him if he would lead us in singing "O, Holy Night." Though very weak, he began singing and we all joined in. However, he was the only one who knew the words beyond the first verse. He sang the whole song. Not bad for a man we thought was dying. The performance brought tears to our eyes.

Joe remained in the hospital for a time and then came home. He was failing fast, but he had plenty of tender loving care from his wife and family. When I didn't come as often as I should have, he'd start asking where I was. What he didn't know was that I hated seeing him so thin and weak.

Joe had a crisis last Saturday evening and we traveling companions rushed to see him. But then he got his second wind. As I left, he gave me a surprisingly hard handshake. "I'll see you tomorrow," I said, never dreaming that he would die in little more than half an hour. "OK," he said weakly.

Not long after, we got a call that he died in Theresa's arms. We were all sure he was in heaven before she knew he was gone.

Joe had a great sendoff. The lines into the funeral home were long and steady over two days. His son Kenneth gave a eulogy at the mass; his son Patrick sang "Danny Boy," the song Joe had sung for hundreds of audiences. There were eight priests at the altar. His grandsons, Billy and

Ryan, helped carry the gifts, and his twin bothers, at 76, served as altar boys.

Jerry Byron and I were among the pallbearers who carried him to his grave. It was hard to fight back the tears on that, our final trip together.

March 26, 1996

CITY'S 7TH MAYOR PART OF HISTORY

A recent airing of the movie, *Andersonville*, reminded me that Scranton's 7th mayor, Ezra H. Ripple, was once a prisoner in that notorious Confederate compound during the Civil War.

Ripple was born in Mauch Chunk, now Jim Thorpe, in 1842, the son of a tavern proprietor. He received a good education by the standards of those days. He went first to public schools, attended Wyoming Seminary for four years, and graduated from Eastman's Commercial School at Poughkeepsie, NY.

Just about the time he was ready to build his own career, operating his late father's tavern, the Civil War intervened.

In 1862 and 1863, he responded to calls for volunteers when Confederate forces were threatening Pennsylvania. Among the battles he participated in was Antietam. In 1864 he joined the 52nd Regiment of the Pennsylvania Infantry. Later that year, in an attack on Fort Johnson at Charleston, SC, he was captured and sent to Andersonville.

In that hellhole of a prison camp, he and others planned and carved out a tunnel that enabled six prisoners to escape. Among them was James Doud, a Union soldier from Scranton. He escaped, but was later recaptured. Ripple, too, was supposed to leave, but he was deathly ill and could not go.

Ripple endured three months in Andersonville, a camp where gangs of Union prisoners preyed on other union prisoners, where the water supply was generally polluted by sewage, where most prisoners were lodged outdoors, where food was constantly in short supply, and where cruelty by guards was ignored.

Ripple, a skilled violinist, was drafted into a camp orchestra that was made to perform at the whim of the camp commander.

After the war, the commander of the prison was tried, convicted, and hanged.

Ripple was moved from Andersonville to another cruel prison camp at Florence, SC. He escaped from there and was hunted down by soldiers with bloodhounds. He was eventually cornered and attacked by the dogs. He carried the scars of the bites through the rest of his life.

Dragged back to camp by Confederate guards, he recuperated from his bites. He was freed sometime later in an exchange of prisoners, and spent the rest of the war at Camp Annapolis in Maryland.

Ripple and his wife and children moved to Scranton, where he became a business partner of William Connell. Over the course of many years, he was president of a company that made wagon axles, was involved in a firm that sold crockery, was a director of various banks, and was on the board of an insurance firm and the International Correspondence Schools. He was also part of management of a street-car firm, a newspaper, and was a partner in the coal business.

In 1877, Ripple organized the "Scranton City Guards," a military unit that would grow in future years into the 109th Infantry of the Pennsylvania National Guard. He became a colonel in that organization —and henceforth was known as "Colonel Ripple."

A Republican, Ripple was elected county treasurer for three terms. He also served a time on the city council, was on the Board of Health, and served as Republican county chairman.

Elected as mayor in 1886, Ripple brought the first electric streetlights to the city. He also was the first to start paving roads. In addition, street-cars began to run during his tenure. After his term as mayor, he became the local postmaster.

Ripple died at home of a stroke in 1909 at the age of 67.

April 20, 1996

MUSICIAN'S CLAIM TO SONG WAS HOKEY

We ran an Associated Press story recently out of Boise, Idaho, telling of the death of Larry LaPrise, an 83-year-old musician who claimed to be the composer of the popular song, "The Hokey Pokey Dance."

I was somewhat amazed by the story, because I always heard that the song—played at most wedding receptions and many other festive events—was composed by two Scrantonians, Robert P. Degen, 89, now of Lexington, KY, and the late Joseph P. Brier.

I called my friend, Ferdie Bistochi, who is still an active musician at the age of 84, and a former music colleague of both Degen and Brier.

"Who wrote 'The Hokey Pokey Dance?' I asked.

Ferdie said that Degen and Brier authorized the number and had it copyrighted. "I never heard of that guy from Idaho," he added.

I expected that reply, because I did a column on Degen last August when he was visiting in Scranton with his wife Vivian, an Arkansas native, and their son, Robert P. Degen Jr., a jazz musician who has won fame in Europe.

In that interview, Degen—a guitarist and former salesman in the old Home Furniture store here—showed me a published songsheet of "The Hokey Pokey" bearing his and Brier's names as the composers. He also told me that he had received $15,000 in royalties in 1994 alone. "It is more popular than ever," he noted.

I called the Degens in Lexington this week, and his wife said her husband was aware of the story about the man from Idaho whose nickname, according to the Associated Press story, was "The Hokey Pokey Man."

Mrs. Degen said a reporter on the Lexington newspaper is also working on the story about who wrote the song.

"He was here yesterday for two hours," she said.

Mrs. Degen said that when Arthur Godfrey was popular in radio and television, he visited Las Vegas and later spoke on the air about a musical group that was attracting huge crowds by laying an original number called "The Hokey Pokey." He said he might have them on his show. She wrote him about her husband and Brier owning the song. He wrote back and said they should be getting royalties. Meanwhile, he decided against booking the group. The Degens and Briers hired a lawyer and established their rights to royalties.

The best proof today that the composers were Brier and Degen is that they or their heirs get the royalties.

Mrs. Degen said her husband got a $1,800 check in February and expects a much bigger one in August.

Mrs. Degen said the royalty checks of years ago were tiny, but Disney enterprises began using the song in recent years and royalties soared.

The song was copyrighted by Brier and Degen in 1944. Yet, the Associated Press story on LaPrise's death said the song was put together by he and two fellow musicians in the "late 1940s" in a nightclub in Sun Valley, Idaho. It added that the group, the Ram Trio, recorded the song in 1949.

Maybe they did make a recording, but Brier and Degen copyrighted the song five years before that.

The "Hokey Pokey" is that dance that begins with the words, "Put your right hand in, put your right hand out," and ends with the words, "Everything is okey dokey when you do the Hokey Pokey, that's what the dance is all about."

The song has nine verses involving various parts of the body that have to be "put in" and then "put out"—with each verse played faster than the last.

While Degen and Brier copyrighted the song and they and/or their heirs get the royalties, the Associated Press story claimed bandleader Ray Anthony bought the rights in 1953 from LaPrise and the Ram Trio for $500 and recorded the song on the "B" side of another novelty song, "The Bunny Hop." Many other recordings were made by other musical groups, it added.

However, Mrs. Degen said the Acuff-Rose song publishing firm in Nashville has the contract to print the sheet music for the song. She said they get a record with each check on where the song is performed. "I remember seeing Japan on a recent accounting," she said to show that the song is performed internationally.

The Associated Press story said that the Ram Trio disbanded in the 1960s and LaPrise—by then the father of six children—went to work in the post office in Ketchum.

If I ever learn more about this story, I'll pass it on.

TORN FROM LAND IN IRELAND, FAMILY PUT DOWN ROOTS HERE

Virtually every town in Ireland has a memorial to a hero who, in some way or another, fought against the English dominance of his country.

In the town of Straide in County Mayo, Ireland, a pageant was held last year to mark the 150th anniversary of the birth of its famous hero, Michael Davitt.

Even Mary Robinson, the president of Ireland, came to pay homage to the man who championed the twin causes of Irish farmers and Irish freedom.

Davitt had family ties to Scranton and came here several times to visit his sister and other relatives, and to pray over the grave of his father Martin in Cathedral Cemetery.

The Davitts were farmers in the days when the island of Ireland was under the British boot. They were tenants in a thatched-roof cottage on the estate of English landowner Henry Joynt.

In good times, they grew enough food to pay the rent and fill their stomachs. However, when the British imposed a "poor tax," Joynt refused to pay, claiming the land was owned by the Anglican Church of Ireland as part of the Straide Monastery. When Joynt's argument was accepted, he then was told to stop renting land he didn't own.

Joynt solved the dilemma by evicting his tenants and razing their cottages.

Davitt was 5 when his family was made homeless. The family migrated to Lancashire, England, where the father, Martin, earned meager wages selling insurance.

At 10, Davitt went to work in a cotton mill. At 12, he was assigned to a machine made for an adult operator. During one of his long work shifts, his clothes became entangled in the machine and he lost his right arm.

After Davitt's recovery, he got a job in a print shop and he sharpened his reading and writing skills. He might have made printing his life's work if he didn't get involved at 19 with a movement to free Ireland. In April 1870, Davitt feared his activities would get his family in trouble. He suggested his parents go to America with their daughters, Anna and Sabina, to live with his oldest sister Mary, who was married to Neil Padden and lived in Scranton.

A month later, he was arrested, charged with treason, and sentenced to 15 years in jail for shipping guns into Ireland.

Paroled after seven years, Davitt probably resumed his anti-British activities but escaped detection. He sailed to America in 1878, but it was too late to see his father. He had died in Scranton a year after settling here.

Davitt also came to preach to raise money for the cause of Irish independence. He visited his sister Mary, who lived on Phelps Street at North Washington Avenue. He also visited his mother and sisters at Manayunk, near Philadelphia. After Martin Davitt died, they moved there and found work in a textile plant.

After a four-month speaking tour, Davitt returned to Ireland and founded the Land League on Oct. 21, 1879, to seek the end of the feudal system of government by landlords. He wanted the nationalization of farmland—a radical idea that most other promoters of Irish independence did not support.

Nonetheless, Irish farmers saw Davitt as a savior, causing the rapid growth of his organization. Once again in 1880, he came to America to visit his family and raised additional money.

While he was touring, his mother died in Manayunk. He knew his activities always worried her. Not being there when she died devastated him.

Whether Davitt raised money for guns is conjectural. However, the British must have suspected that. Shortly after his return to England, he was arrested again.

Paroled again, he continued speaking out for land reforms and was arrested for sedition. While in prison, Davitt was elected several times to the British Parliament. Other Irish members of that body sought gradual change, but Davitt was considered by many as too radical to be effective.

Late in life, Davitt became a journalist. He reported for the *New York American* about anti-Semitism and the massacre of Jews in Czarist Russia, the plight of Dutch farmers in South Africa under British rule, conditions in British prisons, and other causes.

Davitt died in 1906 and is still highly regarded in Ireland, particularly in his home county of Mayo, which is where the vast majority of Irish-Americans here have their roots.

In addition to Davitt's hometown in Ireland honoring his memory last year, the Ancient Order of Hibernians, an Irish-American organization, recently put a marker on the home in which his mother lived in Manayunk. She wanted to be buried in Ireland, but the family could not afford that when she died in 1880. Nor could the family bury her with her husband Martin in Cathedral Cemetery here. Some sort of health rule in that period prevented the reopening of his grave. Thus, she was buried in St. John the Baptist Cemetery in that Philadelphia suburb.

WELSH PIONEERS HAD IMPACT HERE

On this eve of St. David's Day, I am reminded of the impact of the Welsh on Scranton's history.

Welsh in large numbers began arriving here in the 1860s, corresponding with the development of anthracite mining.

What drew the Welsh here?

The early-stock Yankee entrepreneurs who developed coal mining here knew that Wales supplied the British Isles with that fuel. Where better to get experienced miners? Besides, most Welsh could speak English because their conquerors centuries before had forced English on them. Thus, there would be no language problems.

So Welsh miners were wooed to this area to dig the hard coal that crisscrossed in veins under the virgin green pastures and hills of the valley.

They were told they could find a better life here than they had in Wales. Some became mine bosses and did well. However, the majority were miners or laborers who experienced a buildup of coal dust in their lungs that would shorten their lives.

In time, thanks to the sheer number of Welsh families in the city, Welsh Republicans dominated local politics. However, as the anthracite industry grew, more cheap labor was needed. Once again, the owners turned to the British Isles for workmen who spoke English. Irish men, most of them farmers, were told to come here and improve their lives. They came and learned that mining was a harsh way to earn a living.

Unfortunately, there was friction between the Welsh and the Irish. A key reason for that was that the Welsh were here first and were entrenched in the middle-management at every colliery, while the newcomers from Ireland were without mining skills. So there was a caste system that the Irish hated.

As the years passed, more changes occurred. More cheap labor was needed and the mine owners turned to ethnic groups—primarily Italians, Polish, Russians, and other Slavs. Those persons, who couldn't speak a word of English, were at the bottom of the new caste system. Meanwhile, the Irish moved up a notch, especially in local Democratic politics.

Like it or not, the Welsh and Irish miners were in the same boat. The mine owners weren't sentimental when it came to paying wages. On many occasions, the Welsh and the Irish stood shoulder to shoulder during strikes for safer mining conditions, better wages, and other goals. And as they arrived, other ethnic groups joined in. In the early days of this century, union leader John Mitchell was hugely popular with most mineworkers regardless of their origins or religions.

Each ethnic group brought with it its own customs. The Welsh brought their love of choral singing. That was inbred in them in Wales, and it endures to this day. It is indeed an inferior Welsh congregation whose hymns can't be heard a block away.

The Welsh also brought with them their reverence for St. David—known to the Welsh as Dewi—who brought Christianity to Wales. Much of his history is obscure. Even the date of his birth is uncertain. The most traditional claim is that he was born in 466 at Mynyw, now named St. David. His date of death is reputedly to be March 1, 544.

Just as the local Irish honor St. Patrick on March 17, the Welsh honor St. David on March 1. Such celebrations date back to the 1870s, but it wasn't until 1911 that the St. David's Day Society of Lackawanna County was organized and held its first banquet.

I'm looking forward to joining the Welsh at the St. David's Day dinner Friday night at St. Mary's Center.

April 22, 1997

FRANTIC TOURISTS FIND A MIRACLE

Laden with luggage, my wife Betty and I left the Cumberland Hotel, near London's Hyde Park, and traveled by taxi to Waterloo Station to board the Eurostar, the train that would take us under the English Channel to Paris.

The taxi driver took our suitcases out of the trunk and I headed for a porter who was looking for a customer.

With the porter wheeling our luggage on a cart, we went into the bustling station and approached a gate for travelers to board the rocket-shaped Eurostar, the train that now connects the cities of London and Paris.

The porter asked for our tickets. Betty glanced at the cart and said to me: "Where's the carry-on bag?" She was referring to the shoulder bag where we had out our passports, our tickets, and other items that we might need during our move from the Cumberland in London to the Royal St. Honore Hotel in Paris.

I had left the shoulder bag in the taxi and felt weak in the knees. Without the passports and tickets, we could not go to Paris. I ran outside to see if I could catch up with the taxi that had brought us there. The taxis were moving slowly and I ran along the line but I couldn't find our driver. As I returned to the station, more worrisome things came to mind. We'd have to get another hotel in London and we'd probably have to go to the U.S. Embassy to get documents to replace our passports.

If there was any good news, it was that there was no money in the missing bag. Also, we had given ourselves plenty of time to board the Eurostar—so we still had time for the miracle we were seeking through prayers. Finally, our porter, Jimi Oqunsanwo, a native African who went to college in England and spoke with a crisp British accent, could have abandoned us to serve other travelers more likely to pay for his services. However, he said he would stay with us.

First, he took us to an information desk where the girl recommended we go to the office of the transportation police on the top floor of the station.

I had visions of our bag traveling further away while we were getting involved in a bureaucratic maze. Still, we had no choice. We got on a slow elevator and proceeded to the top floor.

The door to the police office was locked and our porter said he would have to wait outside. He rang the buzzer and nothing happened. "What more can happen?" I asked myself.

A minute later, however, a civilian came through the doorway, carrying our bag. He saw us and said: "You're the Flannerys. I've been looking for you."

It was our taxi driver. He had spotted the bag on the back seat shortly after he left the station. He looped around again and went inside looking for us. Then he went to the police station, which is where we caught up with him.

To my regret, I did not get his name because the spare time we once had was almost gone. He identified himself as driver " number 2074." I gave him a five-pound reward and plan to write to London's taxi license bureau to testify to his honesty.

Jimi, our porter, then rushed us to the area where the Eurostar would be boarding. I gave him a five-pound reward, plus the English coins I couldn't use in Paris. Finally, I got the name of his employer so that I could write a letter commending him for his help.

Soon we were traveling almost noiselessly across the English countryside, then under the channel and across the French countryside to Paris.

It was a happy trip, knowing what would have happened if we didn't find our missing bag.

It was nice to know that there are good people in the world like Jimi, our porter, and taxi driver number 2074.

REMEMBERING DAD,
HOPING HE GOT THAT WHITE-COLLAR JOB

I'm reminded on this Father's Day of the hard life of my own father, James Aloysious Flannery, who died at 81 in 1972.

Dad was trained in business school and should have done office work throughout his life, but that didn't happen. There was a scarcity of white-collar jobs in this coal mining area—particularly after the stock market crash of 1929 and the Depression.

Dad was from Carbondale and that's where he and Mom lived during the years after their marriage. During part of that period, he sold insurance. Agents then spent most of their time collecting on policies that were payable as often as each month. One of his customers was a woman who pleaded poverty. When she couldn't pay, he would put in the money for her, which was a violation of the rules. When he finally told her she had to pay, she threatened that she'd report him. He let the policy lapse and the angered woman carried out her threat. He was fired.

He took whatever jobs he could get. During the building of the Irving Theater in Carbondale, he was a carpenter. He also worked for a time in the yards of the Ontario & Western Railroad.

We moved to Jessup early in the Depression because my Mom's family home became available. However, the Depression was in full bloom and Dad found it even harder to find jobs.

He worked for a time in a silk mill. He and two other men opened a mine and got enough coal to get through a winter—but never enough to sell. He picked berries to add a bit of excitement to our simple meals.

We were always on the edge of economic disaster. My parents had a mortgage on the house and sometimes they couldn't make the payments. One time a deputy sheriff tacked a "For Sale" sign on the house. As soon as he left, my mother ripped it down.

We were saved by President Franklin Roosevelt's "New Deal" and the fact that we lived just a few blocks from Mike Lawler, then the Democratic boss of Lackawanna County. When the WPA—Works Project Administration—began building roads and other public facilities, my father got an array of jobs. He cracked rock with a sledgehammer for a new highway. Later, he graduated to inside clerical work. For a time, he sorted out and catalogued the records of the county jail. There were interludes, too, when WPA jobs weren't available. During one such period, my mother went to work as a seamstress in a Scranton store. But there were many times, too, when we signed up for relief.

In the late 1930s, my older brothers went to New York, got jobs in hotels, and sent money home. And later, my sister got a job in Washington and she sent money home, too. After America got into World War II, my brothers went into the service and sent part of their military pay home.

The war also stimulated the local economy. Dad got a job in the Von Storch breaker in North Scranton. We didn't have a car so he went to work on the bus. However, the last bus left the city before his shift ended so he had to walk 7 miles to our home.

Later in the war, Dad got a job with the O & W Railroad, where he had worked decades earlier. Because of all the men in the military services, railroads couldn't get enough help, so he worked seven days a week, with all the overtime he wanted. For the first time in decades, we were no longer impoverished.

After the war, the O & W fell on hard times. Dad went to see Lawler again and he got him a job as secretary at the West Mountain Sanitarium.

It was the best white-collar job of Dad's life. All his years of being a good Democrat finally paid off. He was able to buy a used car—a big step up. Also, my mother was finally able to have our living room furniture reupholstered, to buy new lamps, and to pay off the mortgage. But then she got cancer and died.

Dad retired and drifted into old age. He tried living alone but that didn't work well. He couldn't boil water. For a time, he lived with my brother's family. Finally, he moved back to his family's homestead in Carbondale where his maiden sisters made his life easy.

Mom was the dominant person in my growing-up days. She performed miracles raising a family of five children with never enough money. But Dad did the best he could.

I sometimes have flashbacks of playing checkers with my dad; him alternately smoking and chewing cigars; him taking me to a baseball game that featured Pete Grey, a one-armed outfielder; him blaming me because the muffler fell off his car while I was driving it; him refusing to wear a homburg hat that my brother bought for him, and him—in his old age— giving Kennedy half-dollars to my kids.

My Dad has been dead 25 years. When I stand at his grave I say a prayer that he has a good white-collar job in Heaven.

DANNY FORSOOK FAME FOR HOME

In a 1940 edition of *Downbeat*, a magazine about popular music of that era, there was a listing of the best male band singers in the country.

An up-and-coming guy from Hoboken named Frank Sinatra was 13th on the list.

And an up-and-coming guy from Scranton named Danny Richards was 12th.

That being the case, how come Danny wound up a haberdashery salesman in Samter's old store, and Frank wound up with international fame?

I pondered that bit of trivia after learning that Danny had died recently and reread a column I did on him in 1985 when he was 66 and retired.

Several things happened in Danny's career that sidetracked him.

One thing was that Bunny Berrigan, whose band he was singing with, was afflicted with a drinking problem. There were times the band was without a leader. Eventually, Berrigan dissolved the band, took his trumpet, and went to play with Tommy Dorsey's orchestra. With no job, Danny came back to Scranton and sang with the Four Dukes.

Not long after that, the Dorsey band was booked to play at the Paramount Theater in New York. Mr. Sinatra, then the band's vocalist, had laryngitis. Mr. Berrigan suggested to Mr. Dorsey that Danny could substitute for Mr. Sinatra. However, Danny's confidence level wasn't high enough to handle that. It might have made him a star. But he turned down that invitation.

Mr. Berrigan put together another band. As the singer, Danny became popular, thanks to the personal appearances and Berrigan band recordings. But in 1942 he got drafted and remained in the service until 1945.

After the war, Danny didn't want to become a band singer and travel around the country on a bus, so he went to Philadelphia and sang in nightclubs. However, he began to look for a normal life. He was offered a job in Samter's store. He took it, was married, and raised a daughter.

That's when I first met Danny. I bought a lot of things from him. And he did some part-time singing until recent years—mostly with Ferdie Bistocchi's orchestra.

Danny was blessed with a good voice that might have made him a star. And he was handsome. But he didn't get the breaks.

Still, he had several years in the fast lane, rubbing shoulders with many of the stars of the Big Band Era. One of the stories he told me involved Mr. Sinatra writing the lyrics to the song, "This Love of Mine." Danny liked that number and sang it virtually every night.

One night in Youngstown, OH, the Berrigan and Dorsey bands were playing near each other. The Dorsey band finished first and several of its members, including Mr. Sinatra, went to hear the Berrigan band.

Mr. Sinatra said: "Hey, Danny. Thanks for doing my number." He explained that Mr. Dorsey refused to do the song and he appreciated Danny popularizing it, particularly when the Berrigan band was on the radio.

Danny was pleasantly surprised when a 1970 album, "The Swingin' Days of the Big Bands," was called to his attention. Among the numbers in it was the Berrigan band rendition of "Skylark," sung by him. The recording was made in 1940. While he didn't get any money from the album, he was nonetheless thrilled that his song was picked for the album 30 years later.

I only knew Danny casually. But I did hear him sing and I have a record he made. That he once ranked above Mr. Sinatra on a popularity poll verifies he did, indeed, have talent. But life is funny that way. Some guys make it and others don't.

TWO FAMOUS *LIFE* PHOTOGRAPHS
IMMORTALIZED LOCAL VETERANS

Two of the most famous photographs that came out of World War II involved—I'm convinced—two local men.

Edward J. Regan, an Olyphant native who died on March 2 in Atlanta, was the American creeping through the surf on Omaha Beach on D-Day, in a photo that was printed on the front cover of *Life* magazine after Allied forces landed in France on June 6, 1944.

After the war, Mr. Regan's mother in Olyphant showed him a copy of the photo, asking if it was him. He studied it and recalled that he crawled ashore in that manner. Later, he got additional information from the magazine on where and when the photo was taken. That confirmed that the crawling soldier—later dubbed "Everyman of Omaha Beach"—was indeed Private First Class Regan.

Officials of *Life* agreed, and on the 40th anniversary of D-Day in 1984, flew Mr. Regan to France for a reunion of veterans.

The other World War II photograph that I refer to also was from *Life* magazine. It showed a sailor kissing a nurse on New York's Time Square on Aug. 14, 1945, the day World War II ended.

While *Life* never was convinced of the identity of the sailor kissing the nurse, I was convinced that he was the late Frank S. Conroy, 1337 E. Elm St.

The magazine had identified Edith Shain, formerly of New York and later of California, as the nurse. But it despaired of finding the sailor. Still, the story Mr. Conroy told convinced me he should have been recognized as the hitherto anonymous sailor.

But let me get back to Mr. Regan and his heroism before I explain Mr. Conroy's story.

The *American History* magazine's special issue on the 50th anniversary of D-Day used the picture of Mr. Regan, an admittedly scared 21-year-old, trying to reach dry land amidst dead comrades and withering enemy fire.

The article noted that *Life* photographer Robert Capa landed with the first wave of Americans and took pictures from every angle. One caught Mr. Regan, weighted down with his water-soaked equipment, moving relentlessly toward the enemy.

The article continued: "Regan, crawling shoreward through the maelstrom of lead and shrapnel, did not even see the photographer."

Mr. Regan, retelling the story at the age of 72, said: "Flattened out there in the tide, I found out what fear was. I could see our men getting hit. But I was a rifleman and I had come there to do my duty, as best I could. And that is what I did. I fought back. We all fought back."

Mr. Capa shot three rolls of D-Day photos, but back in London, a darkroom assistant spoiled most of the frames. Of the 106 pictures Mr. Capa risked his life to take, only 10 were salvaged. Among them was the picture of Mr. Regan, which became an icon for all of the GIs who stormed the beaches in the start of what would be a 14-month struggle to defeat Germany.

Mr. Regan was not an overnight celebrity. He didn't know that a picture already taken would, years later, make him famous. With his surviving comrades, he fought his way deep into France. Along the way, an enemy's bullet cut off part of his ear, but doctors later reattached it. On another occasion, he stumbled upon a German machine gun nest and killed the gunners before they could kill him.

After the war, Mr. Regan got a college education and a job with the Veterans Administration. Later, he went with the U.S. Department of Health and Education in Atlanta. He was frequently cited as a war hero of extraordinary courage.

Now, let me get back to Mr. Conroy and his story.

He came into the *Times* to tell me his story about being the sailor who kissed the nurse. He carried with him a copy of the *Life* picture.

That was in 1991 so my first question was, why he didn't say so sooner? He said he was at sea aboard his ship when the photograph was printed, so he never saw it. Also, no one else told him about it because most of his face was hidden as he was nuzzling the nurse. Unaware of the photograph, he came home, resumed his trade as a sheet-metal worker, and raised a family.

Not until the mid-1980s did he see an advertisement of a New York store showing the famous end-of-the-war photo by *Life* photographer Alfred Eisenstaedt.

"Hey, that's me," he shouted.

Subsequently he tried to convince the magazine people that he was the missing sailor. An examination of his height, his huge hands, his ears and his hairline should convince any skeptic, he said.

What he didn't know was that the magazine had done a search for the kisser and wound up with 11 ex-sailors, each claiming he was the one in the picture.

By the time Mr. Conroy made his claim, the magazine said it was no longer seeking the sailor.

He died in 1992, denied the fame that I thought was due him.

May 17, 1998

SWING SESSION FINALLY ENDS,
BUT SINATRA LEGEND WILL LAST

I have long been a Frank Sinatra fan, so I was saddened by his death —particularly because I was preparing to write a column about him.

Back in January, as rumors circulated that Mr. Sinatra was seriously ill, I wrote a nostalgic column about him and my love affair with his music since I was a teenager listening to his songs on WARM's *Swing Session*.

I remember coming home from school and listening to the popular music of the period, including Mr. Sinatra's hits, one of which, "Saturday Night is the Loneliest Night of the Week," was one of my favorites.

I wrote about that in my January column, saying that I didn't want to wait for Mr. Sinatra to die before I wrote something nice about him. His music has given me much pleasure over the years and I wanted to say that while he was still alive.

Back in 1976, I wrote a similar column about Mr. Sinatra. I sent that message to him because he hated a lot of news people and I just wanted him to know that he had a friend in the business in me.

I had just about forgotten that I had sent that letter to him when I got a letter in return.

This is how it began: "Dear Mr. Flannery: I was delighted to receive your letter and read your very thoughtful and generous column in the *Scranton Times*. I wish there were more such 'think pieces' being written so responsibly today to keep all that has happened musically over the past few decades in the proper perspective. Yours is a gem on that score."

It went on to say that, contrary to many stories that claim that he hated the press, most of the news media has been fair to him over the years.

However, he added: "There is always that small section of the press which goes beyond invasion of privacy and deals in garbage. Pure garbage."

He concluded: "But I didn't write this note to get into all of this. Let me end it by thanking you and your thoughtful and generous comments in a column as well-written as any I've seen."

As a fan, I really appreciate the letter.

As Mr. Sinatra advanced in age, I hated the crazy tabloids that kept saying he was nearing death. I saw them as vultures flying over his California home and his words came back to me. Yes, I thought—they do deal in pure garbage.

It was to combat that junk that I wrote my January column. I wrote: "While enjoying Sinatra songs, I often think of the joy his talent has brought to millions of people—not just as concerts but through recordings. Bringing such joy to the world has to be worth something when he gets to the pearly gates."

I sent that column off to Mr. Sinatra, hoping that it would get through the ring of aides who handle all the mail that fans send him.

So much time passed, however, I figured Mr. Sinatra never got my letter and column.

But amazingly, on Monday of this week, I received a letter from an aide, Susan Reynolds.

Much to my delight, this is what she wrote: "Frank Sinatra asked me to thank you for your warm and friendly letter. He enjoyed reading the January column and the trip down memory lane! Barbara Sinatra asked me to let you know your words put a special sparkle in her husband's blue eyes, and that they both were deeply moved by the column."

Ms. Reynolds then invited me to participate in a survey of individuals on their favorite Sinatra songs. People who want to participate can respond on the Internet by logging on to www.sinatra-center.org or by sending them to Frank Sinatra, 8800 Sunset Blvd., Los Angeles, CA, 90069.

Before I could make a choice, Mr. Sinatra died. But I still will do it.

Finally, Ms. Reynolds told me that the annual Frank Sinatra Las Vegas Celebrity Golf Tournament will be held May 29–31 in Las Vegas.

Participants will include celebrities in music, films, television, and sports. Each will also submit their favorite Sinatra song and the reason they love it.

The plan was to give a book listing the favorite songs and reasons of all the participants in the golf tournament.

Proceeds will go to charities which care for abused and neglected children. This is particularly appropriate, because no single person ever raised as much money for good causes as Mr. Sinatra. It is estimated that he raised about $1 billion for various charities.

While Mr. Sinatra will not be around for the tournament, I assume it will still be held.

Four days after I read that letter from Ms. Reynolds, Mr. Sinatra died.

He was, indeed, a great performer. I plan to play a lot of his music as my way of mourning his death.

October 10, 1998

CEMETERY TOUR A WHO'S WHO OF 1800s

As I walked around Dunmore Cemetery on a tour sponsored by the Lackawanna County Historical Society, I wondered whether the people buried there might be upset by this Sunday afternoon intrusion.

The cemetery, which is 160 years old, oozes history. Many of the movers and shakers of the nineteenth century—the ones who turned Scranton into a thriving city—are united in the cemetery, much as they were united in moneymaking enterprises, in building big homes, and in social circles during their lifetimes.

We started at the mausoleum of George Caitlin. I felt that I knew him because he left his home, the Caitlin House, to the historical society. He came from Shoreham, VT, and settled here, because Scranton was a fast-growing city. A lawyer by profession, he founded the old Third National Bank.

The next stop was at the grave of John B. Smith, who came here from Wirtsboro, NY. He was a mechanical draftsman who became president of the Pennsylvania Coal Co. In that capacity, he donated five acres of the coal company property to increase the size of the cemetery.

We then visited the grave of Dr. Isaiah Everhart, a surgeon in the Union army in the Civil War who settled here after that conflict. A collector of birds, among other things, he left $100,000 to establish the museum at Nay Aug Park that bears his name.

After that, we went to the grave of Col. Ezra Ripple, a native of Mauch Chunk, now Jim Thorpe, who was captured in the Civil War in Charleston and wound up in Andersonville, a Southern prisoner-of-war camp. After the war, he got into Scranton politics, became county treasurer, the city's mayor, and later, its postmaster.

Our next visit was to the grave of Cyrus Jones, who came to Scranton from Connecticut. With his brothers, he founded the Grand Union Tea Co., and was a shareholder in several banks. He was the first one I didn't know.

I didn't know John A. Duckworth, either, but I should have. He came from Toronto, and, as an architect, left a lasting impression, designing over 600 buildings, including the Hotel Jermyn, St. Rose of Lima Church in Carbondale, and many public schools. A statue of an angel on his grave had a broken arm that was repaired—the only trace of vandalism on the tour.

John Jermyn, who came from England, became rich by mining at Rushdale, which eventually was named "Jermyn" in his honor. His mausoleum is one of the biggest in the cemetery, probably because he had 10 children. In 1896, he built the Hotel Jermyn. His son John became mayor of Scranton.

Conrad Schroeder, a native of Germany, is in a fine mausoleum. The Scranton Public Library, Moses Taylor Hospital, and the Hotel Jermyn were among buildings he constructed. In 1903, he brought toys for his children from New York. When he was removing them from his bag, a revolver in the bag discharged, accidentally killing him.

Our next stop was at the mausoleum of Col. Henry Martin Boise, who came here from Massachusetts and founded a company that manufactured powder for mining. He also was into banking. His military rank involved a local militia, which explains his resting place looking like a fort.

John Zimmer's mausoleum came next. Another native of Germany, he made money in china and later in furniture.

We then visited the mausoleum of James L. Crawford, a native of Noxen, who rose from a breaker boy to become owner of the Peoples Coal Co. His mansion on Monroe Avenue served as the House of Detention until it was razed by the University of Scranton to build a theatre.

Next came the mausoleum of Thomas Dickson, who formed the Dickson Manufacturing Co., a producer of railroad engines, among other products.

Our visit to the mausoleum of George Scranton, a Connecticut native, made me feel very close to history. With his brother Seldon, he founded the firm that made tracks for the Erie Railroad. That was the start of local industry. He later became a congressman.

That stop tied in nicely with the mausoleum of Joseph Scranton, who came here to pump money into Lackawanna Iron & Coal Co. and other enterprises.

By now, we were starting to lose some hikers and run out of time. We moved quickly past the mausoleum of Frederick J. Platt, who manufactured tools for miners; the grave of Frank Carlucci, who built many famous structures, including the Hotel Casey; the mausoleums of the

Von Storchs, who made their money in coal, and the Krugermans, who produced metal fences, including the one at the cemetery

Our final stop was at the burial site of James Archbald, with its spectacular pink granite columns from Scotland.

It was, indeed, a nice way to spend a Sunday afternoon. And, as I said, I hope all those movers and shakers didn't mind us intruding upon their sleep.

BETTY AND FRANK: TOGETHER AGAIN

I was saddened by the death of Betty Redington whom I first got to know as Betty Brennan, a women's page writer at the old *Scrantonian/Tribune*.

I was a relatively new reporter at the *Scrantonian/Tribune* when Betty was helping Gene Brislin, now deceased, put out what were then called "the women's pages."

Betty, a college graduate and daughter of a physician, had worked for years as the state health department's first hygienic inspector of dental offices.

Her first newspaper job was writing for the women's pages of the *Times*. Later, she went "up the street" to the old *Scrantonian/Tribune*.

I remember her as just "one of the guys" in the male-dominated *Scrantonian/Tribune* newsroom. But that was the way newsrooms were in those days.

Betty turned 40 and seemed destined to remain unmarried. However, sometime in the late 1950s, she began dating Francis Redington, a quiet, soft-spoken individual who ran a Scranton-based furniture sales firm.

Frank and his brother Gerald had inherited J.P. Redington & Co. from their father. In reality, they got little more than the name. They paid for their father's funeral with time payments.

However, they worked hard after that, concentrating on furniture for schools and houses of worship, and expanding their reach to various parts of the country.

As war clouds spread in Asia and Europe, Frank became convinced that it was only a matter of time until the United States would be involved. Knowing that furniture would have a low priority if the country went to war, he suggested the firm buy up furniture and stock it in warehouses emptied by the depression.

And that's what happened. Their business spread to various states, and tidy profits were made on the prewar furniture.

In time, the company gained a fine national reputation. In 1958 it was bought by a New York firm that then realized it needed the brothers to run it.

Success did not change Frank's lifestyle. He kept a low profile. Some time in the 1950s, he and Betty became friends. Not many people foresaw a wedding. However, to the surprise of many, they got married on Dec. 30, 1958, and slipped away on a honeymoon cruise to Nassau and Cuba.

Frank's wealth didn't have much impact on Betty, either. She did give up her journalism job, but not being able to stand idleness, plunged into the real estate business.

In 1972 the brothers bought their company back and ran it for a few more years. Later, they sold it again, once again at a tidy profit. Then they retired.

Betty and Frank went on occasional vacation trips and spent winters in Florida, but the extent of Frank's wealth was not common knowledge. After his death in 1983, Betty confided in me that she was left funds to care for her the rest of her life. Not having any children, she and he had decided to set up a scholarship fund at the University of Scranton with most of the balance.

When Frank—who never went to college—died in 1983, he left about $2.5 million to the school. In memory of his father, who was born in Ireland, he directed that the fund finance the education of youths from Ireland.

Not surprisingly, Betty became very involved in U. of S. affairs.

Last Thursday, Betty planned to eat out with friends at Sibio's restaurant. But she didn't show up. She was found dead in her home, fully dressed for winter weather.

Betty was 81 and still active. I'm sorry to lose her as a friend, but am glad she died peacefully.

JESSE, GI JOE BOUND FOR GLORY

My eyes filled with tears when I saw 10-year-old Jesse W. Barnes in his children's size casket in the Primitive Methodist Church in Dickson City.

He was laid out in a tuxedo, which was given to him for a social event in the distant past. He loved that suit and it was an appropriate garment for a child en route to heaven.

But there was more than that in the coffin. Lying beside him were several "GI Joes," his favorite toys, a signed photo that singer Neil Diamond had sent him with a "get well" message, and a long-stemmed red rose.

Jesse was just one of 700 people in America with Fanconi anemia, a blood disorder caused by flawed genes of both parents.

When I visited Jesse last October, I saw a handsome child with red hair and freckles who looked healthy to me.

However, looks were deceiving. What I couldn't see under his robe was a tube attached permanently to his chest to facilitate the weekly blood transfusions he needed to stay alive.

A smart fifth-grader, he had left school because his condition was getting worse.

I knew there was nothing I could do to help Jesse. He was receiving medical care.

However, I also knew that his mother, Donna Day Barnes, had to take Jesse to Geisinger Medical Center in Danville at least once a week—and sometimes more often—but her 1989 Chevrolet had almost 123,000 miles on its odometer and it had major mechanical problems.

A divorcee with three children to raise with a limited income, she need a newer car to transport Jesse to Geisinger—70 miles each way—whenever his blood needed a boost. Up to then, he had over 200 transfusions and it was possible that he would go on indefinitely.

I wrote a column about the plight of Mrs. Barnes in October and hoped that someone would come to her rescue. Auto dealer Lou Domiano called to say that anytime she needed a car he would loan her one without charge. And John Cardona of South Side Service and Collision offered free repairs for her car.

In the meantime, friends of Mrs. Barnes in Dickson City—Lisa Arthur, Lisa Heater, Sue Sweeney, and Bonnie Ringleben, among others —started a fund drive.

One of their goals was to get her a newer car, so they sent out scores of letters to regional dealers, asking for help. Michael Boyd of Saturn of Wyoming Valley in Hanover Twp. was the only one to respond. He said the agency helps charitable agencies on a regular basis. Using funds set aside for that basis, he said he would sell a completely rebuilt 1991 Ford Taurus, worth $4,000, for just $2,000.

By then, they had over that in the "Jesse Fund" and they bought Mrs. Barnes that vehicle. The timing was great. Mrs. Barnes' car had just died.

As Christmas neared, I asked Sister Adrian of the Friends of the Poor if she had any "GI Joes" for Jesse. She had some, and on Christmas Day, I took them to the Barnes home, but there was no one there.

What I didn't know was that Jesse's condition was worsening, and on Christmas Eve, Mrs. Barnes had to rush Jesse to Geisinger for an emergency transfusion. And because she had no babysitter, she took her other sons with them. They returned home on Christmas afternoon and I delivered the "GI Joes" a few days later.

Meanwhile, Jesse's condition continued to worsen and he died at Geisinger on Jan. 25.

It is the wish of Mrs. Barnes that anyone wanting to remember Jesse can send a donation in his name to the Fanconi Anemia Research Fund Inc., 1902 Jefferson St., #2, Eugene, OR, 97405.

MEMORABILIA THIEVES' ERROR: ITEMS ARE TOO HOT TO HANDLE

When I learned that Factoryville native Christy "Matty" Mathewson made Major League Baseball's All-Century Team, I was reminded of the theft of three of his relics at Keystone College three months ago.

Some time between 10:45 P.M. on Aug. 14 and 6:15 A.M. on Aug. 15, one or more persons broke the Plexiglas and lock on a trophy case in the school's gymnasium and stole a jersey he wore, a contract to pitch for the Giants, and a contract to be a player-manager with the Cincinnati Reds.

I called R. Edward G. Boehm Jr., president of Keystone, to ask if there have been any developments on the case since September, when the school put up a $10,000 reward for the safe recovery of the stolen items.

He admitted that there has not been a breakthrough, but that there have been developments:

Keystone has a Christy Mathewson Hotline (945–6986) on which anyone with information can pass it on without revealing their names, if they choose.

The school has an appeal for information on the Internet.

The state police are still following leads.

The FBI has entered the case on the chance that the stolen articles have crossed state lines.

The leading dealers in the country know the items have been stolen and have pledged to notify the FBI if any show up.

The Baseball Hall of Fame knows of the theft and it will help spread the word to baseball contacts throughout the country.

Dr. Boehm said that he was assured by a major dealer that the stolen items would be spotted by him and other professionals "if they show up now or 50 years from now."

The items were stolen during the annual weekend celebration held at the school to mark the birth of Matty in Factoryville on Aug. 12, 1880.

There were many visitors on campus the evening before the theft. Some came to see a one-man play, *An Evening with Christy Mathewson*. Some came to participate in a baseball roundtable discussion. Some came to view the Mathewson memorabilia. And some came to buy or sell collectibles.

According to Dr. Boehm, the state police checked out all the dealers and others who might have been able to hide in the gymnasium until it closed, then stole the articles and left through doors that could be opened from the inside.

Clearly, the most valuable item stolen was a woolen jersey that Matty wore in 1906 after he helped the Giants win the 1905 World Series.

How good a pitcher was Matty in that period?

The first World Series was in 1903, but not all teams liked the idea of playing beyond the end of their seasons. In 1904, the Giants won the National League pennant but refused to play beyond the end of the season—a decision that angered fans.

When the Giants won the National League pennant in 1905, public pressure forced them to play a seven-game series against the Philadelphia Athletics.

Matty, who had been playing with the New York Giants since 1890, was called upon by John McGraw, the Giants' manager, to start in three games. Incredibly, he pitched shutouts on Oct. 9, Oct. 12, and Oct. 14. In the combined games, he gave up just 14 hits, walked just one, and struck out 18.

When the 1906 season came around, the Giants gave out new woolen jerseys to its players bearing the words "World Champions" across the chest.

Matty found that the sleeve of the jersey interfered with his pitching, so he cut off the right sleeve at the elbow.

Over 30 years ago, Matty's widow Jane decided to share memorabilia of her husband's career with new generations.

The bulk of her collection—including the 1906 jersey—was given to Keystone College, where he studied from 1895 to 1898. Other items were given to the Baseball Hall of Fame, where he was among the first five players to be inducted in 1936, and Bucknell University, where he studied before he decided to make a career of baseball.

Many people regard Matty as the best pitcher in the history of baseball. His old baseball cards, balls autographed by him, and anything else he ever touched—might be worth thousands of dollars.

However, for his jersey and contracts to surface 74 years after his death would raise suspicion and make them too dangerous to market.

If the person or people involved in the crime want to save themselves jail terms, they can send the items to the school anonymously. But if they fear doing that, they can mail them to me at the *Scranton Times*, P.O. Box 3311, Scranton, Pa. 18509. I promise to destroy the wrappings to avoid fingerprint or DNA tracking. Then I will deliver them to Keystone. And I won't want a reward.

November 18, 1999

PRENO'S LEGACY PASSES TO SMITH'S

Bits and pieces:

The closing of Preno's restaurant caused many people, myself included, to grieve the loss.

After all, Preno's was an institution in the downtown ever since it was opened by Russell and Margaret Preno in 1923.

The city bought and closed the place to make way for a new hotel and convention center. That's a good thing, I know, but it does not ease the hurt of losing what was, after 76 years, the oldest restaurant in Scranton.

Incidentally, Mary Jo Preno Yanusauskas, who ran Preno's in its final years, is still debating the possibility of opening a new restaurant under the Preno name, but the last time I saw her, she still wasn't sure if or when she might do that.

Now we have a holder of the "oldest restaurant" title. On a recent stop at Smith's restaurant in South Side, I reminded Ken Smith, the owner, that—with Preno's closed—his restaurant is now the city's oldest.

Smith's was founded in 1934, 11 years after Preno's.

Ken Smith's grandparents, the late James and Mary Smith, had seven children, aged 2 to 14, when he lost his job in the Bellevue Breaker. The family's modest home was in an area that was surrounded by numerous industries, so they converted the front room of their house into a lunch-eonette and began selling meals and soft drinks to workers from the plants.

Ken now represents the third generation of a family's ownership of 64 years. Most of the industries that surrounded the eatery are long gone and the business changed with the neighborhood. Over the years, it gob-bled up the whole Smith family home while evolving into a family restau-rant, complete with takeouts and catering.

Congratulations!

This take is in the realm of what might have been.

When the Wilkes-Barre/Scranton Penguins played their first hockey game in the Northeastern Pennsylvania Civic Arena and Convention

Center in Luzerne County, former Mayor Jim McNulty was among the 8,600 people on hand to see the historic first game.

It was a bittersweet night for the ex-mayor. Back in 1985, when he was in the last year of his first term as mayor, he wanted to build an arena in Scranton's downtown.

The project got as far as being promised by John McMullen, owner of the Jersey Devils, promising a Jersey Devils' farm team for Scranton.

However, if Jim were going to fulfill his dream, he needed to win a second term to complete the project. But he lost to David Wenzel by 121 votes and that ended the project.

Jim, now a television talk show host, didn't give up on the arena idea. He used his TV show on many occasions to promote the Luzerne County project, and on the opening night, he was on hand with his wife Evie to celebrate the region's latest attraction.

Alan Sweeney, president of the Lackawanna Historical Society, told me recently that County Commissioner Joe Corcoran, just elected to a new term, has promised county help with the society's plan to restore the biggest public monument in the county—the Civil War Soldiers and Sailors Monument at Courthouse Square.

Recently, the monument to labor leader John Mitchell on the square was restored to its original beauty by the society, working with labor unions. Also, the Battleship Maine monument at Nay Aug Park has been returned to its original condition. Also, the restored bust of President McKinley will soon be placed in the atrium at the William J. Nealon Courthouse.

Good work, Alan!

January 11, 2000

HEY, KEMO SABE, YOU'LL BE MISSED

I was sad to read that the Lone Ranger—otherwise known as actor Clayton Moore—had died from a heart attack in Los Angeles at 85.

I loved the *Lone Ranger*, first on radio and later in comic strips, comic books, movies, and television.

It was on radio that the Lone Ranger became famous. Young people today might not comprehend the power of radio. It was amazing how words could put images into children's minds.

All that was needed were actors reading scripts, plus sound effect artists making the sounds of running horses, bullets glancing off rocks, and other noises.

Children could easily "see" a masked man riding a white horse accompanied by Tonto, his Indian companion.

And the *William Tell Overture*—a fine piece of classical music—was perfect for setting the mood for the heroics of the Lone Ranger and Tonto.

(Someone once said that people who recognized the music by its true name were highbrows and those who recognized it only as the Lone Ranger's theme were lowbrows.)

Most young people—especially boys—knew the legend of the Lone Ranger. He and five other Texas Rangers were seeking a band of outlaws when they were ambushed in a canyon. Five rangers were killed and the sixth was left for dead.

Later, Tonto came along and discovered that one of the rangers was still alive. He buried the dead and took the survivor to a cave, where he nursed him back to health.

This last survivor and Tonto vowed to seek the outlaws and bring them to justice. And to prevent the outlaws from recognizing him, the recovered ranger began wearing a mask.

There was a time in the 1950s when the *Lone Ranger* was on radio, television, and in movies at the same time. Also, Lone Ranger toys were popular and so were Lone Ranger lunch boxes.

I remember when a kid from Jessup saved the Lone Ranger's life—or so the story was later told.

It occurred during a *Lone Ranger* serial—those segmented stories that were told in weekly chapters.

I was with a bunch of kids who went to Favini's Theater for a 10-cent Saturday double-feature and the latest chapter of a *Lone Ranger* serial.

Among the youths in the theater was a kid named "Frankie" who loved the *Lone Ranger*.

Such films were not produced to win Academy Awards. And parents didn't have to worry about the content. The Lone Ranger and Tonto never said bad words. And now that I think of it, neither did the outlaws.

In the film, the Lone Ranger was climbing a steep hill to catch some outlaws.

He darted from one boulder to another, and managed to dodge all the bullets sent his way. However, he didn't know that an outlaw was hiding behind a boulder off to the side.

It looked certain that the Lone Ranger would soon be in front of the outlaw and in easy range of his rifle.

We were all sitting on the edge of our seats, fearing the worst.

But Frankie couldn't stand the suspense. He jumped up and yelled: **"Look out, Lone Ranger, there's a bad guy behind the rock!"**

And, as silly as it seems, the Lone Ranger heard Frankie—or at least, that's what we thought, because the Lone Ranger saw the outlaw behind the boulder and shot the rifle out of his hands.

Impossible, you say?

Well, the Lone Ranger did survive and was in the next chapter of the serial next week. And we chose to give the credit to our pal Frankie.

January 16, 2000

THROWING IN TWO CENTS' WORTH BRINGS PROPORTIONATE REWARD

I'm really glad to admit that my career in the movies is over.

My most recent check from the Screen Actors Guild—channeled through MGM and United Artists—was for a grand total of 2 cents.

Actually, my earnings totaled 3 cents, but 1 cent was taken out for federal income taxes.

(I have to wonder how the IRS will credit that penny to my federal income tax. But that's another story I don't want to ponder right now.)

My screen career began in 1982 when Scrantonian Jason Miller came home to film *That Championship Season*, the play that 10 years earlier had won him the Pulitzer Prize for drama.

I was excited that Jason had found a movie company that wanted him to direct a film version of the play. But acting in the film was the last thing I expected.

However, when Jason contacted me one day and asked if I wanted to play the role of a news photographer in the film, I was quick to agree.

Jason put together a fine group of actors for the show. They included Robert Mitchum, Martin Sheen, Paul Sorvino, Stacy Keach, and Bruce Dern.

In the summer of 1982, the stars, the crew, and a mobile commissary came to town and began work.

I had to report at 7:45 A.M. at the elephant pen at the old Nay Aug Park Zoo.

Jason said I had to report to my trailer for makeup. I went to the trailers and found the names of Mr. Sorvino, Mr. Keach, and Mr. Dern stenciled on doors of their trailers.

However, mine had my name scribbled on a sheet of paper that was taped to the door of my trailer. That let me know that I was just a bit player in the scene. And after I used the trailer, I was certain that the names of other bit players would soon be taped to the door.

This is the scene that was about to be filmed. Mr. Dern, playing the role of the Scranton mayor, had donated an elephant to the zoo and he just got word that it had died. He feared that he would be accused of foisting off a sick elephant on the zoo. I was a news photographer who gained access to the pen and was taking pictures of the elephant's carcass when Mr. Dern, Mr. Keach, playing the role of a member of city council, and Mr. Sorvino, a businessman who was financing the mayor's campaign, arrived on the scene and chased me from the elephant pen.

I had only one line to say: "I'm just doing my job."

The filming lasted over 12 hours. Scene after scene was shot over and over again. Sometimes it was because actors had bungled their lines. Sometimes Jason wanted to change the dialogue. Sometimes the camera crews wanted to change angles. Sometimes the lighting director wanted changes. And breaks were taken to eat, rest, apply new makeup, and use the bathroom. The slow pace was something I never appreciated about acting.

The extras hired for the movie, myself included, were given limited cards by the Screen Actors Guild and we got union wages for speaking roles.

Much to my amazement, the paymaster gave me a check for $750 for my day's work.

Weeks later, after the film company returned to Hollywood to finish the filming and do the editing, a sound crew came back to the zoo for me to say my one line over and over again. And for that, I got another $750.

The movie, when finally released did not do very well at the box office. However, it later did well in home videos, becoming a cult favorite. In addition, it made money when television networks and independent channels bought the rights for individual showings. And finally, it was successfully marketed in various foreign countries. Thus, overall, the film made money, and actors and others involved received residuals payments every year.

It broke my heart when I learned that my scene had been cut from the film. The reason, I was told, was that the elephant's carcass, carved from foam rubber, did not look realistic. But I felt better when I learned that I would still receive residuals of an actor with lines.

I don't know how much the big stars got, but I received checks as high as $50 in the early years, but as the years flicked by, my checks kept getting smaller.

Still, I was not prepared for the payment of just 3 cents, with 1 cent taken out for taxes.

I'd be ashamed to try to cash a check for 2 cents in a bank. So I am considering having it framed so that my children, grandchildren, and future generations will believe that I once was a journalist *and* an actor right up there with Mitchum, Sheen, Sorvino, Dern, and Keach. And I have the check to prove it.

April 18, 2000

ITALIAN ENVOY TALE JOGS MEMORIES

Last December, Harold Joseph, a reader, asked if I knew about an Italian consulate in Scranton in the 1930s.

I didn't, so I checked with several Italian-Americans and drew blanks. But when I asked Frank Cimini, a former teacher of mine at the University of Scranton, he told me immediately that Fortunato Tiscar, a native of Italy, was the Italian consulate here from 1896 until America went to war with Italy in 1941.

I subsequently learned that Mr. Tiscar and his wife Louisa lived in the 400 block of Quincy Avenue and his office was in the 300 block of Adams Avenue.

He fell in love with America and became a citizen but continued to serve the Italian government. His job was to aid Italian immigrants in 20 counties in this part of Pennsylvania. He advised them on legal, family, and other problems. However, after the war began, he remained loyal to America and continued to serve the regional Italian community, supporting himself by giving speeches at social affairs.

Mr. Tiscar died in 1945 and is buried at St. Catherine's Cemetery in Moscow.

That column brought me several letters. One was from Joseph Bryer, who operates the Genealogical Research Society of Northeastern Pennsylvania in Olyphant.

Mr. Bryer told me he had recently been given a number of Mr. Tiscar's letters. They had been found by a member of the society in a cardboard box left at a curb for garbage collectors. The finder, who did not want to be identified, thought they might have some value to Mr. Bryer. However, it remains a mystery who put them out as garbage. In any case, Mr. Bryer said he is having the Italian translated into English. Still, it is a mystery where they came from and who discarded them.

I also got a letter from Joseph R. Caterina of Peckville telling me that his 89-year-old mother, Mrs. Emmett Caterina—then Clara Agrippina Molinari—served Mr. Tiscar as a secretary for four years. He added that his mother, who could speak and write in English and Italian, was in the first class that graduated from North Scranton Junior High School in 1928 and Lackawanna Business School. To save time on office work, Mr. Tiscar wrote notes and she put them into letter form.

I also had a letter from Mrs. Victor Giacometti of Old Forge—the former Liana Cappuccino. She recalled that her parents were friends of Mr. Tiscar and that he said the eulogy when her mother—Anita Cappuccino—died in 1939.

Dr. Nicholas D. Saccone, an old friend also wrote. He said: "To a first generation American and son of Italian immigrants, Mr. Tiscar was an important person—an acquaintance of my parents. I would wager that many others of my age group know much more than I do about him.

In the wake of my column about Mr. Tiscar, I learned to my amazement that Italy still maintains its link with this area.

Francesco Stoppini of Elmhurst has a job similar to the one held by Mr. Tiscar. He is "consul correspondent" who represents the Italian government and serves six counties under the Italian consul general in Philadelphia.

A few days ago, I had lunch with Mr. Stoppini at Carmen's in the Radisson Hotel. A native of Assisi, Italy, he worked for the American Army in World War II and now operates American Group Travel out of his home, while helping Italian-Americans on Italy-related matters.

Mr. Stoppini, who recently returned from Italy, is a cultured gentleman, very able—I believe—to follow in the footsteps of Mr. Tiscar.

October 22, 2000

FAMILY DUTIES SCUTTLED CHANCE
TO SEE LARSEN'S MASTERPIECE

I assume everyone has had days in their lives they will always remember, and—particularly during this World Series—it seems a good time to recall one of my classic bad episodes.

I was working a 3-to-12 shift on the obit/state police desk of the old *Scrantonian/Tribune*. The date was Oct. 7, 1956.

Chic Feldman, the *Scrantonian/Tribune's* sports editor, was in New York covering the World Series.

The obit/state police desk in the newsroom was equipped with earphones that enabled reporters to type information from funeral directors, state police, and reporters at the scene of stories.

I'd guess it was about 10:30 at night when Chic called with a story about the fourth game of the series, which the Yankees had won to even the series at two games each. He had written it out, and read it slowly enough for me to type it word for word, ready to be sent to the composing room and printed in the morning paper.

In those days, I was a diehard Brooklyn Dodgers fan. That started in the 1940s because my Uncle Mickey Kennedy had been a superintendent of an apartment house in Brooklyn, and its tenants included Dodger first baseman Dolph Camilli.

I was about 14 at the time and was thrilled to meet Mr. Camilli. He was nice enough to provide free tickets to Ebbetts Field to see Dodger games. In addition, he gave me a ball that was autographed by all of the players of the team. Quite naturally, I became a rabid Dodger fan.

I knew the Yanks had won that day's game, so I wasn't happy being the one who had to type Chic's pro-Yankee story about the game. But I did it.

Then Chic asked if I had anything to do the next day. He said he had two tickets for the fifth game and they were mine if I wanted them.

As luck would have it, I was off the next day and was tempted for a moment to accept his offer.

But at that time, Betty and I had our first baby Pat, and our free time was scarce. There was no way I could skip off to New York early in the morning without feeling guilty. So I told Chic I appreciated the offer but I couldn't possibly get away.

Chic didn't want the tickets to be wasted, so he asked me to yell his offer to the staffers in the newsroom. I did, and a colleague, Frank Sempa, said he'd take them. So I let him talk to Chic and arrange a time and place to pick them up.

When I went home that night, I was still brooding over that day's Yankee 6–2 victory, thanks to a crucial run-scoring single by Billy Martin and homers by Mickey Mantle and Hank Bauer.

My day off was used for family tasks, but I couldn't help feeling bad that I couldn't accept Chic's offer. Still, I looked forward to the fifth game, hoping the Dodgers would win their third game and lead once again in the series.

Sal Maglie, once a Giant but traded to the Dodgers, was starting the game for Brooklyn. He was one of the best pitchers of that era. His nickname was "The Barber" because he was famous for very high inside pitches that gave batters the baseball equivalent of a barber's shave. How reckless was he? A sports writer once asked if he would dust his grandmother with a close pitch. "If she's crowding the plate I would," was his immediate reply. He was one tough cookie.

I was looking forward to Maglie giving close shaves to those damn Yankees in that afternoon's game, and was sorry I wouldn't be there to see it.

But I heard most of it on the radio. As expected, Maglie did well. He allowed only two Yankee runs, which ordinarily would have been enough to win.

However, the Yanks had a pitcher named Don Larsen who did much better. He threw 97 pitches and produced the first and only perfect game in World Series history.

Oh, how I regretted not accepting Chic's offer! I could have seen a truly historic game had it not been for my sense of family duty.

Forty-four years have passed since Larsen's 2–0 masterpiece, and I still have never attended a World Series game, let alone a historic one.

The day after Larsen's perfect game, the Dodgers bounced back with a 1–0 victory, thanks to the pitching of Clem Labine and a crucial tenth inning single by Jackie Robinson.

That victory evened the series, 3 to 3. But the roof caved in on the Dodgers in the next game, a 9–0 Yankee rout that made the Yanks the world champions.

I have rooted against the Yanks ever since but to no avail. They continue to win to this day. Now, I'm hoping the Mets will win the current series, but I wouldn't bet a nickel on it.

As near as I can come to a pro-Yankee salute is that I recognize Larsen's perfect game as a piece of historic importance and athletic beauty.

Still, I regret I told Chic I couldn't use his tickets. I could have been a witness to history.

But—like it or not—we all have occasional bad days.

January 27, 2001

CLASSIC WINTER REMINDER
OF SEASONS PAST

Whatever happened to global warming?

After digging out my driveway and sidewalks several times this winter, I'm convinced we're experiencing a classic old-fashioned winter, complete with snow, ice, low temperatures, and all the other discomforting things that I recall from my growing-up days in Jessup.

My memories of winter are not at all fond ones. My father's car rarely started on cold mornings. Water pipes often froze. The task of taking frozen clothes off the line was not pleasant. Huge icicles on the edges of the roof were a hazard. Windows were etched with the artwork of Jack Frost. Wooden bedroom floors were frigid. And arctic air seeping under doors made it prudent to slow the draft with rolled-up rag rugs.

The warmest room in the house was the kitchen. God bless my mother. She got up early and made sure the fire in the kitchen stove was roaring. So we kids got out of bed and raced downstairs to the always-warm kitchen.

What about the furnace?

It was a hot-air heater that had a single outlet on the first floor.

On a really cold morning, it took an hour or more for it to generate heat to reach the second floor.

As the first out of bed, Mom made the hot Mother's Oats or corn-meal mush and a steaming pot of coffee.

If someone wanted toast, a slice of homemade bread was held over the glowing coals with a special tool called a "toaster." But if that tool wasn't available, the bread was held over the hot fire with an elongated fork. But there was a danger with that. The bread could fall into the fire and be cremated.

It was often my job to go out on the porch and bring in the dairy bottle of milk. In those days, dairies apparently didn't know how to prevent cream from rising to the top of the milk.

The cream froze and lifted the lid, creating a Popsicle-like stem of frozen cream.

Modern times have brought many changes that take some of the pain out of winters. Insulation of homes, storm doors and windows, more efficient heating, automatic washers and dryers, plus snowblowers have made our lives more comfortable. Also, when we do go out, we have better garments and better-engineered cars to cope with the cold.

When my father's car wouldn't start or our water pipes were frozen, we called the same guy, Tom Nealon, our plumber, on the phone of a neighbor. (We didn't have a phone.)

Mr. Nealon had cables to start cars and a blowtorch to warm the pipes in our cold basement. Looking back on those days, I wonder why Mr. Nealon's torch didn't burn down our house.

Mom had the task of washing our clothes, bedding, towels, and other items during the winter. She chose mild days she thought the clothes would dry on the outside lines, but sometimes the weather changed and the clothes became as rigid as plywood.

When that happened, we kids were put to work, prying clothes from the lines and bringing them into the house, where they were draped over the furniture.

Some of the frozen clothes amused us. In particular, frozen long underwear took on a spooky lifelike appearance, especially when twilight arrived.

When the weather made it impossible to do a full wash, Mom washed fewer clothes and hung them on a device attached to a kitchen wall that was meant for indoor drying of clothes. It had six wooden rods that folded down from a metal case. The rods could be spread apart and garments could be draped over them for quick drying in the warm kitchen.

It wasn't as efficient as modern dryers, but it helped keep garments clean during subfreezing days.

Keeping the house warm involved a constant care of fires in the kitchen stove and the basement furnace.

Anthracite coal burned slowly, but if someone forgot to put coal on the fires, they went out.

Then it was necessary to start a new fire with crinkled newspapers, bits of wood, and finally with coal.

It also was necessary to remove the ashes from the furnace and kitchen stove and carry them to a mine pit at the rear of our yard.

I especially hated the task of carrying pails of ashes from the kitchen stove or the furnace to the mine pit.

Sometimes, however, if a winter day coated sidewalks and stairs with ice, we used the ashes on the ice to prevent falls.

If there was a plus from winter, it was that our earthen cellar remained cold.

That enabled my mother to keep perishable foods on shelves, where she also stored her bottled chili sauce, stewed tomatoes, and jellies.

And then, of course, there was sleigh riding, building snow forts, and having snowball fights. After a couple hours of that, I loved retreating to home and standing on the metal grill in our living room, directly over the furnace. The warm air wrapped around me and it felt wonderful.

But there wasn't much else about winter I liked. And this winter reminds me of those winters of yesteryear.

July 29, 2001

ONE POTATO, TWO POTATO . . .
SORTING GOOD WORK FROM BAD

On hot summer days, my mind often drifts back over a half century to when two of my high school buddies and I hitchhiked to the Pocono Mountains to seek jobs on our summer vacation.

We went to several resorts and applied for employment, but they had hired their summer help so, quite dejected, we started hitchhiking home.

We put out our thumbs in Mount Pocono and a man in a white Cadillac stopped and asked where we were headed. When we said "Scranton," he said it was our lucky day because that's where he was going.

None of us were used to riding in Cadillacs. I doubt anyone in our hometown of Jessup even owned a Cadillac during the Depression period.

This one was really huge. To this day, I can remember its soft, plush seats. It also had the luxury of air conditioning.

The driver asked what we were doing in the Poconos and we told him we went looking for jobs. "Find any?" he asked. "No," we answered.

After a few miles of silence, the driver asked if we wanted to work for him. He said we would be sorting potatoes and we would be paid $5 a day, big money for high school kids.

We hadn't the faintest idea how potatoes were sorted, but it sounded easy. We met the man at 8 the next morning at a railroad boxcar near the old Delaware and Hudson Railroad Depot on Scranton's Lackawanna Avenue.

The man opened the door of the boxcar and told us to climb in. Once inside, we realized we were going to be working under less than ideal conditions. First of all, it was early in the morning but the sun was already beating down on the railroad car, raising the temperature inside. In addition, there was a strong odor in the car caused by rotting potatoes. Finally, it was obvious that most flies in the city had discovered the boxcar.

We were to dump potatoes from burlap bags onto the floor and sort out the good ones from the bad ones. In addition, he gave us a supply of new burlap bags, plus a supply of cloths to remove the gook from the good potatoes.

And when we had a pile of good potatoes, we were to put them into the empty burlap bags. The man with the white Cadillac told us he'd be back at 4 P.M. and would pay each of us $5. Then he left.

There was no escape. The man was nice enough to give us a ride home the prior evening. Also, we had no other jobs.

So we started opening the burlap bags and pouring the contents on the floor. Some bags had hardly any rotting potatoes and needed little wiping. So gradually, as the day wore on we filled a good number of bags with perfectly good potatoes while we brushed the bad ones and the old burlap bags down to the other end of the car.

We had brought lunches in paper bags and we used the railroad station for toilet facilities. So after a lunch break, we resumed work and filled quite a few burlap bags with good potatoes that people would buy without ever knowing their history.

Unless anyone has spent a day sorting rotten potatoes from good potatoes in a hot boxcar filled with flies, there is little chance of me conveying the job's negatives in mere words. Let's just say it was one of the longest days of our lives. Yet, we stuck it out and worked at the task.

Promptly at 4, the man with the white Cadillac returned and was pleased with the number of bags of good potatoes we had processed. He gave each of us $5 bills and asked if we would return the next day. The money lifted our spirits and we had no other jobs, so we agreed to do so.

"OK," the man with the white Cadillac said, "I'll meet you here at 8 A.M. tomorrow. Though we were filthy from our day's work, we walked over to the Scranton Transit bus station at Penn and Lackawanna Avenues and boarded a bus for Jessup.

However, we didn't realize how socially unfit we had become, until passengers on the bus began changing seats to get as far away from us as possible. Indeed, some chose to stand rather than be near us.

Apparently, our senses of smell had been dulled by our day in the boxcar, but clearly, there was nothing wrong with the noses of our fellow passengers.

Then next morning, we were supposed to meet at the bus stop. However, none of us showed up. Our parents, after seeing and smelling us, decided to terminate our careers as potato sorters. My mother gathered up my clothes and threw them away, and it's likely that the clothes of my colleagues suffered the same fate.

So we never saw the man with the white Cadillac again. From that day to this, no matter what jobs I've held, I have had the consolation of knowing it was better than sorting rotten potatoes. Also, it's another reason why I love writing columns.

May 27, 2001

DEATH, COMMON DENOMINATOR, MULTIPLIES SADNESS BY FOUR

The only thing we can be sure of in this life is that every one of us is going to die. We don't usually know the day or the hour, but we can be sure it's marked down in a book that God keeps on all of us.

Why am I writing about death this holiday weekend? Well, one reason is because Monday is Memorial Day and I will be visiting the graves of my parents and other relatives.

But there is another reason death is on my mind today. Never before have I experienced a period where so many people near and dear to me have died. In a two-week period I suffered the death of four people who were close to me.

First came the news two Sundays ago that playwright and actor Jason Miller had died at 62 of a massive heart attack as he was eating and reading the Sunday paper in Farley's. Because we were old friends, I gave the eulogy at his memorial Mass.

Then came the death last Sunday morning of my beloved niece and godchild, Mary Flannery Matchesky.

On the following day I learned that 91-year-old Mary Brown, my next-door neighbor of over 40 years, had died at the Abington Manor, a nursing home where she was admitted just 21 days earlier. I knew immediately the task of planning her funeral and burial would be mine.

There is an old expression that things happen in threes. So the deaths of Jason and the two Marys fulfilled that prophecy for me. There would be no more deaths impacting on me in the immediate future, I thought.

Then, Tuesday, I read that William T. Cullen, a friend and colleague from the *Scranton Times*, had died at 77 of cancer.

"Please God, no more!" I prayed. But the more I thought of this terrible sequence, the more I knew that from the beginning of time, God knew the minute all four of my friends would die. If there is a common denominator in those deaths, it is that all were nice people who, in one way or another, made me a better person.

I must be honest and explain that the death that hurt me the most was that of my niece and godchild. When I was born, my parents named

337

two godparents to keep an eye on me as I grew up. However, they never worked hard on their job.

So when my brother Jim Flannery and his wife Anne made me Mary's godfather, I vowed to be the best godfather in the world, and I tried to be that as long as she lived. And when it became clear that she might die, I did what I could to boost her spirits with greeting cards and gifts.

Mary never forgot me, either. Over the years, she gave me novelty gifts that I still have, including a yellow cup filled with smiling faces. In addition, every Christmas she gave me a bottle of Crown Royal, which I used for special occasions.

We relatives of Mary bombarded heaven with prayers for a miraculous recovery that would have let her raise her two children to adulthood, but it was God's will to take her into heaven. Those with her when she died said that at the moment she passed away, she smiled. There's no doubt in my mind that she saw her father with his arms out to greet her.

The death of Mary Brown was less traumatic because she had been slipping for months. We used to be pals, but as she entered her 90s, she wasn't always sure who I was. And closer to the end, she had to be spoon-fed and she stopped talking. I never wanted to put her in a nursing home, but did that out of necessity on May 1. I hoped she understood.

In a similar way, I knew that Bill Cullen was dying after a long battle with cancer.

I knew Bill years before I became a journalist, because we had distant family ties. After I joined the *Scranton Times* staff in 1960, we became colleagues. For years, we ate lunch together at Yank's Diner, discussing the day's flow of news with Bob Flanagan and the late Billy Halpin. Then, when Bill gave up his job as associate editor, Pat McKenna and I became associate editors.

Bill fought cancer for years without ever complaining. He dealt with that as though it was happening to someone else.

And he didn't waver. I understand he asked a doctor how he would die. The doctor was probably surprised by the question, but said he would not have pain and would drift off to sleep. Bill thanked him as he might have thanked a person who gave him road directions.

I hope when my time comes, I can be just as casual.

As for the death of Jason Miller, I cherished him as a friend and wrote my column last Sunday about his death and burial. I will miss all four of the people I've lost in two weeks and hope all are in heaven.

I know the date and time of my departure is known to God and I will try to be prepared. But, if God reads this column, I want him to know I'm not in a hurry.

August 11, 2001

A MIRACLE BORN OF GOOSE GREASE, PRAYER

I've always been intrigued by old-fashioned cures, and maybe it's because I owe my life to one.

When I was born my esophagus was blocked, which meant food couldn't get to my stomach. At Mercy Hospital in Scranton, a physician opened a direct line into my stomach, giving me a second belly button that I have to this day.

But that man-made pipeline into my stomach didn't give me nearly enough food to keep me alive. So I was baptized and sent home to die in peace. My parents already had three healthy children, and they prayed for a miracle to keep me alive. However, without food and liquids, my life expectancy was a few days at best.

One evening there was a knock on the door of my family's Carbondale home. The door was opened and Isabelle Gibbs, a nurse, entered with a bottle of goose grease.

She told my parents she had heard about their baby's problem, and maybe she could do with goose grease what doctors had failed to do.

It must have sounded crazy, but my parents had no other options. Thus, they took Mrs. Gibbs to my bed, and she scooped some goose grease from the bottle and pushed it down my throat with her grease-covered middle finger. And again, she put her finger into the grease and shoved more of it down even further into my gullet.

Obviously, I remember nothing about the effort of the nurse to save my life, but stories handed down to me claim I began to scream, cough, gag, and upchuck phlegm. After my treatment, I've been told, I settled down and fell asleep.

Before Mrs. Gibbs left, she told my parents that my esophagus should be normal with all the grease lubricating it. Shortly thereafter, I had my first mother's milk and, within days, I began to gain weight.

From what I have learned since, goose grease is just one of hundreds of quirky cures that were once used to fight almost anything. But I shouldn't make fun of such cures, because goose grease saved my life

after doctors sent me home to die. To this day, I have a great fondness
for geese.

As I grow older, I was introduced to more popular medicines, such
as castor oil, derived from castor beans, but tasting like motor oil, and cod
liver oil, that tasted like fish. When serving up those medications, my
mother mixed them with orange juice. But they still tasted awful. Still, my
mother felt that both were good for whatever ailed you. Thus, it was prudent not to complain about every ache and pain, lest they earn you a dose
of castor or cod liver oil.

In this day of television ads for numerous products for upset stomachs, it might be surprising to learn that a spoonful of baking soda mixed
in a glass of water was a standard cure for a stomachache. Baking soda
could also be used as a substitute for toothpaste.

Another cure of a stomachache involved two or three dinner plates
heated in an oven and wrapped in a towel. The heat of the dishes was
said to be a quick cure for a bellyache.

I have not discarded all the old-time cures. When I feel a cold and
fever coming on, I mix up a concoction of lemon juice, honey, and
whiskey taken with two aspirins. After taking that, I go to bed and sleep
a few hours covered with blankets. The mix causes you to sweat while
sleeping. I don't get colds often, but when I do, that's my old-fashioned
cure.

Once upon a time, every house in America had at least one bottle of
Vicks, a bottle of Mercurochrome, and a bottle of hydrogen peroxide.
The Vicks could be rubbed on one's chest to break up bronchial conges-
tion. Or a tiny amount could be inserted in each nostril to open up nasal
passages. Or it could be melted on a spoon and inhaled.

The Mercurochrome and hydrogen peroxide were used for cuts and
bruises. Mercurochrome was bright red so that when it was put on a cut,
you got a lot of sympathy. The hydrogen peroxide fizzed on a cut, and I
always imagined that bubbling was a battle between the good medicine
and the bad germs in the cut.

There were also many cough syrups on the market, many spiked with
alcohol. So if your cough was not cured, at least you felt happier.

Beyond those products, other cures involved everyday items. For
instance, bits of wet bread could make it easier to cut an ingrown toenail
or make it easier to draw slivers to the surface. But granted, it made a
bulky bandage.

For some reason I do not know, the popular mix of sulfur and molasses was often billed as a "winter tonic." Thank God, I never had to take it.

Before antibiotics came along, whooping cough was a dangerous ailment. One cure for that was a bag of charcoal from a gas plant. The fumes were said to cure whooping coughs.

And then there was the belief that cobwebs could heal cuts or other skin sores.

I don't believe in most of those cures, but if you have some, send them along.

However, I do believe in goose grease.

A WELL-DESERVED CELEBRATION FOR HEROIC SCRANTON COUPLE

My wife Betty and I recently attended a surprise 50th wedding anniversary party at Finelli's in Dunmore. The couple being honored was Joe and Catherine Walsh of 2048 Cedar Avenue.

Everyone kept the secret, and the couple was absolutely surprised when a friend, who had taken them to a movie conned them into having a meal at Finelli's, where family and friends awaited secretly their arrival.

But I'm getting ahead of my story. So let me back up.

My involvement with the Walshes began one day in 1982 when my telephone rang and I answered it with a bit of annoyance over being interrupted in my work.

The caller was Catherine Walsh, who told me she was the foster mother of an 11-year-old child who was disabled by cerebral palsy.

Mrs. Walsh was aware that from time to time I wrote sympathetic columns about sick people in desperate need of financial help. She said she needed help to buy for Bobby, her foster child, a computer that would help him communicate.

"What would that cost?" I asked.

"$5,000," she said.

I froze. That was a large sum 20 years ago and I didn't think I could get that much by writing a column. But she wasn't taking "no" for an answer. "Would you come out to see Bobby?" she asked.

I had run out of excuses, so I said I would drop by. And that's how I met Bobby, who couldn't walk, talk, or use his hands, but certainly knew how to smile.

Mrs. Walsh told me that Bobby was smart but he was behind in his education because he had no way of communicating. But, she said, she had read about this computerized machine that disabled people could use with pointers attached to their heads to spell out words and numbers.

I don't know whether it was Mrs. Walsh's pitch or Bobby's smile, but I agreed to write about what I saw.

A day or two later, I had a call from Bill Nellis of the Kiwanis Club, who said the club would be pleased to start a campaign to raise funds for Bobby's computer. So I wrote about the cause and the money poured in.

As soon as Bobby got his machine, his long-delayed education took off like a helicopter. His foster parents went further to give Bobby a sense of security. They adopted him, making him their seventh child. I recall writing that, at an age when their own children were raised, they would be excused if they went on a cruise to celebrate their freedom.

Instead, they took on the task of parenting a severely disabled child. To me, the father of six, that was truly a decision of heroic proportions.

As the legal parents of Bobby, they were anxious to give him the education he had missed in institutions. However, the Scranton School District was dubious at first because it had never let such a severely disabled child into regular classes.

But the Walsh couple didn't want Bobby to be a second-class student. They wanted him to have social contacts with classmates instead of being isolated. So he was allowed to attend classes, and soon showed he was smarter than anyone could have guessed. He breezed through the elementary grades, and in 1992 graduated with honors from West Scranton High School.

By then, Bobby was convinced he could handle college. He enrolled at Marywood University and breezed through there, too. After graduation, he became a computer programmer for county government and still works there today.

When the Walsh couple neared their 50th wedding anniversary, he was one of the Walsh kids who planned the surprise party for their parents.

So who was chosen to give a speech? His brothers and sisters voted for him.

Bobby has an electronic voice machine that is attached to his wheelchair. So he programmed a speech that silenced the room and brought tears to the eyes of many guests, including his parents and myself.

This excerpt will provide the flavor of his message: "My parents put love, caring, and passion into my life. They have been supporting me for 20 years. I know they are my best cheerleaders. God gave me those two angels when my life was filled with uncertainty."

The Walshes are extraordinary. And so are their natural children who welcomed Bobby into the family. Bobby was a foundling who spent his early years in institutions, classified as learning-impaired. If Joe and Catherine had not made him part of their family he could still be looking out institution windows instead of being a 30-year-old computer whiz who supports himself, serves as a lector at his church, and now studies for his master's degree at Marywood.

Joe and Catherine, I'm proud to know you, and wish you many more years of wedded bliss.

SOMETHING FISHY
ABOUT THE SNAKE STORY

A number of years ago, I did some research into the legend that St. Patrick banished snakes from Ireland. With the St. Patrick's parade today and St. Patrick's Day coming a week tomorrow, I thought this would be a good time to revisit the tale.

I probably heard the story of St. Patrick and the snakes from my Irish-American parents and accepted as holy dogma that the man who converted the pagan Irish to Catholicism also banned reptiles from their island. But as I grew older, I began to wonder if the story was true.

"How could snakes be banned forever from an island?" I often asked myself. It made no sense to me that such a ban could remain in effect for over 15 centuries. So I asked a friend from Ireland if the St. Patrick story was true, and he said it was. But I delved deeper. I asked, "What would happen if I put a snake or two in a suitcase, took them with me to Ireland and released them in some wooded area? Would they live or die?"

But the Irish have ways of eluding questions they don't want to answer. My friend replied: "Joe, you'd never get your bag past customs."

Some time later, I decided to make a more serious inquiry, so I wrote letters to the Consulate General of Ireland in New York, the Zoology Department of the University of Dublin, and the Royal Zoological Society. Each replied that snakes can and really do live in Ireland.

Ironically, the letter from the official from the Royal Zoological Society had an Irish stamp on the envelope that showed St. Patrick cleaning out a den of snakes with his bishop's staff.

As long ago as 238 A.D., Salinus, a Roman historian, wrote that Ireland had no reptiles other than the common lizard, but he didn't say why. Six hundred years later, the Venerable Bede, an Irish monk, arrived at the same conclusion but was more imaginative as to why. He wrote: "No reptiles are found there and no snakes live there and no snakes can live there, for though often carried thither out of Britain, as soon as the ship comes near the shore and the scent of the air reaches them, they just die."

Wow! Just the scent of Irish air could kill inward-bound snakes! No wonder I began to doubt the story.

However, a more scientific reason why Ireland originally had no snakes was given to me from the director of the Zoological Society of the University of Dublin. In his answer to my question, he wrote that as the Ice Age was ending in Europe, animals migrated from the continent across a land bridge to England and then to Ireland.

However, the land bridge between England and Ireland eroded before reptiles, slow travelers by nature, had time to reach that island.

To clinch his case, he wrote that no fossils of snakes have ever been found in postglacial deposits of peat or in the many mountain caves in Ireland.

So why does St. Patrick, who brought the Catholic faith to Ireland in the fifth century, get the credit?

Well, in the twelfth century, Jocelin, a monk at Furnes, Belgium, wrote a very flattering biography of St. Patrick. He claimed that St. Patrick ended a plague of "reptiles, demons, and magicians" during his mission to Ireland. That included "earthly serpents, demons from hell, and pagan priests endowed with the power of darkness."

Perhaps Jocelin had heard the tale that St. Patrick studied for the priesthood at a monastery on an island just off the coast of France. Many years earlier, snakes had been cleared away by eliminating a swampy area where they bred. In his zeal to glorify St. Patrick, he may have given St. Patrick the credit for clearing the snakes.

In fact, there are snakes in Ireland today. Some have been imported from other countries for Irish zoos. Others are in the wild. So from where do they come? They could be escaped pets or animals that got away from circuses or carnivals. Once free, they found a climate hospitable to breeding. And they could have arrived from foreign countries and slithered their way to freedom from ships tied up to Irish docks.

While St. Patrick did not chase the snakes from Ireland, he did bigger things. When he landed in Ireland, its inhabitants were pagans who had never heard of Christ. By the time he died about 460 A.D., most inhabitants of the island were Christians. And his influence still is felt today. Ireland today has 3,539,000 people, with 93 percent of them Catholics.

Most historians have accepted the story that he used the shamrock to illustrate the Holy Trinity. And he probably performed miracles like curing the sick that the Vatican accepted before he was declared a saint. But St. Patrick did not chase the snakes out of Ireland.

P.S.—Many years ago, I sold this story about St. Patrick and snakes to *Sign*, a national Catholic magazine. But I figured enough time has passed to do it as a column.

May 12, 2002

POWER OF MOM'S INFLUENCE
RESONATES OVER HALF CENTURY

I could not let this Mother's Day pass without thinking of my mother, Clare Martina Reap Flannery, who died 50 years ago, but who lives on in my memory as the person who did the most to mold my character. Mom's father died of miner's asthma, and as the oldest of eight children, she had to leave school and go to work in a silk mill.

In time, Mom became a self-taught seamstress and hired herself out to families that needed dresses, shirts, and other garments and had the money to pay her. On occasion, she stayed overnight in homes to make the most of her time.

Meanwhile, as the oldest of the Reap children, she became dominant among her siblings, all of whom worked when their ages allowed.

I'm not sure how many years Mom went to school, but she could read, write, and do simple arithmetic. And she could make clothes from complex patterns with ease.

Then she married James Aloysius Flannery of Carbondale and bore five children, four boys and our princess, Clare.

While fathers were dominant in many ethnic groups, it wasn't that way in Irish homes. She was the boss in our home and that was taken for granted, even by my father.

Consider how she solved the problem of getting coal into our coal bin. Our house was perched upon a hill, and for years our coal had to be carried up the hill in baskets. Mom pestered my father for years to dig out a driveway, which trucks could use to deliver our coal. But my dad's motto was accepting things the way they were.

Mom finally ran out of patience and hired a contractor to dig out the driveway with a power shovel. The day the shovel arrived, Dad disappeared after saying, "We'll be the talk of the town!" So my Mom spent the day outside, overseeing the job.

Despite Mom's determination, she remained a classy person who was deeply religious, deplored off-color language, hated idle gossip, was devoid of prejudice, dressed well in clothes she made herself, and styled her hair to imitate movie actress Claudette Colbert.

Mom never shirked her duties. She enforced curfews on a theory that nothing good was going to come of being out late at night. And the same rule applied to Dad.

The Great Depression made life miserable for millions of American families, but that was when Mom was at her best. She could make a grand meal out of a soup bone, a bag of rice, homemade bread, and a cake or pie that she made without measuring ingredients. I can still taste the ginger cookies she could whip up in 15 minutes or so, and her biscuits melted in my mouth.

She also cut our hair, made our clothes, and forced medicine upon us when we were sick. And she was the first one up in the morning to get the fires going in the winter. And she didn't go to sleep at night unless everyone else was in bed.

She also was an amazingly creative person. With paint, wallpaper, and material for drapes, she could change the appearance of a room to match one she saw in a magazine. Or she could see a dress she saw in a magazine and recreate it on her sewing machine without the help of a pattern. Also, if the lump coal needed to be cracked, she could do that too when there was no male around. And if the collar of Dad's shirt was ragged, she could take it off, turn it around, and sew it back on again.

Like most housewives of that era, she was a slave to her duties. She did her washing with a wringer washer, ironed all our clothes, and emptied the water in the pan under the icebox. She also could strip a piece of furniture and repaint it, make slipcovers for the living room chairs, and mix a batch of cement to patch some cracks in the sidewalk.

A hard as she worked, she remained very feminine. She dressed well, usually in clothes she made herself. For a holiday like Easter, she could make a hat out of a few pieces of felt and a few feathers, and dye a pair of shoes to match. She did her own hair in curlers and painted her own fingernails to convert herself into an attractive woman.

After prosperity returned to America, Mom finally began to enjoy the luxury of new appliances, occasional visits with my Aunt Kitty in New York, and a few extra dollars in her purse. But just about the time it seemed she could enjoy her life, she was stricken with cancer and died. I was married by that time and not making a lot of money. I would have loved to take her out to dinner, to a Broadway show, or a concert. But that never happened.

Nonetheless, I often include her in my prayers, because I am absolutely certain she is in heaven with my dad and two older brothers. Thanks, Mom, for all you did for me. And happy Mother's Day.

May 19, 2002

AREA SHOULD COMMEMORATE OWN GREAT ONE, JASON MILLER

It's hard for me to believe that Jason Miller has been dead for over a year.

A huge homegrown talent, Jason became a famous playwright on Broadway and a famous actor in Hollywood, but he loved the slower pace of life in Scranton and gave up California's Malibu beach for Scranton's downtown.

Among his habits was having brunch at Farley's with the Sunday papers and his girlfriend Dana.

On Sunday, May 13, 2001, Jason was eating, chatting, and reading when he suffered a heart attack. It's likely that he was dead before he hit the floor.

Jason was just 62, relatively young by today's standards. He had more things to do and seemingly lots of time to do them, but none of us knows when God will pull the plug. So in an instant, Jason was gone.

At the time of Jason's death, he was working on a script called *The Great One*, about his former father-in-law, Jackie Gleason, whose waistline was matched only by his ego.

Jason married Linda Gleason on March 9, 1963, at St. Patrick's Church in West Scranton, his hometown parish.

Mr. Gleason never liked Jason, but Jason knew talent when he saw it, so he respected his father-in-law as an entertainment genius. I really thought Jason's tale about his deceased father-in-law had the potential to put him on top once again. He soared to fame in 1972 when his play, *That Championship Season*, won him a Pulitzer Prize in drama and followed that by earning a nomination for an Oscar for his portrayal of a priest in the film *The Exorcist*.

Jason was equally skilled as a writer and actor. He had written a number of plays, but while they won a few awards, the blockbuster that he was seeking eluded him. During those lean years, he and his wife lived in modest flats in New York City. While he worked as a waiter, a doorman, bartender, and other low-paying jobs, his wife helped by passing out free samples of cigarettes on street corners. Then came *That Championship Season*, a story of a Scranton Catholic high school basketball team that won a state championship in Philadelphia. Jason knew Joseph Papp, the president of New York Public Theatre, so he took his script to him and asked if he would read it. Mr. Papp, always seeking new talent, read the play and liked it. However, he also suggested changes, such as adding more locker-room language for what was originally a rather pristine script. Jason did as he was told and the show opened off-Broadway and won rave reviews. Later, the show as moved to Broadway where it continued to win praise. In the same time period, Jason was given a role in *The Exorcist* and he won praise for his acting. For the first time since he left Scranton, Jason was a big star. But it did not endure. He continued to write and act and earned a decent living. Periodically, he would sell a script or get a part in a movie or television drama. For instance, he was nominated for an Emmy for his portrayal of F. Scott Fitzgerald on television. But his marriage fell apart and he came back to Scranton, leaving his ex-wife and four children in Hollywood, where one son, Jason Patric, grew up, changed his name and became a star.

In Scranton, Jason was the artistic director of the Scranton Public Theater. Among his accomplishments was a production of *Inherit the Wind* that was a hit here and in Philadelphia.

Then, 10 years after *That Championship Season* opened on Broadway, one of Jason's dreams came true. A new film company decided to make a movie of that play, with Jason as the director and such stars as Robert Mitchum, Martin Sheen, Paul Sorvino, Stacy Keach, and Bruce Dern. A hit movie would have made Jason a millionaire.

However, the film company chintzed on the budget, and the film was dribbled out to a few theaters at a time and was horribly under-advertised. So it did not make Jason rich. After that disappointment, Jason continued to get acting roles in movies and television and worked with the Scranton Public Theater.

Then he got the brilliant idea of writing a script about the Jackie Gleason he knew as a father-in-law. He also knew many of the Gleason family's secrets through his ex-wife. I was sure this project would have made Jason hot again. But I don't think he finished the script. Even if he did, the Gleason family might not want the dark side of Mr. Gleason done on film or television. So that last dream of Jason is not likely to materialize.

Still, I hate to let the local fame of Jason die. Maybe a state historical marker should be erected in his memory. Or some of his friends could get together to put a plaque on the Brooks Building where he lived. Or maybe the University of Scranton, where Jason got his bachelor's degree, could put a plaque on the wall inside or outside the Royal Theater at McRae Center, where he acted in his one-man play, *Barrymore's Ghost*, just two years ago.

May 26, 2002

LOVE, BABIES ARE LOVELIER
THE SECOND TIME AROUND

I've fallen in love again. Her name is Kiera Rose. She has jet-black hair, dark blue eyes, and a lovely soft and pink complexion.

So why am I, a senior citizen, broadcasting a new love affair? Isn't it going to cause a bit of trouble with my wife Betty at home?

No, it isn't. Actually, my wife also loves my new girlfriend.

Wow! That's a surprise! Let me get this straight. You, a married man, have a girlfriend, and the wife actually knows and likes her? Isn't she jealous? Not a bit.

I don't understand that.

Why would my wife be pleased by my falling in love again with a girl many years younger than I am?

Well, I may have confused you by not disclosing that Kiera Rose is my three-month-old grandchild. Her arrival gives us a total of 11 grandchildren spread over three states.

My wife and I raised six children and we shared the tasks of giving them bottles, burping them, walking the floor with them, and holding them close until they fell asleep. And once you master those things, they stay with you for life.

Born on Feb. 12 to my son and daughter-in-law, Tom and Karla Fabri Flannery, Kiera Rose is a beautiful child who I love to hold close to my chest and feel her breathing. I can sit in a chair with her in my arms and feel the warmth of her body for an hour or more. It's a nice feeling.

That doesn't mean that a new baby can't get mean. When Kiera Rose awakens and is hungry, she lets you know. She can exercise her lungs and vocal chords to get her message across that she wants her formula and she wants it NOW!

That's another thing I enjoy. Giving Kiera Rose her bottle. I love looking at her as she rhythmically sucks on the nipple. She gets it fast enough at the start, but later she slows down and pauses occasionally. Sometimes she empties the bottle and sometimes she doesn't. After that, it's time to get her to burp. I usually carry her around the living room and dining room table, tapping her gently until, "BURP," she expels the gas that was bothering her.

With that done, she usually is ready to fall asleep. I walk with her, gently patting her on the back. Soon I can feel her head resting on my shoulder. With luck, I can then sit in a chair with her for a considerable amount of time.

God knew what he was doing when He invented new babies. They need tender loving care, and parents and, yes, grandparents are programmed to provide that service.

That is not to say that tiny tots can't be irritating at times. If they have a bellyache, a fever, or some other thing that makes them uncomfortable, they can let go with a demanding cry. And the later it is at night, the more demanding they can be. But since Kiera Rose spends her nights with her parents and sister Alyssa, I don't have to get up at night to quiet her down.

But I do recall such duty when my children were tots. My wife and I usually took turns caring for our babies. For some reason I can't explain, I recall one winter night when I had to go down to the kitchen to heat a bottle of formula to soothe a hungry tot. It was about 3 A.M. and the kitchen was chilly because the house heat was turned down. I recall looking out the window and seeing snow whirling about, which chilled me even more. A glass bottle was in a pot of water on the electric stove and it seemed the water would never boil. Finally it did, of course, and the water heated the formula and the crying infant got the formula he or she was crying for.

Now, of course, the microwave heats plastic bottles in a matter of seconds, making the task much easier than what it was in the age of glass bottles.

When Kiera Rose falls asleep in my arms, it reminds me of when my children were tots. All babies are programmed to cry when they are hungry. I learned that as a father. Usually, after they are fed and burped—and maybe provided with a fresh diaper—hey are easy to lull back to sleep.

I love feeding Kiera Rose, walking her around, and tapping her on the back to make her burp. With that done, I know she will soon go to sleep. I walk with her and tap her gently until I feel her head droop to my shoulder. But it is important not to sit down with her too soon. Tots like being carried around, and if you sit too soon there is a danger of them waking up. So to be sure she is sound asleep, I walk her another few minutes and then sit gently in a chair and let her body heat radiate onto me.

Yes, I love Kiera Rose and look forward to many more sessions of feeding her and holding her close as she sleeps.

And while she hasn't told me yet, I think she loves me, too.

July 13, 2002

WILLIAMS' DEATH STIRS IRISH MEMORIES

The recent death of Ted Williams, one of baseball's best hitters, caused me to think of Thomas "Irish" Langan, a South Side saloonkeeper who died 13 years ago. So what's the connection between Williams and Irish?

Williams was no angel. He had a volcanic temper that caused him to throw bats, make obscene gestures, and spit at fans when they booed him and harangue sportswriters who criticized him.

Yet, when Irish called him a "bush leaguer," a real insult in baseball, Williams laughed and said, "You're the bush leaguer, Irish." And as their friendship deepened, both called each other "Bush."

How did this unlikely friendship begin?

On June 14, 1948, when the Boston Red Sox came here to play their Scranton farm team in the stadium on Monroe Avenue in Dunmore, Irish was a county detective who was assigned to keep the fans away from the big leaguers.

Scranton won that game, 2–1, and Williams went 0 for 3. However, in a pregame home run derby with other power hitters, he knocked one of the allocated five pitches each batter got over the fence and into the woods that once existed on the hillside beyond the fence.

Irish was never bashful. For instance, he became a buddy of Admiral Chester Nimitz, who was directing American naval forces in the Pacific from Hawaii in World War II. Irish was a chief petty officer whose job was to stage morale-building athletic events for sailors. But sometimes his sailor-athletes made trouble in bars, and Irish had to ask Admiral Nimitz to get them out of jail. At one point, Nimitz said to Irish: "I spend 90 percent of my time getting your guys out of jail and 10 percent of my time fighting the enemy!"

So when the Boston team came here, Irish assigned himself to Williams, and before the event ended, he invited him and his pals to Langan's bar for drinks and steaks. They came, and Irish, with his brash humor, made them all laugh when he called them "Kuz," "Stiffs," "Bums," "McGoose," and when he really couldn't remember a name, "Joe Goss."

The Boston players, including Williams, had fun that night. And more importantly, Williams and Irish became good friends.

Over the years, when Williams was driving from Boston to Florida after the season ended, he would stop at Irish's home and spend a day or two there before continuing his journey to his home in the Florida Keys. In addition, the thrice-married Williams sometimes called Irish when he was lonesome or when he had a funny story to tell. And sometimes Irish called him and regaled him with stories. That's when they started calling each other "Bush."

In the 1950s, Williams gave Irish two tickets to the All-Star Game in Baltimore, and Irish and Snap Nagelberg of Scranton made the trip to Baltimore in Snap's car. After the game, Williams said he had to go to Washington on business, and Snap and Irish said they would drive him there. Midway between Baltimore and Washington, Snap's car ran out of gas on a busy beltway, and Irish and Williams had to get out to push it off the fast traffic lanes.

A kind motorist saw the men pushing the car and pulled up behind them. He was astounded when he was introduced to Williams, one of the most famous baseball players of all time. The man took Snap to the nearest service station, where they bought gasoline, and then he took them back. They poured the gasoline into Snap's car and resumed their trip to Washington.

Williams wasn't a bit upset, Snap assured me, adding: "He thought it was funny."

Back in those days, Snap was selling encyclopedias, and Williams bought a set to quench his real thirst for trivia. Sometime later, Snap met Williams in an airport, and Williams told him that a tropical hurricane had ruined his home in the Florida Keys, and that his encyclopedias were ruined. Snap sent him another set without charge.

After Williams retired, he did some television commercials for a cigarette company. In the ads, he was in a boat fishing, smiling, and holding a lighted cigarette. When Irish saw the ad, he noted that Williams wasn't holding the cigarette the way a real smoker would hold it. He picked up his phone and called him in Florida. This is approximately what he told Williams, according to his daughter, Patsy Healey: "Hey, you bush leaguer. Why are you doing that cigarette ad? You don't even know how to hold a cigarette. If you're that hard up for money, come up here and I'll feed you."

Williams couldn't stop laughing, but Irish noted that Williams stopped advertising the cigarette shortly after that.

Bernie Blier, a friend, also told me that when the Scranton Chamber of Commerce was organizing the Lackawanna Industrial Fund Enterprise in the 1950s, it was seeking celebrities to do radio commercials, and Irish got Williams to do one. "He'd do anything for Irish," Bernie said.

When Williams died, I expect Irish welcomed him into heaven like this: "Bush, it's about time you got here!" And Williams replied: "Bush, it's good to see your ugly face again."

August 17, 2002

NEW YORK GREAT PLACE TO VISIT, EVEN WITH EXORBITANT PARKING

My wife Betty and I love New York, and we go there as often as we can, particularly on our wedding anniversaries.

What's the connection between New York and our anniversaries? We visited New York on our honeymoon and listened to the music of Xavier Cugat on the roof of the old Hotel Astor. And the memory lives on.

My ties to New York go back to my childhood, when we Flannery kids from Jessup visited our Aunt Kitty and Uncle Howard in Astoria, just across the East River from Manhattan. I remember standing on the third-floor roof and marveling at the New York skyline while Aunt Kitty hung clothes on the line.

It was in my tenth year in Jessup High School that Helen Lyons, my English teacher, planted a seed in my mind. "You have a writing talent and you should think about getting into journalism after high school," she told me. Since no one had ever given me such a suggestion, I took it to heart, and after graduation I moved in with Aunt Kitty and Uncle Howard and became an office boy in the Manhattan newsroom of the *United Press*. Miss Lyons was right. I loved the atmosphere of the busy newsroom.

But my dream of becoming a journalist in New York was dissolved one day when a veteran *United Press* reporter told me that journalism was changing and college degrees were becoming more important in getting jobs.

I was crushed. I couldn't afford college. So I went to my big brother Tom, to cry on his shoulder. He was doing well selling cartoons to New York magazines and told me to go home, register at the University of Scranton, and send him the bills. So I did that and went back to New York, where I became an office boy again, this time with the *New York News*. I wanted to become a cub reporter, but the competition was tough. I was up against guys with degrees from Columbia, Fordham, NYU, and other high-profile schools.

Then a miracle happened. I got a call from the managing editor of the old *Scranton Tribune* and he offered me a job as a neighborhood correspondent. I practically ran home and went to work for peanuts, but within 6 months I was a staff reporter, and shortly thereafter, Betty and I were married.

Years later, I was hired by the *Scranton Times* and did well enough to take frequent visits to New York with Betty, especially on our anniversaries. This year's trip was great. We got in line at Times Square, where tickets to Broadway shows with empty seats are sold for half price. So we waited in line for an hour or so and bought half-price tickets to see *42nd Street*.

We also went to Jimmy Neary's restaurant on 57th Street, our all-time favorite place to eat on our New York visits. In addition, we found another restaurant that we will put on our list for future meals. It's Patsy's Italian Restaurant on 56th Street, which was a favorite of Frank Sinatra whenever he was in New York. The food was good and the prices reasonable.

Understand, the U.S. dollar isn't worth much in New York. But if you are careful, you can have fun in New York without going bankrupt. The day we arrived, we took a deep walk into Central Park and sat on a bench in the shade, watching New Yorkers walking, running, playing baseball, and sunning themselves. That didn't cost a cent.

I also love watching people on the sidewalks of New York. That's a show unto itself. The ethnic diversity is amazing. So is the diversity of dress. Some business people can look real cool even on a 95-degree day. And then there are the youths in their baggy pants, with earrings in their noses. A few feet farther there are guys or girls selling purses, wristwatches, ties, or framed pictures of the twin towers. And then there might be a beggar asking for a donation.

On our visit last weekend, we stayed an extra night to go to the Metropolitan Museum of Art Monday morning to see an exhibit of paintings of Paul Gauguin, who fell in love with the South Pacific islands, particularly Tahiti, in the 1890s. We checked out of our hotel and drove up Madison Avenue to the 80s and sought a parking garage. After driving around for a time we found the 8 Street 83rd Garage, which had a sign that said "Museum Parking."

We figured we'd need two hours and were stunned that it would cost $23. I winced but felt helpless. So we walked to the museum.

Upon our arrival, we saw signs that said, "Closed on Mondays." We went back to the garage and told the attendant our problem. I figured he'd charge us a few bucks and we'd be on our way home. However, he said we had to pay the minimum fee of $15 for an hour because we were already in the computer and he had to show a payment.

I was furious because the "Museum Parking" sign outside had deceived me. But he said $15 was the minimum parking fee and I had to pay that. So I did. I guess we'll never see that Gauguin exhibit.

But for sure, we will return to New York. And I'll never forget that the museum is closed every Monday.

September 15, 2002

HERE'S TO YOU MRS. ROBINSON
FOR YOUR VISION, SUCCESSES

I have long believed the late Mina Schimpff Robinson was an amazing woman who should be included in every history of Scranton.

"Never heard of her," you say?

I can understand that. Eighteen years before women in America could vote, Mrs. Robinson was a successful entrepreneur in South Scranton.

Her husband, Philip Robinson, whose roots were in Germany, decided to build a brewery, but when the project was only half completed, he died and left her with 11 children. While American women were conditioned then to believe that their place was in the home, circumstances dictated that Mrs. Robinson, who also had German roots, complete her husband's brewery and run it. In time, she made enough money on beer that she let it be known in South Scranton that loans were available from her on low-interest terms.

Mrs. Robinson's success caused a number of South Side businessmen to wake up to the fact that their rapidly growing part of the city needed a real bank. A committee was formed with ex-Mayor Benjamin Dimmick as the temporary chairman. At the first meeting, the committees agreed the proposed financial institution should be called the South Side Bank, and that a minimum of $60,000 in capital stock would be needed to start it.

No doubt, because Mrs. Robinson was a woman, she was not invited to the early meetings, but her importance could be judged in that the founders rented two rooms in a building she owned on Cedar Avenue for $50 a month. So the clever Mrs. Robinson became the first person to make a profit from the new bank.

The following 13 businessmen, many of whom have family names prominent in Scranton's history, served on the original board: Conrad Schroeder, who also became the bank's first president; Richard J. Bourke; ex-Mayor Dimmick; Ambrose Herz; Stephen S. Spruks; Henry Belin Jr.; Frank J. Dickert; John F. Gibbons; Frank Hummler; George Scheuer; Charles H. Welles; and Henry J. Ziegler Sr.

But women's lib had not yet surfaced. Thus, the board was all male. Indeed, it wasn't until 1983 that Emily S. Perry became the first female on the board.

The original board drew bank rules, including that it would accept minimum deposits as small as 10 cents, and its passbooks on saving accounts would be printed in English, German, and Polish, the dominant immigrant languages of the South Side.

The bank opened on Oct. 2, 1902. On the first day, the deposits totaled $44,472.01, which pleased the founders in a period when most people saved their money under their mattresses. And whose name was on the first business account? It was that of Mrs. Robinson. And who was the first cashier? It was F. J. Helriegel, her son-in-law and a future president of the bank.

From the first day, during wars, recessions, and other crises, the bank was a success. In 1913 it bought Mrs. Robinson's building for future expansion. In 1929, when some banks were collapsing, it bought the assets of the Dollar State Bank and Trust Co., a purchase that was an omen. In 1931 the bank moved into its new building on the site of the old Robinson structure and thrived.

Decades later, a period of expansion began under the direction of attorney Robert Johnson, a grandson of Mrs. Robinson. In 1966 the National Bank of Moscow was incorporated into the South Side Bank and Trust Co. Two years later, the bank leased its first computer and entered a new era. In 1971 the bank's name was changed to Penn Security Bank and Trust Co., and the East Scranton State Bank became a branch of Penn Security. Five years later, Penn Security opened an office in Moscow.

Also in 1976, while some big banks in central city were downsizing, merging, or closing, Penn Security opened a major downtown branch in the Mears Building. Several departments and executive offices were moved from the original South Side quarters.

In 1977 the North Pocono office was moved into a new building. The old structure was donated to Moscow borough to serve as a health center. In 1983 the bank opened branches in Gouldsboro and in South Abington Twp.

In 1998 the Green Ridge Bank, founded in 1914, became a branch of Penn Security, while a new branch was added in East Stroudsburg.

When Mina Robinson began loaning money to South Siders, the seed was planted for a bank that is marking its 100th anniversary this year. Even now, links between her and the bank continue. Her great-grandson, attorney Otto P. Robinson Jr., became president of the bank on Nov. 25, 1975, and continues in that post.

As a widow who raised 11 children. Mina must be looking down from heaven as she observes in wonderment the banking business she spawned.

November 3, 2002

LONG-SOUGHT MONUMENT
RISES TO HONOR CIVIL WAR HEROES

Here's a test.

Who are these guys? Patrick Delacy? John Carroll Delaney?

You say you don't have a clue?

Well, you haven't been paying attention, because I've been writing about these men because they were local residents who became heroes in the Civil War. Our Celtic Medal of Honor Committee was formed to raise money to erect a monument on the Courthouse Square, so that future generations will know about the bravery that earned them the Medal of Honor, our nation's highest honor.

So why am I writing about them today?

Because, after more than a year of begging, our committee finally raised enough money to erect a monument that will be unveiled Wednesday at 11 A.M. near the monument erected years ago for Gino Merli and Joseph Sarnoski, heroes of World War II, who also earned the Medal of Honor for heroism in combat.

As the originator of this monument project, I'm inviting everybody who wants to come to be there for the ceremony.

Before the program, the Greater Scranton Black Diamond Pipe Band will play American and Irish melodies on their bagpipes. Keith Martin, a Scranton native, a retired National Guard general, and the top newsman at WBRE-TV, will give the main address, and Billy Mattison, a freshman at Scranton High School with a beautiful voice will sing patriotic American and Irish songs. Also, John "Star" Kelly, the committee chairman, will be master of ceremonies and will sing a song he composed for the ceremony. Mayor Chris Doherty said he will be there, and we will expect other dignitaries to show up.

Given the fact that winter is on its way, I'm hoping the program will be short and sweet. Later, we will have a light lunch at the Banshee restaurant.

I regret that state Sen. Robert Mellow and state Rep. Gaynor Cawley will not be able to attend, because they have to be in Harrisburg that day.

We asked all our state legislators with help with our funding, but they are the two that got us state grants. Without their help we would still be begging.

I also want to thank the county commissioners, especially Joseph Corcoran, for letting us put the monument on the Square and setting up a podium for the dedication.

Why did we start the project? We thought it would serve history to let future generations know that during the Civil War, our nation's bloodiest conflict, these local men helped the United States to remain one nation instead of breaking into two smaller nations.

Who are these men?

Captain DeLacy was born in Carbondale of Irish immigrant parents on Nov. 24, 1835. After the Civil War began, he volunteered to serve in the Union Army. In the Wilderness Campaign in Virginia on May 6, 1864, he ran ahead of his comrades during a charge and shot the flagbearer of the oncoming Confederates. With no flag to follow and the battlefield covered with smoke, the rebel line broke and the Union forces prevailed. After the war, he settled in Scranton, became police chief, postmaster, a state representative, and an alderman, among other jobs. While friends wanted him to run for mayor, he preferred to busy himself with veterans' affairs. He died on April 27, 1915, and is buried in St. Catherine's Cemetery in Moscow.

Capt. Delaney was born in Ireland on April 22, 1848, and came to America with his parents as a child. He was living in Honesdale when the Civil War began. He lied about his age, joined the Union Army, and might well have been the youngest wartime recruit. He earned his Medal of Honor on Feb. 6, 1865, when he might have been just 16. During the battle of Danby Mills, VA, he saw a wounded comrade who was about to be burned in a fire in the brush. Ignoring the Confederates who were firing his way, he ran to his friend, picked him up, and carried him back to safety.

After the war, he settled in Dunmore and later became superintendent of buildings and grounds at the state Capitol in Harrisburg and then inspector of factories in the state. Later he got a federal job in Washington. He died on April 4, 1915, at Chevy Chase, MD, and was buried in the National Cemetery at Arlington, Virginia.

I realize that thousands of men from our county have fought heroically in our nation's wars. So why pick out two for a monument on Courthouse Square? Because we should cherish our history, and Mr. Delacy and Mr. Delaney became part of our history when they received the nation's highest award. Decades from now or even a century from now, people walking through our Courthouse Square will be reminded that these men from our county fought heroically in America's worst war.

All donors to our $29,000 project should be proud they helped this patriotic cause.

TEACHER SPARKED 52 YEARS OF WRITING

After 52 years in journalism, I plan to retire this weekend. But before I get to that, let me tell the story of how I became a journalist.

It began one day in 1944 when the late Helen Lyons, my English teacher at Jessup High School, asked me to stay after class.

I walked to her desk and she said: "Joseph, what do you want to do with your life? "

I couldn't come up with an answer. I was a junior in high school but my only goal in life was to become a senior. Beyond that, I had no master plan. So I gave her an honest answer: "I never gave that much thought."

So she tried again: "You did very well with that essay assignment, and I wondered if you ever thought of becoming a journalist."

It was the first time anyone had ever said I was good at something. So as I walked home from school, I kept rolling over the idea of becoming a journalist. It pleased me that I had a talent that my teacher thought was worth developing. So from then on, my goal was to become a journalist.

For a time I forgot that my parents had no money to send me to college. Miss Lyons was the daughter of a physician. Clearly, she could afford college to become a teacher. But I didn't dwell on my problem. I just told myself over and over again that sometime, somehow, I was going to become a journalist.

A year later, I graduated from Jessup High School and went to the State Employment Office in Scranton, where I filled out a form saying I wanted to be a journalist.

However, I was sent to the Morris White Pocketbook Factory in Scranton, where I was taught the craft of cutting leather to make handbags. I put metal dies on large pieces of leather, and then I caused a flat steel hammer to hit the dies with enough force to cut cleanly through the leather.

Doing that eight hours a day bored me out of my mind. Indeed, I hated my job so much that I refused to go to bed early, because to do so brought me back to the factory quicker. So I stayed up late every night.

Fortunately for me, my brother Tom was working in New York City as a freelance cartoonist. I hitchhiked to New York and told him how unhappy I was in the factory. I asked if there was any way he could get me a job that might get me into journalism.

Tom had been a cartoonist for *Yank* magazine in London during World War II, and he met a lot of newsmen who were back at their old journalism jobs in New York. Through one of them, he got me a job as an office boy with *United Press*. I answered telephones, ran errands, and went out to buy coffee and Danish pastry for the staffers. But it was a newsroom, and it excited me to think I might get a break and become a reporter.

One day a boss came to me with a *Westbrook Pegler* column that the *United Press* distributed to Latin America.

"Get some carbon paper and make me 10 copies," he ordered.

I was terrified.

"I can't type," I confessed, never mentioning the fact that the column was written in Spanish.

"You can't type?" he said. "Who hired you?" Before I could think up some answer, he said I had 10 days to learn to type or I would be fired.

I do believe that God sometimes intervenes when someone prays hard enough. I rode the subway home to the apartment of my aunt and uncle in Queens, where I was boarding.

While in the Grand Central subway station waiting for the train to Astoria, I spotted a thin booklet hanging on a hook where a man was selling newspapers and magazines. "Learn to type in 10 easy lessons," the booklet promised. As I recall, the booklet cost just 50 cents, so I bought it and began reading the lessons.

That weekend, I went home to Jessup and borrowed a portable typewriter from my sister Clare. For the next week or so, when I wasn't eating and sleeping, I was teaching myself how to type, and kept my job with the *United Press*.

I loved the electricity of the newsroom and hoped that someday I could become a reporter. But my hopes were dashed when one of the old veterans called me over one day and asked if I was serious about becoming a newsman. I said I was. He said that journalism was changing and I would need a college degree to get a job.

That shattered my dream, because college was still beyond my means. I went to see my brother Tom, and told him what I had been told. He told me to go home, enroll at the University of Scranton, and send him the bills.

I was thrilled and got my degree in three years. But the door to journalism still didn't fly open.

December 1, 2002

AFTER 52 YEARS, 4,000 COLUMNS, JOE X. OPTS TO TURN THE PAGE

This is my final column before retirement. Yesterday, I detailed how a high school teacher's suggestion steered me into a 52-year career in journalism, including 35 years as a columnist. The column ended with me working as an office boy with the *New York News*.

One afternoon in that newsroom, I was told I had a telephone call. It was B. B. Powell, the managing editor of the old *Scrantonian/Scranton Tribune*. He said he had an opening for a regional correspondent, which could develop into a job as a reporter in the future. I ran home and was promoted to reporter within six months.

One of the first times I realized the power of the press was when I was sent to the old Maloney Home, now the Holy Family Residence, to interview the Little Sisters of the Poor about a state demand that they install a new heating system to replace the old boilers that were in danger of exploding. To solve their problem, the nuns put a plank between the boilers and put a statue of St. Joseph, their patron saint, on the plank to keep them from exploding.

However, the state inspector didn't have that much faith in St. Joseph and gave them a deadline to install new boilers.

My story, accompanied by a picture of the statue on the plank, started-ed a deluge of donations to the Little Sisters. And after the wire services picked up the story, more donations arrived. In a few weeks, the nuns had about $28,000, enough to put in a new heating plant and to buy the very first television sets the institution had.

Weeks later, I received a telephone call from an official of *Strike It Rich*, an early television show that offered money to contestants with sad stories. I was told I was the first journalist to win a $500 government bond for raising money for the nuns to buy new boilers. My wife and I were flown to New York and interviewed on the TV show. That bond became the first deposit in an account to buy our home. After that, I often wrote sad stories when people were in need of help.